Flintridge Pr

Politics and Religion in France and the United States

Politics and Religion in France and the United States

EDITED BY ALEC G. HARGREAVES, JOHN KELSAY,
AND SUMNER B. TWISS

LEXINGTON BOOKS

A division of
ROWMAN & LITTLEFIELD PUBLISHERS, INC.
Lanham • Boulder • New York • Toronto • Plymouth, UK

LEXINGTON BOOKS

A division of Rowman & Littlefield Publishers, Inc.
A wholly owned subsidiary of The Rowman & Littlefield Publishing Group, Inc.
4501 Forbes Boulevard, Suite 200
Lanham, MD 20706

Estover Road
Plymouth PL6 7PY
United Kingdom

British Library Cataloguing in Publication Information Available

Library of Congress Cataloging-in-Publication Data

Politics and religion in France and the United States / edited by Alec G. Hargreaves, Jojn
Kelsay, and Sumner B. Twiss.
    p. cm.
 ISBN-13: 978-0-7391-1929-7 (cloth : alk. paper)
 ISBN-10: 0-7391-1929-X (cloth : alk. paper)
 ISBN-13: 978-0-7391-1930-3 (pbk. : alk. paper)
 ISBN-10: 0-7391-1930-3 (pbk. : alk. paper)
 1. Religion and politics—France. 2. Religion and politics—United States. 3. France—
Politics and government—20th century. 4. United States—Politics and government—
20th century. 5. France—Religion. 6. United States—Religion. I. Hargreaves, Alec G.
II. Kelsay, John, 1953– III. Twiss, Sumner B.
 BL65.P7P638 2007
 322'.10944—dc22   2007032109

Printed in the United States of America

Contents

Acknowledgments

The editors gratefully acknowledge the assistance of Sophie Romeuf, Administrative Coordinator of the Winthrop-King Institute for Contemporary French and Francophone Studies, in support of the conference from which this volume grew; of Matthew A. Kemp, who co-translated the texts of French contributors while completing his doctorate in the Department of Modern Languages and Linguistics at Florida State University; and of Joseph W. Williams, a doctoral candidate in American Religious History in Florida State University's Department of Religion, for his assistance in the copyediting and indexing of the book. We are also deeply appreciative of the financial support of the Ada Belle Winthrop-King Memorial Fund.

Introduction

Alec G. Hargreaves, John Kelsay, and Sumner B. Twiss

The events of September 11, 2001, and their aftermath focused the attention of the world on the role of religious forces in both national and global politics. While the relationship between politics and religion has undoubtedly taken a new turn since 9/11, the interface between these two spheres has of course a deep and complex history. The present volume explores a range of contemporary issues with reference to France and the U.S., where seemingly similar controversies have in recent years emerged over matters such as the tension between secular and religious institutions, the role of religion in the public square, challenges to the civil rights of religious minorities, expressions of prejudice toward religious and ethnic minorities, the impact of international events on domestic religious thinking and behavior, and the possible effects of economic and cultural globalization on domestic religious and political attitudes and behavior, to mention but a few. The book grew out of an international conference on Politics and Religion in France and the United States, sponsored by the Winthrop-King Institute for Contemporary French and Francophone Studies in association with the Department of Religion at Florida State University, held in September 2005. The rationale of both the conference and the resulting book was premised on the perception that while sharing significant similarities as multicultural democratic societies, France and the U.S. might be usefully compared on the subject of the intersection of religion and politics at a time when both countries grapple with the phenomenon of ever growing religious diversity. Indeed, such a comparison might yield important lessons for each country on how best to interpret and respond to this phenomenon in their respective contexts. We thought that a controlled case study (or set of case studies)—focusing mainly on selected traditions in France and America and employing scholars of law, history, sociology, and religion—might have the advantage of bringing to the fore subtle nuances of the interactions between religion and politics that would otherwise be missed or go underappreciated. Additionally, given the long history of French and American political relations—including both its ups and more recent downs—it appeared to be a propitious time for trying to enhance their respective understandings of each other, for if political allies cannot understand and appreciate each other, what hope is there for mutual comprehension among other societies in the world, particularly over their constitutive political and religious identities?

The analytical plan for the conference and the consequent volume was built on the pairing of experts on France and the U.S. respectively in relation to a series of frames of reference, beginning with the historical and constitutional (or more broadly, legal) frameworks of both societies. The four traditions of Protestantism, Catholicism, Judaism, and Islam were then scrutinized for their relations with the political institutions and dynamics within their respective national settings. The analysis concluded with sustained comparative observations that took into account the preceding studies. This plan, of course, did not preclude specialists on faiths in particular national contexts from making comparative allusions of their own in the course of their analyses.

As befits any published collection of original scholarly essays, a few introductory words are in order pertaining to the overarching questions and issues addressed and the character of the particular contributions themselves. The volume begins with two essays that sketch the historical and constitutional frameworks for considering the problematic of religion and politics in the U.S. and France respectively. Jeremy Gunn, who adopts both an internal comparative perspective within America and (to a lesser extent) an external perspective between the U.S. and France, limns two sides of the American debate that he calls "liberal" and "conservative," respectively, developing these as heuristic ideal types for the purposes of discussion, while eschewing claims about their precise historical or political accuracy. Roughly speaking, the liberal side emphasizes the secular foundations of the U.S. Constitution and Republic, opposing state endorsement and funding of religion, while the conservative side emphasizes religio-moral values as being crucial to the foundation of the Republic and its laws, supporting as a consequence state endorsement of some religious expression and (to a lesser extent) funding. The liberal side views official endorsement of religion in any form as discriminatory, while the conservative side views American identity as inherently religious and accuses liberals of being overly secular and even hostile to religion per se.

Interestingly, suggests Gunn, despite their differences, these two sides do in fact share a number of presuppositional commonalities, especially when compared with the French context. For example, both sides agree on the fundamental legal relevance of the U.S. Constitution (and therefore Supreme Court) to religious matters, while in France controversial religious and public issues are referred to the Council of State (an administrative court) or Parliament (a political body) for adjudication. Both liberals and conservatives in America vest high priority in the right to religious freedom, and both therefore resist official infringement on this right, while in France considerations of public order often prevail over rights of religious expression. So also, in the U.S., liberals and conservatives agree that religious groups should be able to attain legal personality, along with tax and other benefits, without prior state evaluation, whereas in France it is left to each prefect to decide on a case-by-case basis whether a group is "authentically" religious and therefore entitled to legal and tax benefits. What, then, do the differences between liberals and conservatives come to in the American context? Here Gunn argues that the differences reflect a struggle by the two sides over how to interpret not only the Constitution but also and more deeply what constitutes America's very identity—as either secular or religious (in a disjunctive manner)—in the past and present and for the future.

With respect to historical and constitutional matters in France, Rémy Schwartz, after carefully defining the meaning of *laïcité*, gives some flesh to Gunn's characterization of the French situation by discussing the content of the law of December 9, 1905, its implications, and its recent applications. The 1905 law codified the French system of *laïcité* involving the separation of church and state and the recognition of freedom of religion and conscience, thereby rendering in principle a position of equality for all religions in France. Although this law did not define religion, the subsequent emergence of non-traditional religions (other than Protestantism, Catholicism, and Judaism) resulted in the Council of State defining religion as a belief in divinity put into practice by a community through ceremonial ritual activity, with the stipulation that a religious association must have worship as its sole purpose in order to gain access to certain tax and other advantages. Additionally, although the 1905 law prohibits state subsidies for religions per se, it does vest in state and local authorities the responsibility for the maintenance of cathedrals and churches (that is, the edifices themselves) in existence at the time of the law (though not those built subsequently), as well as permit state subsidies for faith-based schools. Moreover, the law carried the implications that public officials acting in their official capacities must display strict neutrality regarding religious belief and that religious expression in public places and in public services must not be proselytizing, nor, of course, disruptive of the public order. Although Schwartz himself does not say so directly, these implications appear to contrast strongly with the evidently less stringent regulation of religious expression in the U.S.—for example, public officials' display of their religious beliefs; and a more open-textured understanding of what constitutes a religion and what its adherents may do in public, for example, wearing religious dress in public schools.

It is a manifest fact that Protestantism had differential histories and effects within the American and French republics. The modern French Republic emerged, for example, from a background of Catholic monarchy—indeed, France was once known as the Roman Church's "eldest daughter"—whereas the American Republic was founded by a largely Protestant population, with the Reformed tradition being deeply influential in its history and development. In the latter regard, David Little appears to trace much of the liberal versus conservative debate cited by Gunn to a deep tension (or apparent contradiction) within the heart of the Reformed tradition itself, that is, to John Calvin and his early American successors. This tension is between, on the one hand, freedom of religion and conscience assertable against the state (within limits, of course) and, on the other, the view that the civic order requires as its condition "proper" religious belief and practice encouraged by the state. Little demonstrates that this tension is not only inherent in Calvin's theology but also played out in various phases of American history, ranging from Roger Williams of Rhode Island versus the leaders of the Massachusetts Bay Colony, to the "Protestant establishment" of the nineteenth and early twentieth centuries (brought to a symbolic end by a 1940s Jehovah's Witnesses legal case), to and including recent political "awakenings," to the perceived public importance of Christian moral values, and disagreements between Congress and the Supreme Court over state limitation of religious practice. None of this is meant to imply that traditions other than Protestant or of Reformed background are not also caught up in and contributory to this dynamic tension, but it does suggest that at a very deep level the inherent Protestant tension still greatly affects the broader relations between religion and politics in America.

By contrast to the American situation, the persecution of the Huguenots in the seventeenth and eighteenth centuries accounts in part for the later French Protestant embrace of *laïcité* (and all that this implies) so as not to have to endure ever again a Catholic-dominated state. Sébastien Fath is eloquent on this point but also equally subtle in identifying three phases in the Protestant reaction which he casts in riveting terms—(1) "No" to the "city of God" (1905); "No" to a "city without God" (the past decade), and (3) "God in the city" (most recently emerging). In the first phase, although Protestant groups can be differentiated in how warmly they embraced the 1905 law, all did accept it for fear of Catholic resurgence in French politics. In the second phase, during which Christianity in general was perceived as being under attack as antimodern and also as being challenged by the deregulation of the religious marketplace, Protestants began to worry about the prospect of a "pagan" France, devoid of all religious values. So, in the third phase, Protestants are moving self-consciously into the public sphere by developing institutional and media strategies to keep God "in" the Republic and thereby strengthen its moral fiber. Somewhat ironically to be sure, this modest Protestant voice in France appears to echo the more dominant conservative (for example, evangelical) Protestant voice in the U.S.: according to these voices, both republics need religious values and a "pox" on a city without God at all (extreme secularism or *laïcité* to a fault).

Whereas Catholicism was—and, according to some, continues to be— influential in France due to its prominence since the time of the monarchy, this tradition has had a less dominant role in America, although such a claim is becoming less and less true as the population swells, for example, with largely Catholic immigration from Latin American countries; 25 percent of the U.S. population and 30 percent of the electorate now identify themselves as Catholic. Indeed, it is only within the past few decades that the tradition has been seriously studied in a non-parochial way in the field of American religious history, thus remedying an important lacuna in the subject. Scott Appleby focuses particular attention on the internal religious changes within American Catholicism as well as the significant trends exhibited in the voting behavior of Catholics, especially since the time of the New Deal in the post-Depression era. With respect to internal religious changes, he observes that in their thinking and behavior Catholics taken as a whole have been increasingly secularized as well as being gradually fragmented into groups with differing degrees of distinctive Catholic identity. He traces some (if not all) of this diffusion and fragmentation to not only the breakup of "classic" ethnic neighborhoods (for example, Irish, Italian) and other economic and social factors but also the influence of Vatican II leading, for example, to more individualistic conceptions of moral and religious conscience.

On the political side, Appleby notes that during the time of Franklin D. Roosevelt's administration and through that of John F. Kennedy, Catholics (particularly ethnic Catholics) tended to vote for the Democratic Party (perceived to be the party protective of immigrants and the marginalized as well as oriented to a "welfare state" political philosophy). But, as Catholics have become upwardly mobile economically, they have increasingly tended to vote Republican (a party perceived to be economically conservative, pro-business, and less welfare-state oriented), even though they remain sensitive to controversial social issues as reflected in some of their Democratic voting behavior. The big exception to this trend to vote Republican on economic issues and Democratic on social issues are the Catholic evangelicals who appear to reverse this trend because of their perception that the Republican Party's social platforms are more supportive of Catholic moral family values and the Democratic economic platforms are more supportive of Catholic socioeconomic teachings. In spite of this exception, however, Appleby is clear that within contemporary American Catholicism there is a general fragmentation into an internal pluralism, ranging from a relatively weak Catholic identity among many to a strong one in the case of the evangelicals.

Blandine Chélini-Pont observes a similar solubility or dissipation of Catholic identity on the French political scene, with, for example, *laïcité* becoming the cultural norm for most Catholics and with the disappearance of a unified Catholic voting bloc. By the same token, however, she also contends that there may be discernable Catholic imprints on French politics both in the cautious attitude of the population to a general European swing away from substantive social welfare policies and in certain worries about the legal status and benefits of same-sex couples who raise children. In both cases, it might be argued that there are traces, respectively, of Catholic socio-economic teachings and Catholic gender and family values. We might remark that these possible traces appear to echo precisely the concerns of evangelical American Catholics, so the similarity may well indicate a distinctive religious influence at work in both cases.

With respect to Jews and Judaism, the next section of the book considers what is manifestly a minority tradition in both France and the U.S., but their histories of development appear quite different at least up to the contemporary period. In the American case, Michael Berenbaum argues that only in America has the government itself been officially neutral regarding religion from the colonial period onward, thus making Jews and their tradition only one of a series of "outsiders" ethnically speaking and furthermore one that was less despised than others. Compared to Europe generally, Berenbaum contends that anti-Semitism was not a large problem in America, at least regarding equality of citizenship, although more "private" social exclusion was encountered up through the 1960s. According to Berenbaum, over time there has been a high assimilation rate of Jews into mainstream society with the rule of (social) emancipation once being "Be a Jew in the home but universal in the street." That rule has been "rescinded," so to speak, and Jews now feel free to be themselves *as* Jews in all public settings. Berenbaum also contends that distinctively American values have greatly influenced the traditions of American Judaism itself, ranging from forms of liberal Judaism barely distinguishable from certain Protestant phenomena to the fact that even ultra-Orthodox Jews use typically American practices in marketing their religious values.

Although there clearly has been a renaissance or revival within American Judaism—indeed, Judaism has tracked the great "awakenings" in American religious history generally—especially in recent years with respect to more "fundamentalist" Jews feeling threatened by secular values within American society, it is, for Berenbaum, an open question as to whether Judaism as a whole will remain a distinct and viable religious community. As in the case of American Catholicism, there are shades of fragmentation with respect to American Judaism as well. He notes—as does Michel Wieviorka in the French context—that the renewal of Jewish identity was greatly influenced by memories of the Holocaust and pride in Israel as a Jewish state brought into international public view by the 1961 trial of Adolf Eichmann and the 1967 Six-Day War. Berenbaum also notes, in contrast with Appleby's observations about the voting patterns of upwardly mobile Catholics, that Jews have largely not moved to the Republican Party with their own economic advancement, though he concedes that Orthodox Jews do in fact follow the voting patterns of evangelical Christians and the religious Right, due most likely to the shared perception of the importance of religio-moral values for the welfare of the broader society.

Berenbaum's own excursus on recent anti-Semitism in France constitutes an appropriate segue into Wieviorka's discussion of French Jews. Wieviorka begins by noting that up to the Second World War, Jews were relatively self-effacing in France and thought of themselves as simply Israelite French citizens on par with other citizens in the Republic. This self-image was, of course, denied by the anti-Semitic actions of the Vichy government during the Nazi occupation of France. The status quo ante was restored, at least outwardly, after the end of the war. What Wieviorka calls the "great change" came about following the Eichmann trial and the Six-Day War, resulting, as in the American case, in a sense of constructive Jewish identity as a people capable of self-defensive action. French Jews at that time began to become more visible in politics and, with Charles de Gaulle's public distancing of France from the State of Israel, became even less certain of the protective cover of the republican political model. Renewal of Jewish cultural and religious traditions followed, resulting in what Wieviorka characterizes as a "new model" for Jewish involvement in the public sphere, namely the apparent embrace of what the French call *communautarisme*—assertive ethnic identity politics and institutional development. Like Berenbaum's excursus, Wieviorka concedes a recent upsurge of anti-Semitism in France to which Jews have reacted publicly and that has led to an increased emigration by Jews to Israel, as well as the public phenomenon, fueled also by other immigrant groups and their problems, of competitive victimhood among different religious and ethnic minorities.

While the presence of Islam in America dates back to the nineteenth century, Liyakat Takim focuses largely on Muslims in the twentieth century. Here he identifies two main phases. The first involves the nostalgic phenomenon of immigrant Muslims' "back home" orientation: the hope of return to their original societies combined with their refusal to integrate into the general population, a general distain for American culture, and a greater interest in foreign rather than domestic political issues. These features, suggests Takim, are marks of a conservative form of (mainly Sunni) Islam. The second phase—no doubt spurred by second and subsequent generations of Muslims born in the U.S. as well as by immigration—represents the increasing indigenization of American Islam since the middle 1960s, with the identification of America as a permanent home and the appropriation of distinctly American cultural values. This second phase, however, in recent years has also been marked by the aftereffects of the events of September 11, 2001, resulting in the need for Muslim institutions to combat prejudicial and discriminatory attitudes toward Muslims among sectors of the general public, due also in no small way to Bush administration rhetoric about and actions taken against this religious group, ranging from the earlier language of a crusade against Muslims abroad to more restricted immigration and detention policies at home. The "silver lining," if one can call it that, in this unfortunate situation is that Sunni Muslims in America are becoming more active politically, ranging across voting behavior, formation of civil-rights action groups, and even the fielding of candidates for elected office. The exception to this development is the Shi'i Muslim population, which still exhibits an aversion to American politics, though certain components of this population sponsor public events and conferences on issues of peace and religious toleration. There is some data, says Takim, indicating a growing Shi'i cooperation with Sunni Muslims in the American public sphere.

While Muslims constitute a relatively small minority tradition and population in America, they are proportionately larger in France, which accounts for fully one-third of all the Muslims in West Europe. This phenomenon is in part due to the earlier French colonization in Africa (notably Algeria), a fact that lies behind the immigration of Algerian Muslims into France proper. Catherine Wihtol de Wenden, somewhat like Takim regarding America, focuses on the Muslim presence in France in the latter part of the twentieth century onward. She discerns three phases of development. The first (1974-84) begins with the history of Muslim immigrant workers having little cultural and religious expression and then extends to the second generation that began to protest, through newly formed associations, against police violence, deportation, racism, restricted citizenship, and related phenomena. The second phase (1984-94) is marked by various political gains in this regard as well as by agitation for the right of religious expression in the work place. Although integration progressed during this period, there were also setbacks—for example, sparked by the 1989 Salman Rushdie and headscarf affairs—resulting in the need for Muslim counteraction to increasingly negative public attitudes toward Islam in general. Indeed, says de Wenden, this period was marked by the often asked question, "How can one be a Muslim in France?" The third phase (1994-2005) saw the paradoxical phenomena of both the rise of a radical Islam *and* the increasing integration of Muslims in France. De Wenden suggests that Islamic fundamentalism in France is more of an invention of a new way to be Muslim rather than a self-conscious return to ancestral forms of religious practice. She notes that Muslims have on occasions scored political successes in, for example, helping to force the government to rescind a 2005 law requiring high schools to teach students about France's "positive" role in colonialism. Yet one is inclined to wonder whether this success is not muted somewhat by the recent stricture against wearing conspicuous religious symbols (notably headscarves) in public schools.

Thus far, we have seen both pointed and subtly nuanced similarities and differences between the U.S. and France regarding the intersection of religion and politics. Some of the broad similarities appear to be these: (1) a parallel between the American "liberal" position regarding the separation of church and state, on the one hand, and the French 1905 law and *laïcité*, on the other; (2) the general dissipation and fragmentation of Catholic identity in both countries, with certain remnant traces pertaining to family values and socioeconomic teachings; (3) the revival and renewal of Jewish identity in both countries following the global impact of events in the State of Israel; (4) the growth of a generalized concern by conservative religious groups (of all traditions) in both countries over the loss of religio-moral values supposedly undergirding state and society; and (5) the increasing integration or indigenization of historically minority religious groups within both societies. By contrast, some of the broad differences between the two countries are these: (1) radically different religious influences in the foundations of the two countries—Protestant for America, Catholic for France; (2) the political power of conservative religious voices in America, as compared with the lesser power of analogous voices in France; (3) the relatively more stringent regulation of religious expression in the French public sphere than in the American; and (4) a differing degree of religious prejudice (especially anti-Semitism) in the two countries due in part to their differing histories. These observations are, of course, hardly exhaustive, nor are they intended to be definitive, since justifiable qualifications and subtleties abound. Instead, they are intended only to provoke thought and reflection on the part of readers as they work their way through the essays in this volume.

Indeed, the concluding essays by Jean Baubérot and Amanda Porterfield nuance considerably the above generalizations as well as add important points of their own regarding similarities and contrasts. Baubérot effectively traces the infrastructural implications of France's founding references to the Roman Catholic Church and to the French Revolution for the subsequent relations, tensions, and conflicts between religion and politics, dividing into periods, successively, of outright conflict, reconciliation through *laïcité*, and re-emergent tension especially between religious minorities and political authorities. While focusing largely on Catholics in France and their shifting fortunes, he also explains the differential voting behavior of religious groups vis-à-vis the proposed European Constitution as a marker for deeper issues of religious identity of these groups.

For her part, Porterfield draws a rather strong contrast between, on the one hand, the French government's predilection for using reason and rational analysis as the means for social reform regarding its treatment of religion and, on the other, American openness (at all levels) to appealing to religion, individual conscience, and self-government as the means to solving social differences. In developing and explaining this contrast, she adds significantly to our understanding of why and how the U.S. and France are so culturally different in handling issues arising from religious diversity and multiculturalism. To remark on these differences, however, is not to gainsay that the two societies have much to learn from each other's respective experiences and experiments. Quite the reverse, since Porterfield argues eloquently for a rapprochement between flourishing and vital religious pluralism, on the one hand, and the use of reason, on the other— that is, hospitality to religious voices and insights combined with rational analysis of the pragmatics of conflict, reconciliation, and social reform.

At this point, we invite our readers into their own direct encounter with astute, informed, and often inspiring essays aimed at the comprehension and appreciation of religion and politics in France and America. We wager that the result of such perusal will be eye-opening for both self and cultural understandings of all who pursue this course.

Part I: Historical and Constitutional Frameworks

Chapter One
Religion, Politics, and Law in the United States in Comparative Perspective

T. Jeremy Gunn

Every country in the world regulates religion in a unique way. In order to help explain the variety of approaches that states take, scholars will sometimes identify three basic models of the relationship between the state and religion. The first may be described as the "separationist" or "secular" model. Examples of the secular model typically include, despite their striking differences, France, the United States, and Turkey. The second basic model, that of the "established church" or "state religion," is illustrated by the examples of Great Britain, Norway, and, until 2000, Sweden. Non-European cases might include Iran and Sudan. The final model, sometimes described as "cooperationist," includes such countries as Spain and Germany. While such basic models no doubt have some heuristic value, they also run the risk of obscuring what may be the most interesting and revealing idiosyncrasies of any particular country. They may also unintentionally suggest that when the laws and practices of a state are not fully consistent with the ideal "model," there has somehow been a failure of legal reasoning (at best) in the country or blatant hypocrisy (at worst). Viewed from a European perspective, there might, for example, appear to be many such apparent contradictions in the United States as a supposedly "secular" country.

On the one hand, the United States appears from a foreign perspective to be a strictly secular country that employs as a guiding metaphor the "wall of separation between church and state."[1] The United States Constitution of 1787 articulated the radical principle (at the time) that "we the people" are to be the source of laws rather than God, a king (acting through divine right), or the church. The Constitution explicitly prohibits a religious test for public office (Article VI), and the First Amendment, drafted in 1789, provided that "Congress shall make no law respecting an establishment of religion or prohibiting the free exercise thereof." Unlike most European countries, the state is strictly prohibited from providing (or even permitting) sectarian religious education in public schools. Unlike secular France, where the state owns all churches built before 1905, the state does not own religious buildings (other than the important exceptions of religious buildings on military bases and non-denominational chapels located in some state buildings and airports). Also unlike France—and many other European countries—the Christian cross is typically not displayed prominently on or in public buildings, schools, or on state property (although there are some peculiar exceptions).[2]

But on the other hand, again from a European perspective, the United States appears to be a country that has infused its own style of religion into politics, law, and government. Public opinion polls repeatedly show that, of the developed countries in the world, the United States is the most actively religious. One of the most salient manifestations of this fervent American religiosity from the perspective of skeptical European observers is the pervasive "God" rhetoric used by political figures and that is exemplified by the now traditional conclusion of a presidential address with the words "God bless America." Each legislative day the Senate and House of Representatives begin with a paid chaplain offering an invocation to the Almighty followed by the formal recitation (typically in a sparsely populated chamber) of the Pledge of Allegiance, which declares that the United States is "one nation under God." The president traditionally takes the oath of office with his hand placed on a Bible, although the Constitution makes no such requirement. Since 1998, with the adoption of the International Religious Freedom Act, the U.S. State Department has been promoting "religious freedom" beyond American shores and legislators and now the president have succeeded in blocking, for religious reasons, the use of American funds abroad for contraceptives and abortions. The rhetoric of President George W. Bush has led some in the world to believe that he leads a cabal of fundamentalist Christians that are perfectly happy to use military power either to open countries for Christian missionaries or to hasten the last days with the battle of Armageddon (or both). From the outside, there seem to be few restraints on the ability of hucksters and gurus to launch their own new and peculiar religions.

Thus the constitutional restraints regarding religion in the United States may appear to be starkly secular in comparison with those of Germany, Spain, Poland, England, and Norway, while at the same time American political life is awash with religiously infused rhetoric that may sometimes resemble the religious rhetoric of Iran and Sudan (though American law differs substantially from those of the two Islamic republics).

I do not believe that these apparent contradictions between an ostensibly secular state and a country that is permeated by religious politics are superficial or that they can be reconciled if only we were to arrive at a more enlightened or deeper understanding of American law and culture. Rather, these contradictions

themselves are manifestations of lively—and sometimes hostile—internal debates about American values and national identity. Though I will not argue it at
length here, I suspect that these apparent contradictions with regard to religion,
law, and politics are not unique to the United States, but that they exist (albeit in
very different ways) in most countries as they are forced to grapple with their
competing national values and ideologies. In France, for example, the famous
1905 law on the separation of churches and the state provides that the state shall
"recognize no religion" at the same time that state officials are required to decide whether religious groups are to be recognized by the state as "religious bodies" (*cultes*) and thereby be entitled to receive bequests from donors and obtain
tax benefits from the state.[3] Rather than think of the United States and its laws as
exemplifying either a failing secular model or a rising proto-theocracy, it is
more appropriate to understand the people of the United States as grappling with
differing notions about their identity. The struggle is less a formal debate about
the proper legal interpretation of the First Amendment religion clauses and more
a debate about the images and symbols that Americans want their country to
promote. Indeed, we can speculate that religion is frequently tied to notions of
perceived national identity in most countries of the world—and that conflicts
over religion and law are particularly volatile exactly because they are so closely
tied with deeply felt personal and national identities.

Before focusing directly on the United States, it is perhaps worth making
two observations that apply not only to the United States, but can be generalized
to other countries as well. First, it is not possible to understand the legal relationship between religion and state solely by examining the principal legal texts
that theoretically lay the foundation for the relationship. The guiding principles
are found less in the general words of the foundational texts, whether the U.S.
Constitution or the French law of 1905, but in understanding the history of how
the fundamental texts have come to be interpreted over the years—
interpretations that may be so distant from the texts as to make the words seem
almost irrelevant. Second, despite the lack of legal clarity, and despite the often
volatile internal debates about religion and the national identity, Americans (like
others) are largely satisfied and even proud of how their country has resolved
religious issues. Each country of the world thinks of itself as having the best of
all possible laws regarding religion in the best of all possible countries.

I will explain the American approach to religion and the state in three steps.
First, I will identify what could be described as two competing ideological tendencies, loosely "liberal" and "conservative," that argue for differing theories
about the proper relationship between religion and the state. Second I will identify three important areas where American liberals and conservatives largely
agree and that to some extent differentiate the American approach from that of
other countries. And finally, I will identify some of the most contentious issues
between liberals and conservatives, and suggest that the core of this disagreement ultimately is less about technical interpretations of constitutional provisions and more of an "identity" dispute about what people believe their country
is—and should be.

"Liberals" and "Conservatives"

The scholars, jurists, and opinion makers in the United States who engage in the debate about the constitutional mandates regarding religion and law can loosely be differentiated between two ideological tendencies that I will describe as "liberal" and "conservative." There are many problems with using these two terms, just as there would be if any other terms were substituted in their place, and the terms will accordingly be used principally as shorthand descriptions rather than as rigid groupings. Those whom I place in the "liberal" category will often share a cluster of beliefs that relatively stress the secular foundations of the American Constitution and Republic, oppose state endorsement of religious expressions and symbols, and oppose state funding of religious entities and activities. (It is important to note, particularly for non-American audiences, that "liberal" as used here does not refer to classic liberal economic thought. So American liberals, as the term is used here, typically would disagree with many European "liberal" political parties.) Those whom I place in the "conservative" category typically emphasize the purported religious values of the American "founders" who are alternatively imagined to be the leading figures of the constitutional period (1785-91), or sometimes the figures of the revolutionary period (1774-83), or even those who settled in the Americas during the seventeenth century. The conservatives often will speak of the necessity of religion (or moral values) underlying law, and they typically favor state endorsement of religious expressions and advocate state funding of faith-based charitable activities. The debates between these liberals and conservatives take place in the public media, legislatures, law schools, and the judiciary.

Agreements between "Liberals" and "Conservatives" in the United States

The Hound of the Baskervilles was one of Arthur Conan Doyle's most famous murder mysteries. While some characters in the novel examined existing physical clues to help solve the crime, Sherlock Holmes understood that the most important clue was something that did not happen and that had left no trace. Holmes deduced that the decisive clue for solving the crime was the fact that the victim's dog did not bark, signaling that the murderer was someone known to the hound. Americans who engage in the sometimes heated debates over the proper constitutional relationship between religion and the state often do not realize that one of the most revealing insights into the American system is where the often polarized sides silently agree with each other—and that it is in these mutually agreed, though often unarticulated positions, where the differences between the United States and other countries can perhaps best be seen. I will identify three areas where, for most practical purposes, there is widespread agreement in the United States about religion and law issues. While it cannot be said that everyone agrees—a feat impossible in a country of nearly 300 million people, consisting of one federal government, fifty state governments (and the District of Columbia and other territories), and thousands of local jurisdictions (including school boards)—those factors identified here are where most American liberals and most conservatives overwhelmingly agree.

First, Americans overwhelmingly agree that not only *does* the Constitution ultimately decide religion and state issues, but also that it *should* be the law.[4] The debates in the United States are thus not whether the Constitution should control the outcome, but only over how it should be interpreted. Similarly, both conservatives and liberals will often appeal to the "founders' intent" with regard to the religion clauses of the First Amendment, with the debate then turning to "what *did* they actually intend?"[5] This of course differs from France where neither the constitutional language nor the decisions of courts are thought to prevail. So the debate in the United States is one of *interpretation* of constitutional language and norms and not whether the Constitution should play the decisive role.[6] The final arbiter of constitutional language is almost universally acknowledged to be the Supreme Court, which is one of the reasons that confirmation of justices has becoming increasingly contentious. In France, to the contrary, the fundamental touchstone in religion and state issues is not the Constitution of 1958, but the vague doctrine of *laïcité*, with the ultimate interpretation of the meaning of *laïcité* entrusted not in judges and courts, but in the parliament that is understood to express the will of the people.[7] For example, in the debates leading up to the enactment of law no. 2004-228 of March 15, 2004, which banned students from wearing "conspicuous" (*ostensible* in French) religious attire in public schools, there was virtually no public debate about the meaning of the Constitution of 1958 nor its protections of freedom of conscience. The debate was largely confined to the meaning of *laïcité* and it was assumed that the parliament was the appropriate branch of government to determine it.[8]

A second value that is widely shared by Americans is that religious freedom, as embodied in the free-exercise clause of the First Amendment ("Congress shall make no law . . . prohibiting the free exercise [of religion]") is a particularly important right that is entitled to a great deal of deference. While there are disagreements in the United States regarding the proper interpretation of the free-exercise clause, from a comparative-law perspective, liberals and conservatives in America are notable for their relative lack of disagreement. A book by the scholar Marci A. Hamilton indeed argues that this overwhelming consensus in America regarding rights of exercise of religious freedom is a serious problem that weakens the American polity. Hamilton argues that American laws in fact give too much leeway even to questionable religious practices—a viewpoint that is frequently shared by foreign observers of the United States.[9] An interesting illustration of this broad liberal-conservative consensus was the immediate popular reaction against the Supreme Court's decision in *Employment Division v. Smith*, 494 U.S. 872 (1990), where the Court held that the state could regulate religion if it had a reasonable basis for doing so (which would correspond roughly to the French model). In the ensuing uproar, the principal liberal and conservative groups joined together to press a virtually unanimous Congress to adopt what became the Religious Freedom Restoration Act. In France, the very basic notion of the *ordre public* (which can perhaps best be translated as "public policy") is generally understood to prevail over rights of religious expression and perhaps even rights of conscience—a position anathema to the vast majority of Americans.[10]

A third, and closely related value shared by American liberals and conservatives alike, is that religious groups should be able to register with the state and thereby obtain legal personality automatically and without any substantive state evaluation of their beliefs or practices. In addition, such religious groups also should be permitted to obtain tax-exempt status virtually as a matter of right and self-declaration. The liberality of such policies and laws, which are surprising to most outside observers (and which is disturbing to Professor Hamilton), is nevertheless pervasive. In France, as was mentioned above, although the 1905 law declares that the state does not recognize any religious body (*culte*), each *préfet* has the authority to decide, on a case-by-case basis, whether a religious group is entitled to tax-exempt status and whether it can receive bequests. For the most part, Americans take such rights for granted and do not even think about them or debate them. Thus one of the religion and law issues that is the most difficult and troubling in many countries—the procedures by which a religious group obtains legal personality—does not even arise as a question for debate or meaningful discussion in the United States. Whereas most countries will struggle with the complex issue of defining what is and is not religion and which groups should and should not be permitted to register as such and thereby obtain legal personality, it is a subject largely ignored in the United States because there is such a wide consensus.

Sharp Disagreements between Liberals and Conservatives

The liberality of religious practice and the widespread consensus in America on these issues really is quite stunning from the international or comparative perspective. Given the degree of consensus on the very issues that are often highly controversial outside of the United States, it should be surprising to foreign visitors to observe the vehemence and ofttimes hostility that arises regarding issues that might even be deemed trivial from a foreign perspective: government endorsement of religious expressions and activities (religion in public schools, the positing of the Ten Commandments, and declarations about being "one nation under God").

The most controversial legal issues in the United States regarding religion and the state arise from the interpretation of the establishment clause of the First Amendment of the Constitution: "Congress shall make no law respecting an establishment of religion." As suggested above, there tends to be relatively fewer conflicts regarding the free-exercise clause because most Americans, unlike their French counterparts, typically tolerate wide-ranging religious practices and unconventional beliefs. While there are certainly disagreements about the scope of the free-exercise clause, they produce relatively small conflicts. Not so with the establishment clause, which often provokes heated debate.

Several of the leading figures that are associated with what has generally been called the "religious Right," including Jerry Falwell, Billy James Hargis, Pat Robertson, James Dobson, and others, autobiographically date their entry into politics as a reaction to two Supreme Court decisions in the early 1960s: *Engel v. Vitale*, 370 U.S. 421 (1962) and *Abington School District v. Schempp*, 374 U.S. 203 (1963). In *Engel*, the Supreme Court held that the state could not draft prayers for public schools, and *Abington* held that schools could not teach the Bible as if it were sacred literature. Although the decisions were somewhat modest in scope, they were immediately and widely characterized to the public as taking prayers, the Bible, and God out of schools. People affiliated with the Religious Right have even suggested that those two decisions have been responsible in part for the moral decline in America and have provoked a rise in school violence and the drug culture. Such assertions rarely include any rigorous statistical data to support the claims, but they are widely believed in a significant part of the American population—regardless of the absence of meaningful data. For many, the causal link is so obvious as to obviate the need to provide any evidence at all. The misleading cries that "the Supreme Court has taken prayers, the Bible, and God out of public schools" continues to be a staple of conservative rhetoric and fundraising appeals.

In 1954, at the very time that Joseph McCarthy was making some of his broadest and most controversial allegations about spies in the State Department and the Department of Defense, the U.S. Congress decided to focus its energies on amending the Pledge of Allegiance to add the two words "under God" so that it would read that the United States was "one nation under God." Almost fifty years later, when a divided panel on the United States Court of Appeals for the Ninth Circuit held in 2002 that these two words were an unconstitutional establishment of religion, there was an immediate outcry in the United States. Although Congress's powers, which are strictly enumerated in Article I, Section 8, provide no authority for it to make theological findings or declarations, the decision provoked sufficient outrage among conservatives that even most liberal politicians felt obliged to denounce the decision. Many declarations were made in the media and in Congress about the fundamental importance to the country of children reciting the words "one nation under God" at the beginning of the school day. (The inflamed rhetoric makes one wonder how the Republic managed to survive prior to 1954 when the words were inserted.) It is of course telling that those who have decried the supposed decline in America since the 1950s do not trace the decline to the addition of "under God" in the Pledge. Their post hoc, ergo propter hoc argument that is used with great certainty and fanfare with regard to the link between banning official school prayers and the decline of American civilization is not imagined to apply to the insertion of "under God" and the supposed decline of American civilization.

A third issue that seems to provoke public conflict involves displays of religious expression on state property. Although the law is clear that governments may open up public property to all expression (*Capitol Square Review and Advisory Board v. Pinette*, 515 U.S. 753 [1995]), where religious and non-religious opinions may be displayed, the controversy continues where some seek endorsements or sponsorship of some religious expressions (to the exclusion of others). Thus a recurring controversy is whether and under what circumstances a county commission, for example, may erect a monument displaying the Ten Commandments or permit a Christmas display of a crèche.

A fourth issue that continues to stimulate legal controversy in the United States involves prayers before meetings of governmental bodies, including legislatures and commissions. Although the courts generally have accepted as constitutional non-sectarian (or generic) prayers, there is a continuing controversy involving specific invocations to "Jesus Christ" or "our Savior" in meetings of county commissions and state legislatures. While the wish to use governmental bodies for such invocations might seem incomprehensible to Europeans, they are very much a part of the wishes of many in the United States. A related controversy involves private groups sponsoring quasi-official "prayer breakfasts" where political officials are exhorted in highly religious terms to follow the teachings of holy scriptures.

The permissibility of these activities deeply divides Americans along religious and ideological lines. Conservatives typically argue that such activities are fully consistent with both the wishes of a majority of Americans and that the activities are consistent with practices that have been followed in America since its founding (whether in the seventeenth century, the revolutionary period, or the constitutional period). Wherever these issues are successfully advertised to the public as "religion versus non-religion," a majority of the population probably sides with the rhetoric of the conservatives—much to the dismay of the liberals who are frequently unsuccessful in conveying the broader message that the government should not be discriminating among religions and ought not be getting mixed up with theological issues. As a consequence of the conservatives' success in framing the issues, it is probably fair to say that during the last twenty to thirty years there has been an increasing willingness to allow governmental expressions supporting these religious activities.

In addition to the government sponsoring or endorsing religious expressions as described above, there is yet another arena that provokes controversy between liberals and conservatives, although to a lesser extent: state financing of religious and quasi-religious institutions. Traditionally the battleground for this has been state financing of religious schools. This subject has been treated in numerous Supreme Court decisions where the basic, albeit wavering, guideline has been that the state may provide funds to the *parents* of students who attend religious schools but it may not provide direct funding to the religious schools themselves. This has led to a series of cases where some states have proposed "voucher" programs that give parents of non-public school students a specified amount of money each year for their children's school tuition that can be paid to the religious schools. Whereas liberals typically characterize this as a cosmetic change that indirectly transfers funds to religious schools, conservative supporters of the programs emphasize that the money goes to the schools only by means of the voluntary and permissible choice of the parents. This conflict in the United States may be contrasted with a supposedly "secular" France, which freely provides direct state funding for sectarian religious schools. Although in France such financing does evoke some controversy, it is permitted and it continues in spite of any doctrines of *laïcité* that might have been assumed to prohibit it.

Finally, beginning in the administration of President Bill Clinton and growing under President George W. Bush, there have been heightened efforts to provide state funding for faith-based charitable organization that provide social services to the public. Although the state has long provided such funds to organizations that administered the programs in entirely secular ways, the walls have to some extent broken down. At the beginning of his term in 2001, President Bush's proposed "faith-based initiative" legislation was designed to facilitate federal funding of activities of faith-based charitable institutions. But the measures were so controversial that they were not able to be enacted even in the Congress that was controlled by the president's own Republican Party. Avoiding the legislative route that had proved to be unsuccessful, several federal agencies, including most notably the Department of Health and Human Services, the Department of Education, the Department of Housing and Urban Development, and the United States Agency for International Development (USAID) have issued guidelines and have conducted outreach programs that encourage faith-based institutions to seek federal funds to perform services. While the majority of Americans typically do not object to the programs in the way that they are described by their supporters, they become more dubious when they learn that the federally funded programs discriminate on the basis of religion in their hiring and employment practices and that some have used federal funds to promote their particular religious beliefs. Presumably, the federally funded programs will be prevented from discriminating on the basis of the religion of the recipients of aid, but these areas continue to develop.

When considered from an outside perspective, such as from France, the United States would seem to present a peculiar set of obsessions and idiosyncrasies. But what is perhaps of greatest interest is that the most volatile and provocative conflicts pertain to governmental religious expressions and endorsements of religious activities: prayers in schools, posting of the Ten Commandments and religious symbols on state property, and ritual statements about being "one nation under God" and "in God we trust." One of the greatest peculiarities in the conservatives' efforts to promote governmental endorsement of religious expressions and symbols is the inflammatory rhetoric that they use against the liberals who oppose governmental endorsement of religious expressions and symbols. The conservatives frequently accuse liberals of being "hostile" to religion or "demanding that any trace of religion be removed from the public square"—an accusation that is bizarre when seen from a comparative perspective and when understood in light of the widespread support for personal religious expression and activities by liberals in the United States. Indeed, the accusation is often so vituperative and so far from reality that the question arises as to why (some) conservatives believe that liberals' opposition to governmental endorsement of religious expression means that liberals are "hostile" to religion. Would they say that if the U.S. Congress does not pass a resolution endorsing the Roman Pontiff as the leader of the Christian world that this means that the U.S. Congress is thus "hostile" to Christianity, or Catholicism, or to the pope? When conservatives equate "opposition to endorsement of religious expressions" with "hostility to religion," it suggests something far deeper and more personal is involved than a mere disagreement about the proper interpretation of the language of the Constitution.

The explanation for the provocative power of these symbols and the culture clash that they engender is probably found in the competing senses of national identity. The conservatives want to be able to say that their country is religious and that religious and moral teachings are a part of its fabric. If the courts prohibit the erecting of Ten Commandments monuments and prohibit state schools from promoting prayers, this is felt to suggest not that the state is neutral with regard to religion, but that the state is actually hostile to religious expression. For the conservatives, these religious symbols are expressions of who they are— of their identity as citizens of a country that has particularly been blessed by God.

Liberals, on the other hand, reject official endorsements of religious positions for various reasons. They argue that such endorsements necessarily are discriminatory because they improperly divide people on the basis of their religious beliefs rather than their qualities as citizens. The state, they further argue, has no business choosing one religious value system over another. While such arguments are perfectly logical—and perhaps even compelling—this does not necessarily account for the strength of the emotional reactions of the liberals. It would seem that for liberals, as for the conservatives, a good part of the emotional impetus for the struggle is that they too see the struggle as one of identity. For the liberals, *their* country is secular and does not discriminate on the basis of religion and does not endorse religious messages and they too are offended by a state that seems to be wandering away from its proper mission and that has become involved in endorsing and promoting religious beliefs.

Notes

1. In reality the Supreme Court has not explicitly used the "wall" metaphor favorably since *Larkin v. Grendel's Den*, 459 U.S. 116 (1982). The Court does, however, continue to hold on to many of the underlying principles that go under the rubric of "separation of church and state."

2. The Pantheon in Paris, the great and most prestigious monument of French *laïcité*, is in fact a converted church that retains a Christian cross atop its dome and that is filled with religious paintings. For my own prior inquiries comparing France and the United States on this and related themes, see T. Jeremy Gunn, "Religious Freedom and *Laïcité*: A Comparison of the United States and France," *Brigham Young University Law Review* no. 2 (2004): 419-501; and T. Jeremy Gunn and Blandine Chélini-Pont, *Dieu en France et aux États-Unis: Quand les mythes font la loi* (Paris: Berg International, 2005). The most comprehensive French texts to analyze religion and law are: Alain Garay, Emmanuel Tawil, and Xavier Delsol, eds., *Droit des Cultes: Personnes, activités, biens et structures* (Paris: Juris-Service, 2005); and Francis Messner, Pierre-Henri Prélot, and Jean Marie Woehrling, eds., *Traité de droit français des religions* (Paris: Editions du Juris-Classeur, 2003).

3. As another example, although German law requires that all religious groups should be treated "equally" by the state, the laws in fact establish a hierarchy of three different levels of religious organization with varying privileges, rights, and responsibilities for each type. From the perspective of minority or non-mainstream religions, the hierarchical system is blatantly discriminatory. From the perspective of many within the larger and more traditional religions, the laws are not discriminatory and simply reflect the different functions, responsibilities, and historical roles of different types of religious groups. Similarly, while much of German society is proudly "secular," the Constitutional Court decision that provoked the greatest popular hostile reaction was when it held, in the *Bavarian Crucifix Case* (May 16, 1995), that Christian crosses could not be placed in public school classrooms.

4. For several examples, see T. Jeremy Gunn, *A Standard for Repair: The Establishment Clause, Equality, and Natural Rights* (New York: Garland Publishing, 1992), 3-7.

5. The most elaborate "liberal" historical interpretation of the "original meaning" of the religion clauses is found in Justice Hugo Black's opinion in *Everson v. Illinois*, 330 U.S. 1 (1947). Its "conservative" equivalent is the dissenting opinion by Justice Rehnquist in *Wallace v. Jaffree*, 472 U.S. 38 (1985).

6. Following some controversial decisions of the Supreme Court over the meaning of the First Amendment, there have been calls for amendments to the Constitution. For example, with draft amendments to permit school prayer, proponents typically argue that the Supreme Court misinterpreted the correct meaning of the Constitution and that the amendment is designed not to correct the Constitution, but to correct the wayward interpretation of judges and restore the original intent of the founders.

7. The term can roughly be translated into English as "secularism," but the term evokes much more in France than does the English equivalent in the United States.

8. The French Conseil d'État, the highest administrative court in France and the body ultimately responsible for applying the law in French schools, had spoken rather clearly on the constitutional right of Muslim schoolgirls to wear the headscarf (as long as they did not use the headscarf to disrupt the schools) in a series of almost fifty decisions between 1989 and the enactment of the religious attire law in 2004. The Conseil d'État

decisions, however, were almost completely ignored by the parliament and the public in the debates leading to the headscarf ban. Although the 2004 draft law *could have been sent* to the Conseil Constitutionnel for an opinion on whether the headscarf (and other religious symbols) ban complied with French constitutional rights, neither the president, prime minister, nor members of parliament made any such request—even though the Conseil d'Etat had earlier declared that there was a constitutional right involved.

9. Marci A. Hamilton. *God vs. the Gavel: Religion and the Rule of Law* (New York: Cambridge University Press. 2005).

10. There are difficulties in translating the French *ordre public* into English. The literal translation. of course. would be "public order." But in American and English law "public order" is the bulwark against disruptions, social conflict, and disorder. The French notion of *ordre public* is much broader, and suggests something along the line of the public ethos or good public policy. Thus an American looking into "public order" might ask whether wearing a headscarf prompted students to be disruptive in class or provoked fighting, whereas a French person looking at *ordre public* might ask whether the headscarf "fits" with the atmosphere that one would wish to have in secular classroom.

11. The leading case is now *Zelman v. Simmons-Harris.* 536 U.S. 639 (2002).

Chapter Two
Historical and Constitutional Relations between Churches and the State in France

Rémy Schwartz

France is *une République "laïque"* (a "secular" republic). This notion, which structures French thinking, now enjoys a widespread consensus. But the term *laïcité* (secularism) is relatively recent in relation to France's long history. It appeared for the first time in dictionaries only in 1877. Originally, the term *laïc* (layperson) simply denoted a church member who was not a member of the clergy. The word *laïcité* was later created to signify the separation of the religious and the profane, keeping the religious separate from the public. The religious was no longer allowed to interfere with the functioning of political institutions. *Laïcité* therefore signified first and foremost the separation between churches and the state.

Under the monarchy, although France was often referred to as *la fille aînée de l'église* (the church's eldest daughter), there were political conflicts with the church. The kings of France always affirmed their total independence from the Vatican, sometimes to the point of allying during wars with Protestant princes or with the Ottoman Empire against Catholic states. French kings even imposed their control over the French church—and Napoléon strengthened that control. Thus the temporal had always asserted its independence over the spiritual, but *laïcité* went beyond that. It also meant asserting the independence of society in the face of the Catholic Church. The church would no longer be allowed to exert an influence over personal choices or over the development of society. Citizens

15

would decide their future themselves. Secularism was conceived as a way of ensuring the freedom of all citizens in their personal choices. In the 1880s, the Republic secularized its schools, removing the Catholic Church from them. Then came the major law of December 9, 1905, which ensured the *laïcité* of French society. Firstly, this law affirmed freedom of conscience. Then it set forth the principle of the separation of church and state and went on to ensure that all would be free to express their beliefs. These principles have been applied during the course of the past century by the nation's judicial system, primarily by administrative courts. Under the system of French jurisdiction, ultimate juridical authority is divided between the Cour de Cassation (Final Court of Appeal) in matters of civil and criminal law on the one hand and on the other, the Conseil d'Etat (Council of State) in matters relating to administrative courts, relations between individuals and the state, and relations between different arms of the state. The rules set out by the law of December 9, 1905, defining French *laïcité*, established the framework for relations between the state and religions, and this framework was interpreted essentially by the Council of State, the supreme court of French *laïcité*. It is therefore through its jurisprudence that I will examine relations between the state and religions in "secular" France.

Complete Freedom of Conscience

The law of December 9, 1905, separated church and state. But before that it affirmed: "The Republic assures freedom of conscience" (article 1). Never again would there be an official or recognized religion imposing its views and its choices on French society as a whole. The state does not recognize "a" religion; rather, it recognizes them all. Everyone is free not to believe, or to believe, in the religion of his or her choice. The individual is totally free. He defines himself by himself and by his choices, and not by a declared or supposed allegiance to a religion. Hand in hand with this total liberty comes the absence of any official definition of religions or institutions of worship. These are placed in a situation of theoretical equality. In law, no form of worship can benefit from more rights than any other. Everyone is free to believe in the religion of their choice, and all religions are theoretically of equal value. The courts have drawn the consequences of this leveling of values and of the universalism of freedom of conscience. When confronted with new religions or with religions newly implanted in France, they have reaffirmed the equality of all religions under the law.

For a long time, the question of defining a religion was not posed. Religions tracing their origins back to the Bible were present in France and in the colonies. The need to define religions is recent, linked to the arrival in France of religions that had not, up to this point, been present in France, or to the emergence of new Christian churches. In particular, Jehovah's Witnesses and the followers of Krishna led to legal rulings on this question.

In outlining a definition of religion, the Council of State based itself on the notion of doctrine. A religion was defined in terms of a belief in a divinity practiced by a community through collective ceremonies. "Associations claiming the status of associations for religious worship must have the practicing of a religion as their sole purpose, that is to say . . . the exercising, by persons joined by the same religious beliefs, of certain rituals or certain beliefs."[1] This is the reason why a Union of Atheists, which considers God to be a myth, cannot claim to be a religion.[2]

Jehovah's Witnesses now benefit from recognition as a religion, though initially the Council of State had considered that the activities of one of their associations, taken as a whole, could not be classified as constituting a solely religious association. This suggested that its activities included some of a religious nature but did not consist exclusively of those.[3] But later the Council of State recognized an administrative court appeal ruling according to which an association of Jehovah's Witnesses was a practicing religion and that in view of this it was exempt from property tax.[4]

The followers of Krishna also benefited from recognition as a religion, provided they joined together as a community to practice, through ceremonies, a belief in a divinity.[5]

Thus every religion, provided it meets the shared definition of a community of believers worshiping a divinity through celebrations or rituals, is "recognized" under the law. This does not imply any value judgment here. Any religion, that is to say any group of worshipers meeting the general definition given above, is therefore entitled to claim the status of an *association cultuelle* (association for religion worship), thereby gaining the right to certain tax advantages, including exemption from property taxes on buildings open to the public, the possibility of receiving donations and bequests without restriction, the possibility for donors to benefit from tax deductions equal to 50 percent of donations up to a limit of 10 percent of taxable income for individuals and 3.25 percent of turnover for companies. The restrictions are that, firstly, an association for religious worship must exclusively have the practicing of religion as its sole purpose in order to benefit from this status;[6] secondly, the association must not carry out activities contrary to public order.[7] Thus an association whose founder had been the subject of a number of criminal prosecutions and which had close links with other associations convicted of serious violations of urban regulations was refused the status of an association for religious worship on the grounds of public order violations.[8]

This universally valid freedom of conscience has been accompanied by a separation between the churches and the state.

The Separation of Church and State

This separation, essentially between the Catholic religion (which was hegemonic in 1905) and the state in the sense of all public bodies (the central state and local authorities) manifested itself in a refusal to subsidize any religion and in the absolute neutrality of the state.

The Absence of Subsidies for Religions

Article 2 of the law of December 9, 1905, prohibits all subsidies for religions: "The Republic does not recognize, pay for or subsidize any religion." This prohibition had contentious implications. But at the same time, the state and local authorities were given responsibility for the maintenance of cathedrals and churches, whose exclusive use for acts of religious worship was protected by the law.

The Banning of Public Financing for Associations of Religious Worship

An association for religious worship, in the sense of the 1905 law, must have as its sole objective the practicing of religion, that is, the construction, purchase, or renting of a place of worship or the support or training of ministers of the religion. An association not having this as its objective is excluded from the provisions of the 1905 law. The recognition of the religious nature of an association is therefore dependent on the recognition of the existence of a religion and on the condition that the practicing of this religion is its sole purpose.[9]

Courts take into account not only the statutory purpose of the association, but also the reality of its activities, which could lead to it being denied the status of an association for religious worship. An association for religious worship that also engages in other activities cannot be recognized as a religious association in the sense of the December 9, 1905, law.[10] It must be remembered, as has already been indicated, that an association whose activities disrupt public order cannot be granted the status of a religious association.[11]

An association for religious worship, thus defined, cannot receive public funds, and a "mixed" association that has both cultural and religious activities cannot benefit from the status of the 1905 law and cannot receive public funding. And even if the association does not have religious status under the terms of the 1905 law, it cannot receive public subsidies if it engages in religious activities.[12] These aspects of jurisprudence therefore encourage a clear distinction between, on the one hand, associations for religious worship whose purpose is religious, and on the other hand, other associations which can receive public funds provided they do not engage in any form of religious activity.

We can see, on this point, the jurisprudence is quite recent. There is no doubt that the question of the public financing of religious activities did not arise for a considerable period of time. The prohibition of this was strictly respected.

The arrival in France of religions that had not, up to that point, been present, or that had had only had a minor presence, led to these issues being brought before the courts.

The Management of Places of Worship

The state and local authorities do not directly finance religions, but they contribute indirectly to their financing by maintaining places of worship built prior to the 1905 law. In contrast to the question of subsidies for religious associations, which has only recently been at issue, the question of the management of religious buildings arose immediately.

In the absence of recognized associations for religious worship, churches and their contents became the property of local authorities. Churches are thus a part of the public domain belonging to local authorities.[13] Those authorities must ensure that the buildings are used solely for religious purposes, place them at the disposal of believers, and cover the financial costs of their upkeep.[14] The public authorities pay these costs without having any right to interfere in what takes place within these buildings. The use of churches belongs to priests who alone control what takes place within them,[15] except in cases of disruption to public order that could lead to the intervention of the competent police authority.

Places of worship constructed after 1905 are private buildings, constructed through private funds. Although they belong neither to the state nor to local authorities, subsidies can be paid to religious associations to support the maintenance of buildings that they own and use for religious worship. Privately owned places of worship can, therefore, be maintained by public funding in the same way as publicly owned places of worship.

State Neutrality

Strict Neutrality on the Part of Public Officials

Public service must be absolutely neutral. It cannot give the impression of favoring any particular conviction or philosophical orientation, and must treat all users equally, whatever their convictions may be. The service cannot give the appearance of tending to favor some and not others. For example, religious emblems such as a crucifix cannot be displayed in the interior of a public building except for those buildings dedicated to religious or sepulchral purposes.[16]

For this reason neutrality is strictly imposed upon public officials. They cannot, through their behavior or through a display of beliefs, leave users in any doubt over the neutrality of their service. Neutrality in the form of respect of *laïcité* is important for entry into public service and throughout the careers of public servants.

With regard to entry into service, very early on the Council of State confirmed the refusal to admit priests into public service, since through their behavior they were deemed unfit to perform the functions for which they were applying.[17] It is true that this jurisprudence was made during a period that has now gone, during which priests were obliged to wear priestly clothes, which was in itself incompatible with the neutrality of the exercising of public functions. But if, for example, the simple fact of having studied in a religious establishment did not legally permit him to be refused employment as a teacher,[18] it would still be possible, in principle, to refuse the admittance of an individual to a public position if he had, through his previous personal or political behavior, shown an incapacity to perform the functions that were required.[19] I am aware of no new jurisprudence since the end of the Second World War refusing to admit persons into public employment due to their religious convictions and/or expressions of them. But we cannot exclude such a possibility in the event of extremist religious behavior showing an incapacity to perform public functions with due respect for republican neutrality.

In terms of career path, in an opinion published on May 3, 2000, the Council of State underlined the strict neutrality which public officials must respect.[20] Whether they are in contact with service users or not, officials are not allowed to express their religious convictions or wear any religious symbols when carrying out their functions.

Respect for the Freedom of Conscience of Public Officials

Outside of their official duties, public officials are free to act as they wish provided they do not behave or express themselves in ways which could have repercussions on the exercising of their functions. This is where their duty to discretion comes into play. The more officials rise within the administrative hierarchy, the greater the duty of discretion that is imposed upon them.

There have been few court cases over measures taken by the administration due to the religious expression of public officials outside of their official duties. One must go back to May 3, 1950, to find a Council of State decision relating to a measure taken against a public official due to their religious convictions. In a ruling on Mlle Jamet, the Council of State cancelled the disciplinary action taken by an academic inspector against a temporary teacher who had been dismissed solely on the grounds that "she frequented, during her free time, a group of a religious nature."[21] The woman involved had never infringed the neutrality of service in the exercise of her functions.

Since then, no further court cases have been brought against public officials due to the expression of their religious beliefs outside the exercise of their functions. Freedom of religious expression, which is constitutionally protected, has not been challenged by the administration on account of off-duty behavior. However, one cannot exclude the possibility of extremist religious behavior by a public official while off duty having repercussions for public service. If the duty to behave discreetly were neglected, this could lead to disciplinary action or even dismissal.

Allowing Free Expression to Everyone

The December 9, 1905, law separates church and state in order to ensure freedom of thought and of conscience: "The Republic assures freedom of conscience. It guarantees freedom of religious worship" (article 1). The neutral state must, therefore, be attentive to everyone's right to religious expression in order to facilitate this. But we need to distinguish between freedom of expression in public spaces and the rights enjoyed by users of public services.

Following the December 9, 1905, law, administrative courts operated on the principle of proportionality between the necessities of public order and respect for freedom of religious expression. In this respect, public authorities obviously have no right to intervene in private spaces. In churches, the clergyman in charge has sole authority for "maintaining religious order" except in cases of disruptions to public order necessitating the intervention of the competent police authority.[22] Problems may arise from religious activities on public highways or in public spaces more broadly. These may take the form of processions or the ringing of bells, which have been addressed according to the principle of proportionality.

Measures banning external activities—traditional processions, or ceremonies of a religious nature relating to the dead—expressed in general terms and not motivated by public order needs, were of course overturned.[23] Even expressed in non-general terms, banning orders against ceremonies conforming to local traditions were overturned provided they were not required on the grounds of public order.[24] Similarly, bans motivated by policing considerations were cancelled, for example, with reference to public highways, if they applied only to religious manifestations.[25] And traditional processions could only be banned in cases where the risk to public order was of such gravity that the mayor would be unable to maintain order with the police forces normally at his disposal.[26] Conversely, bans have been approved on public order grounds in the case of exceptional processions not founded on local traditions.[27] But if there was no danger to public order, the banning of ceremonies that did not conform to local traditions was overturned.[28]

The ringing of bells has also been dealt with by local regulations. The need to regulate bell ringing through local bylaws, in order to assure *la tranquillité publique* (public calm), was recognized very early on,[29] notably when this regulation conformed with existing local practices.[30] But the courts overturned regulations that would have abolished the ringing of bells for religious services, thereby infringing freedom of religious expression,[31] or where there was no public order necessity.[32] In accordance with their duties, the courts have validated regulations on bellringing when these do not damage freedom of religious worship[33] while overturning regulations judged to be too restrictive in relation to public order requirements.[34]

Court cases of this kind were relatively short-lived, demonstrating the decline, and then the disappearance, of conflicts relating to exterior displays of religious worship. Today, churches and the public authorities find it easy to reconcile religious demonstrations in public spaces (processions, open air ceremonies, ritual slaughterings unique to the Islamic religion, and so forth) with respect to public order without any problems. There are virtually no remaining points of contention in this respect in France.

The situation regarding religious expression in public services is just the opposite. Except for some cases relating to the creation of chaplainships, there were initially no conflicts between public service users and providers over religious expression. Users seem to have rigorously respected the neutrality of public services and the strict imperatives associated with *laïcité*. Conflicts arose more recently at the end of the 1980s.

For public services that users interact with for relatively brief periods of time, such as public transport or the postal service, no particular requirements have been imposed on users. Difficulties have arisen in public services that bring together users of diverse natures over sustained time periods, requiring them to live together—essentially the army, teaching establishments, hospitals, and prisons. The difficulties here have been twofold.

Firstly, when users of these services use them over a sustained period of time, they may encounter difficulties in exercising their religious freedom. Boarding school pupils, hospital patients, or prisoners could find themselves deprived of their religious liberty. For this reason the 1905 law made an exception to the separation of church and state: the law provided for the state to cover the costs of a public service for religious worship in the form of chaplains who are public officials.[35] Thus the state can legally take any measures aiming at ensuring freedom of worship, such as allowing the construction of places of worship within student dorms.[36] Beyond the question of chaplains, public services must permit their users to respect religious festivals. In the domain of national education, the service must therefore allow students to participate in large traditional festivals, but cannot systematically excuse a student from attending class on a given day if this would prevent the accomplishment of tasks inherent in his or her studies.[37]

Secondly, difficulties may arise from the cohabitation of very diverse populations: believers and non-believers, Catholics, Protestants, Jews, or Muslims. In reality, up to the beginning of the 1980s, the question of the religious expression of users of public services (except for the matter of chaplains) did not arise. The question appeared, for teaching establishments, with the wearing of religious symbols by students at the end of the 1980s. The wearing of religious symbols by Muslim girls was completely new and resulted from the religious and political fallout of the Islamic Revolution in Iran. When asked by the government to pronounce on this matter, the Council of State ruled that as the law stood, notably with reference to France's international engagements, but more particularly with reference to the framework education law of July 10, 1989, granting freedom of expression to pupils in school establishments, it was not possible to place a blanket ban on the wearing of all religious symbols by pupils.[38] This opinion was confirmed in the overturning of expulsion orders against pupils that had been based exclusively on the wearing of religious symbols, independently of the conditions surrounding each case.[39] However, the 1989 opinion and the rulings that followed strongly restricted this right in order to ensure the normal functioning of the public educational service, and to avoid conflicts between pupils. Commentators at the time neglected to clarify for the public the firmness of this jurisprudence. Actions could be taken against pupils if a number of conditions posed were not fulfilled:

> in [public] school establishments, the wearing by pupils of symbols by which they intend to display their belonging to a religion is not, in itself, incompatible with the principle of *laïcité* to the extent that it constitutes the exercise of freedom of religious expression and freedom to display religious beliefs, but this liberty does not permit pupils to wear symbols of religious belonging which, by their nature, by the conditions in which they are worn, individually or collectively, or by their ostentatious [*ostentatoire*] or assertive nature, would constitute an act of pressure, provocation, proselytism or propaganda, would prejudice the dignity or freedom of the pupil or other members of the educational community, would compromise their health or security, would disrupt the running teaching activities or the educational role of teachers, or would disrupt order in the establishment or the normal functioning of public service."[40]

In this way, exclusion orders were confirmed against pupils who refused to stop wearing their veil during physical education or technology lessons, with the court ruling that appropriate clothing was necessary for these lessons.[41] Also confirmed were court orders ruling against pupils who had held demonstrations in teaching establishments and seriously disrupted their normal functioning, even if such demonstrations had as their purpose the claiming of the right to express their beliefs.[42] Finally, the court ruled against pupils who had infringed attendance rules by refusing to go to gymnastics classes.[43]

But this jurisprudence, based on the statutes then in force, was insufficient in the face of the problems arising in teaching establishments and the need to respect individual freedom. The case-by-case treatment implied by this jurisprudence was, in practice, extremely difficult. The line between an "ostensible," proselytizing symbol, and legally admissible symbols was unclear. And, concretely, school heads were placed in a situation of permanent discussion and conflict. In addition, too many pressures were being exerted on young girls to force them to wear religious symbols in violation of their personal freedom. Because the wearing of religious symbols was not, in itself, forbidden, groups—most often groups of young men—imposed their vision of the world and of women upon young girls. Following the report of the "Commission to consider the future of *laïcité*" in 2003, parliament therefore modified the framework education law in order to ban the wearing of all ostensible symbols, that is, all religious symbols except for those worn "discreetly" such as medallions and pendants which are worn not to be seen, but as the symbol of a personal link with a religion. The personal freedom of girls was thus assured. Concordant evidence supports this: women's defense associations were warmly thanked by girls who were now free not to wear the veil in school.

Conclusion

It is apparent that the problematic that concerns us has evolved over the course of the last century. The questions that arose frequently and with intensity at the start of the twentieth century are no longer the subject of legal arguments. Conversely, new conflicts over *laïcité* have led to new forms of jurisprudence. The situation has changed with the arrival in France of new religions or new forms of religious practices, changes in individual behavior, and an upsurge of politico-religious demands. But the principles of the law of December 9, 1905, have remained unchanged, and jurisprudence still assures the scrupulous respect of these principles. The courts have remained faithful to the careful balance struck in law, constantly ensuring public order and the provision of public services while at the same time ensuring that every one is free to exercise freedom of worship peacefully. This balance remains essential today. France remains the "eldest daughter of the Catholic Church," welcomes dynamic Protestant churches, and has the largest Jewish and Muslim communities in Europe. Living together is necessary in society and in public services, and when conflicts appear, when individual liberties are threatened, it is by firm rules and prohibitions that freedom is ensured. Against the law of the jungle, the law of the strongest, democracies have the rule of law: at certain moments it is necessary to introduce a ban, which is obviously limited in its scope, to ensure the liberty of everyone, and most notably of the youngest and weakest.

Translated by Matthew A. Kemp and Alec G. Hargreaves

Notes

1. Conseil d'Etat (CE), October 24, 1997, Local Association for Worship of Jehovah's Witnesses of Riom.

2. CE, June 17, 1988, Union of Atheists.

3. CE, February 1, 1985, Christian Association of Jehovah's Witnesses.

4. CE, January 13, 1993, Budget Minister v. Christian Congregation of Jehovah's Witnesses of Puy.

5. CE, May 14, 1982, International Association for the Conscience of Krishna.

6. CE, October 9, 1992, District of Saint-Louis v. Association Siva Soupramanien de Saint-Louis.

7. CE, October 24, 1997, Local Association for Worship of Jehovah's Witnesses of Riom; and CE, June 23, 2000, Minister of Finance and Industry.

8. CE, April 28, 2004, Association of the Triumphant Vajra.

9. CE, October 24, 1997, Local Association for Worship of Jehovah's Witnesses of Riom; and CE, October 29, 1990, Religious Association of the Armenian Apostolic Church of Paris.

10. CE, January 21, 1983, Fraternity of Servants of the New World Association, which also engaged in publishing and related activities in respect of its doctrines; CE opinion, November 14, 1989; and CE, October 24, 1997, Local Association for Worship

of Jehovah's Witnesses of Riom.

11. CE, October 24, 1997, Local Association for Worship of Jehovah's Witnesses of Riom; and CE, April 28, 2004, Association of the Triumphant Varja.

12. CE, October 9, 1992, District of Saint-Louis v. Association "Siva Souprama-nien" de Saint-Louis.

13. CE, June 10, 1921, Commune of Montségur.

14. For example, CE, June 20, 1913, Father Arnould; or CE, February 17, 1932, District of Barran.

15. CE, February 24, 1912, Father Saralongue; and CE, April 11, 1913, Father Somme.

16. Administrative Appeals Court of Nancy, February 4, 1999, Civic Association Joue Langueur, and others.

17. CE, May 10, 1912, Father Bouteyre.

18. CE, July 25, 1939, Mme Beis.

19. CE, December 11, 1987, Interior Minister v. Paterna; or CE, January 27, 1992, Interior Minister v. Castellan.

20. CE, May 3, 2000, Mlle Marteaux.

21. CE, May 3, 1950, Mlle Jamet.

22. CE, May 24, 1938, Father Touron.

23. CE, January 27, 1911, Father Chalmaudron and others; CE, November 22, 1912, Father Plisson; CE, May 1, 1914, Father Didier; CE, June 16, 1926, Rochette and others; CE, November 17, 1926, Claverie; CE, November 23, 1932, Father Richob; and CE, December 12, 1934, Father Chatel.

24. CE, December 22, 1928, Father Desmarest; and CE, July 26, 1932, Father Vroman.

25. CE, December 4, 1925, Charton; and CE, August 3, 1927, Town of Quincy.

26. CE, January 31, 1934, Rennus; and CE, July 2, 1947, Cuiller.

27. CE, May 5, 1928, Father Rerolle.

28. CE, March 5, 1948, Independent Christian Youth.

29. CE, August 5, 1908, Leclercq and Gruson; and CE, July 7, 1912, Father Gary.

30. CE, March 10, 1911, Tival.

31. CE, August 5, 1908, Morel; CE, July 8, 1910, Father Carlin; and CE, January 12, 1923, Sieur, Lebrun, priest of Harancourt.

32. CE, January 13, 1911, Father Savarin.

33. CE, November 25, 1925, Father Le Dain.

34. CE, October 28, 1931, Penanduer; and CE, May 24, 1938, Father Touron.

35. On the public service status of chaplains nominated and revoked on the recommendation of religious authorities, see CE, October 17, 1980, Pont; CE, October 9, 1981, Beherec; CE, May 27, 1994, Bourges; and CE, May 7, 1997, Minister of justice v. Dodu.

36. CE, March 7, 1969, City of Lille.

37. CE, April 14, 1995, Koen; and CE, April 14, 1995, Central Consistory of Israelites in France.

38. CE opinion, November 27, 1989.

39. CE, November 2, 1992, Mr. and Mrs. Kerhouaa; CE, March 14, 1994, Ms. Yilmaz; and CE, May 20, 1996, Minister of education v. Ali.

40. CE opinion, November 27, 1989.

41. CE, March 10, 1995, Mr. and Mrs. Aoukili; CE, October 20, 1999, Minister of National Education, Research and Technology v. Mr. and Mrs. Ait Ahmad

42. CE, November 27, 1996, North Islamic League and Mr. and Mrs. Chabou.

43. CE, November 27, 1996, Mr. and Mrs. Wissaadane and Mr. and Mrs. Chedouane.

Part II: Protestantism

Chapter Three
Religious Freedom and American Protestantism

David Little

This is a big subject that wants limits. I shall meet this constraint by putting forth a general thesis, illustrating it historically with reference to the Reformed tradition in America, which is the part of American Protestantism I know best, and giving particular attention to the colonial period because (in my opinion) of its special importance. In conclusion, I shall then reflect on the thesis, as exemplified in the light of some recent American legal developments in the field of religious freedom.

The general thesis is this: *There is a deep tension, if not an outright conflict, over attitudes toward religious freedom that lies at the heart of the Reformed tradition, and that has been highly influential on the course and character of American Protestantism. Furthermore, some of the divergent beliefs about religious freedom articulated during colonial times, and variously influential thereafter, are of the profoundest importance for contemporary controversies.*

Specifically, the Reformed tradition—that part of European Protestantism deriving principally from John Calvin (1509-64), the Genevan reformer—presupposes, on the one hand, an essential distinction between an "internal forum" of conscience and an "external forum" of civil authority, between a "law of the spirit" and a "law of the sword," and ascribes a certain priority to the "internal" or "spiritual" aspects of human experience. In fact, such an evaluative distinction implies the idea of the "sovereignty of conscience," according to which the jurisdiction of the state is firmly limited in deference to what is taken to be a fundamental right to the free exercise of conscience in religious belief and practice.

On the other hand, the same tradition also assumes an inseparable connection between the civil order and "proper" religious belief and practice, and therefore affirms that the state has a strong interest in and responsibility for defining and enforcing what is regarded as proper religious belief and practice.

The story of the Reformed tradition in America, as well as, I believe, the story of much of the rest of American Protestantism, is a chronicle, right up to the present, of the continuing competition between these two conflicting lines of thought.

Origins

From the beginning, the idea of conscience, and its freedom, was important to Christians, particularly as expressed in the Pauline literature. The influential notion of conscience as a private, internal tribunal, adjudicating the probity of an individual's religious and moral beliefs and practices, is referred to in Romans 2:14-15. The passage speaks of non-Jews possessing "by nature" a moral law "written on their hearts," to which their "conscience" (*syneidesis*) "bears witness," and in relation to which their "conflicting thoughts accuse or perhaps excuse them . . . ," all under the authority of God who "judges the secrets of everyone." The idea that this moral law is universal, according to which "the whole world may be held accountable," is affirmed in Romans 3:19-20. In the context of a discussion in 1 Corinthians about tolerating conscientious differences, there is the additional suggestion that the conscience is fundamentally free, since one person's conscience cannot control anyone else's.[1]

Furthermore, given that God is understood to be the ultimate judge of conscience, the conviction arises in early Christian experience that an important part of the freedom of conscience is its independence from and superiority to human judgments, including those of the civil authority. Some have even interpreted Paul's words in Romans 13:5, enjoining political obedience "for the sake of conscience," to imply a right to stand in judgment concerning the behavior of governments, particularly in the light of his preceding claim that "rulers are not a terror to good conduct, but to bad" (Rom. 13:3).

Classical texts used to support what later came to be known as the doctrine of the "sovereignty of conscience" are Acts 5:29—"We must obey God rather than human beings," and Mark 12:17—"Render unto Caesar the things that are Caesar's, and to God the things that are God's."

John Calvin and his Reformed followers made a great deal of the doctrine of the sovereignty of conscience, as hinted at in the New Testament, even if they were far from united in their understanding of it. Calvin himself caused the original problem by saying what appeared to be contradictory things on the subject. On the one side, he proclaimed the freedom of conscience and the separa-

tion of the "spiritual power" and the "power of the sword," notions linked in his
mind to a critical distinction between two forums or tribunals, the "internal" or
conscience, and the "external" or civil authority.[2] On occasion, Calvin spoke of
these as "two worlds," over which different kings and different laws have authority, requiring that they "always be examined separately."[3] In addition, he
strongly supported the idea of the superiority of conscience. Even under the
conditions of human sin and ignorance, "this tiny little spark of light remained"
recognizing "conscience to be higher than all human judgments."[4] "[H]uman
laws," he added, "whether made by magistrate or church, even though they have
to be observed (I speak of good and just laws [!]), still do not of themselves bind
conscience."[5]

On the other side, Calvin proceeded, without batting an eye, to veer sharply
in the opposite direction. Speaking both as a theologian and as a community
organizer frustrated with widespread insubordination and religious dissent, he
assigned to the Genevan authorities the right to impose on the unruly masses
"the outward worship of God" and "sound doctrine of piety and the position of
the church."[6] And then, having declared that the "church does not have the right
of the sword to punish or to compel, not the authority to force, not imprisonment, nor the other punishments, which the magistrate commonly inflicts," he
contrived an arrangement with Genevan officials to use none other than the
"sword, force, and imprisonment" to enforce his doctrines across the city.[7]

Calvin equivocated on yet one other crucial idea, drawn from Paul's allusions, mentioned above, to a universal moral law that applies to all human beings regardless of their religious or ethnic identity or commitments. On the one
hand, he distinguished between two orders of human experience: "higher
things," that is, strictly religious matters referred to in the first table of the Decalogue and the "things of this life," the moral and civil sphere, involving questions of life and death, protection of property, reputation, and certain crucial
institutional responsibilities and obligations that are referred to in the second
table of the Decalogue.[8] Whereas human beings, because of their shortcomings,
are, if left to themselves, incompetent and almost totally dependent on divine
assistance, they nevertheless retain effective, if limited, competence in their
moral and civil dealings because of vestigial access to the universal moral law. It
is, in theory at least, the "things of this life," and not the "higher things" that are
subject, in Calvin's mind, to the jurisdiction of the state, further underscoring
the distinction between the "internal" and "external" forum. Calvin reiterates
this point in his commentary on Romans 13. Because, he says, magistrates are
entrusted to be "guardians of peace and equity," all who desire to preserve the
rights of "every individual," and to "live free from injury," must support the
political order. Above all, he goes on, Paul makes clear that magistrates have
only to do with "that part of the law which refers to human society. There is no
allusion at all here to the first table . . . , which deals with the worship of God."[9]

On the other hand, Calvin appears to forsake these limitations by regularly
endorsing, both in Geneva, and in other settings where Reformed faith took root,

quite extensive forms of the civil enforcement of religion for which Calvinism is notorious.

Colonial America

During most of the seventeenth and eighteenth centuries, American colonial experience was profoundly affected by the tension over attitudes toward religious freedom that we have just outlined.

It all began in 1620s and after as New England was being settled. The competing camps who set up shop on American soil reflected deep divisions already present in England. Prior to and during the English Civil War (1642-48), and then during the commonwealth and protectorates (1649-60), mostly under the leadership of Oliver Cromwell, Puritan descendants of Calvin and others sharply opposed one another over questions of religious liberty and "freedom of conscience," among other things. The idea that Puritans, whether English or American, had the same view on these questions is one of those widespread and stubbornly held convictions that seems impervious to the most unmistakable counterevidence.[10]

On one side of the religious and political leadership of the Massachusetts Bay Colony were John Cotton (1584-1652) and John Winthrop (1588-1649). In keeping with Calvin's "establishmentarian" sentiments, they favored the civil enforcement of religion on the grounds, as Cotton put it, that the civil order's primary task of regulating "the bodies and goods" of citizens ("things of this life," in Calvin's words), could only properly be fulfilled by providing in addition "spiritual helps to their souls" and preventing "such spiritual evils" as might obscure the fact *"that the prosperity of religion among them might advance the prosperity of the civil state."*[11]

It is not that Cotton and Winthrop and their followers had not objected to what they regarded as the violation of their rights to religious freedom in England, or that they rejected in general the idea of freedom of conscience and religion, or due limitations on state authority. It is just that for them there is a crucial difference between "true" or "proper" and "false" or "improper" religion: The "establishment of pure religion, in doctrine, worship and government, according to the word of God, and also the reformation of all corruptions of any of these," directly concerns the promotion of civil peace and welfare. "For if the church and people of God fall away from God, God will visit the city and country with public calamity."[12]

Moreover, it is not that they deny the importance of honoring conscience. In fact, for Cotton the state properly shows its respect by punishing people whose consciences are, by the state's reckoning, misguided. The fundamentals of true religion "are so clear" that a person "cannot but be convinced of the truth of them after two or three admonitions." If, therefore, a person, once exposed to the truth, "still continues obstinate," that person is self-condemned, and if punished, "is not punished for . . . conscience, but for sinning against [it]."[13]

Nor does Cotton reject the idea of an independent moral law that is naturally available to all human beings, regardless of religious disposition. Rather, he, like Calvin, has a highly restricted view of its reliability in practice. When it comes to acting on the moral law, particularly in the public sphere, Cotton and his allies are profoundly skeptical. Such is the depth of human fallibility that it requires extensive political as well as spiritual remedy. Citizens simply cannot be trusted to live up even to their "natural" moral obligations. "Never look for true dealing" from heretics who stand "against the Gospel, and against . . . conscience." "If they deal not truly with God, they will not deal truly with [their fellows]."[14]

The opposing side of Puritan attitudes toward freedom of religion and conscience was memorably represented by Roger Williams (1603-83?), one of the founders in 1635 of the Rhode Island colony, an experiment Sydney Ahlstrom has called "the first commonwealth in modern history to make religious liberty . . . a cardinal principle of its corporate existence and to maintain the separation of church and state on these grounds."[15] Williams, it should be remembered, wound up in Rhode Island in the first place because, with the help of some Indian friends, he escaped there after being officially banished from Massachusetts Bay and condemned to punishment in England.

Williams affirmed an array of offending beliefs, which eventually provoked his expulsion. One was his challenge to the right of the English monarch to allocate colonial land, a conclusion apparently inferred from his belief in the "natural and civil rights and liberties" of all human beings. Since, according to "natural right," Native Americans, and not the king, are the true owners of the lands of the New World, it is from the former alone that land must be acquired.[16] Another (with which Cotton was not altogether unsympathetic) was his claim that the English flag should be shorn of the prominent red cross at its center because, as a religious symbol, its presence serves to confuse civil and spiritual spheres. Related to that was his opposition to public oaths, particularly when imposed on unbelievers, together with his advocating (against Cotton) a very stringent restriction of civil jurisdiction to the "bodies and goods" of human beings, namely, to their "outward state,"[17] and *not* to their spiritual affairs.

These and other highly controversial views all touched various aspects of Williams's radical commitment to the right of "soul liberty," as he called it. Basically, his general position was simply an elaboration and intensification of one side of Calvin's thoughts on religious liberty and freedom of conscience, and an explicit repudiation of the other.[18] He began by assuming Calvin's central distinction between two tribunals, two forums—conscience and civil authority—that are parallel in some ways, though differently administered and enforced; the one by the "law of the spirit" and the other by the "law of the sword."

There are in Williams's mind several grounds on which to draw this distinction. One is clearly religious. He spends considerable time interpreting Christian scripture, and particularly the image and impact of Jesus to prove that authentic

Christianity favors a distinction between spirit and sword. But he also relies on reason and experience. To try to convince a person of the truth of something by threatening injury or imprisonment is to make a mistake about how the mind and spirit work. It is futile, writes Williams, to try "to batter down idolatry, false worship, and heresy" by employing "stocks, whips, prisons, [and] swords" because "civil weapons are improper in this business and never able to effect anything in the soul."[19] Civil efforts to coerce conscience lead either to defiance and thus the probability of extensive bloodshed and suffering, or to hypocrisy, neither of which advances the cause of conscience.

There are various compelling reasons, then, for believing in the existence of an internal forum and its right to freedom: "Only let it be their soul's choice, and no enforcing sword, but what is spiritual in their spiritual causes. . . . I plead [on the part of the civil authority] for impartiality and equal freedom, peace, and safety to [all] consciences and assemblies, unto which the people may as freely go, and this according to each conscience [in keeping of course with the requirements of civil order]."[20]

Again following Calvin, at least in part, Williams invokes the idea of a universal moral law available to all, regardless of religious identity, as the proper basis for protecting the "common rights, peace and safety" of all citizens, which is, he says "work and business, load and burden enough" for political officials without presuming "to pull down, and set up religion, to judge, determine and punish in spiritual controversies."[21] There exist common moral standards that are available to all sorts of people other than Christians, so that "civil places need not be monopolized [by] church members, (who are sometimes not fitted for them), and all other [people] deprived of their natural and civil rights and liberties."[22]

These common and naturally available moral standards place important limits on tolerable religious practices. He holds that civil magistrates are entitled to punish religiously authorized behavior that violates what he took to be the fundamental conditions of public safety and order. For example, he approved of the outlawing of human sacrifice, even though practiced for conscience's sake.

Williams considerably sharpens Calvin's utterance about the restricted function of government, about the focus on temporal social concerns to the exclusion of religious affairs. Williams means it when he writes that although God authorizes civil government in a general way ("the world otherwise would be like the sea, wherein men, like fish, would hunt and devour each other, and the greater devour the less"), particular governments "have no more power than fundamentally lies in the [body of people who appoint them], which power, might or authority is not religious, Christian, etc., but natural, humane and civil."[23] In strong contrast to Calvin's work in Geneva, this was precisely the image of civil government Williams endeavored, with some success, to institute in Rhode Island.

Another striking contrast between Williams and Calvin was the remarkable degree of religious and cultural tolerance that Williams both espoused and implemented. Not only was an amazing diversity of religious groups welcomed and respected in Rhode Island, but Williams, despite his own fervent Christian convictions, resolutely refrained from evangelizing Native Americans because, among other reasons, they mostly lived under a colonial system that denied them genuine freedom in matters of religion and conscience. Based on his commitments to "impartiality and equal freedom," as well as "peace and safety" for all "consciences and assemblies," he attempted to deal honestly and equitably with Native Americans, seeking unsuccessfully to achieve what one historian has called a "respectful relationship" between colonists and Native Americans.[24]

Also worth mentioning in this connection was Williams's extraordinary willingness not only to promote freedom *of* religion, but freedom *from* religion as well. Even atheists and people altogether indifferent or hostile to religion should be equally respected. He considered the objection, undoubtedly widespread at the time, that if the state does not enforce religion, people are likely to drift away from religion and "turn atheistical and irreligious," as he put it. Such an outcome, he concedes, is a risk that must be run; "however it is infinitely better, that the profane and loose be unmasked, than to be muffled up under the veil and hood as of traditional hypocrisy, which turns and dulls the very edge of all conscience either toward God or man."[25] Beyond that, he was fully prepared to grant equal freedom to religions like Judaism, Islam, and Roman Catholicism, so long, of course, as adherents are willing to accept citizenship on Williams's general terms. It is "known by experience," he said that "many thousands" of Muslims, Roman Catholics, and pagans "are in their persons, both as civil and courteous and peaceable in nature, as any of the subjects in the state they live in."[26]

Finally, since there has been considerable misunderstanding of this point, it must be stressed that Williams sought to protect *both* religious organizations and government from abuses caused by enforcing religion. He did not just care about religion.[27] He believed that *neither* religious groups *nor* states function properly so long as one illicitly interferes in the proper activities of the other, and he is passionately concerned about the corruption of the state. He says that it is "against civil justice for the civil state or officers thereof to deal so partially in matters of God, as to permit to some the freedom of their consciences and worship, but to curb and suppress the consciences and souls of all others."[28]

Throughout the eighteenth century, Reformed Protestantism continued to manifest in a dramatic way the deep tension over attitudes toward religious freedom exhibited in the conflicts between Cotton and Williams. For example, the Presbyterians, who, early in the century, became a force to contend with alongside the Congregationalists, Baptists, and others identified with the Reformed tradition, divided over the subject of religious freedom. This was particularly true in Virginia where they became prominent as the result of extensive Scotch-Irish immigration.

The issue was sharpened with the passage in 1786 of Thomas Jefferson's Statute for Religious Freedom by the Virginia legislature. Its language is remarkable in the light of Williams's ideas. "No man," declares the statute, "shall be compelled to frequent or support any religious worship, place or ministry whatsoever, nor shall be enforced, restrained, molested, or burdened in his body or goods, nor shall otherwise suffer on account of his religious opinions or belief." It continues to state "that all men shall be free to profess, and by argument to maintain, their opinions in matters of religion, and that the same shall in nowise diminish, enlarge, or affect their civil capacities." It further states that "the rights hereby asserted are of the natural rights of mankind," and adds that "it is time enough for the rightful purposes of civil government, for its offices to interfere when principles break out into overt acts against peace and good order." The statute also announces that permitting the magistrate to intrude on matters of religion is to corrupt both religion ("by bribing, with a monopoly of worldly honors and emoluments those who will externally profess and conform to it") and state (by permitting public officials to abuse their office by making their opinions "the rule of judgment, and approve or condemn the sentiments of others only as they shall square or differ" from that rule).[29]

Predictably, there were Virginia Presbyterians who worried about this language. The views of Stephen Stanhope Smith, president of Hampden-Sydney Academy and later of Princeton University, were influential and helped dilute Presbyterian support for the statute. While favoring a diversity of religious confessions, he nevertheless elevated the importance of state-supported public religion on grounds that "religion is necessary to national prosperity," as the title of a characteristic sermon declared. "When a nation has abandoned religion, the firmest basis of civil government is dissolved. Voluptuousness and effeminacy, avarice and prodigality, a restless ambition, dark treacheries, and a universal disregard of justice" are "the natural consequences of a general impiety," and "accumulate every species of misery on a wretched people, forsaken of God, and lost to virtue."[30]

However, by 1785, Virginia Presbyterians were veering away from Smith's position, and joining the Baptists in support of the statute, which depended for its passage on that joint support. Presbyterians shared with Baptists the memories of discrimination and abuse under an Anglican establishment that had prevailed in Virginia until 1786, and a majority of them eventually adopted a position that sounded very close to Roger Williams. A statement on the subject by the Hanover Presbytery called upon legislators to remove "every species of religious, as well as civil bondage." "There is no argument," they went on, "in favor of establishing the Christian religion but what may be pleaded, with equal propriety, for establishing the tenets of Mohammed by those who believe in the Koran. . . . We ask not ecclesiastical establishments for ourselves; neither can we approve of them when granted to others."[31]

In 1789, the Presbyterians went further and substantially revised their traditional approach to religious freedom, which dated back to the Westminster Confession of 1647. Under the leadership of John Witherspoon, president of Princeton University and signatory to the Declaration of Independence, the church now proclaimed that "God alone is Lord of the conscience," and, therefore, "the rights of private judgment in all matters that regard religion" are "universal and inalienable." Moreover, the new statement held that the civil magistrate had no authority to initiate action against heresy, to convene a church synod, or "in the least [to] interfere in matters of faith. Its only responsibility was to protect all religious groups from "molestation," presumably in "outward" matters.[32]

Witherspoon was an interesting case; despite his strong endorsement of the freedom of conscience and religious pluralism, he also retained something of the contrasting opinion of Stephen Stanhope Smith to the effect that national prosperity and survival depended on "the knowledge of God and his truths." It is, he said, "in the man of piety and inward principle, that we may expect to find the uncorrupted patriot, the useful citizen, and the invincible soldier,"[33] nor did he doubt that the government might properly "make public provision for the public worship of God, in such manner as is agreeable to the great body of society," all the while tolerating dissenters.[34] On balance, he seemed to hold out for some kind of "multiple establishment" whereby the state might provide financial and other forms of aid on an impartial basis. The tension characteristic of Reformed Protestantism is sometimes held together within the same individual.

The fact that the more liberal Presbyterians, along with other religious people, were committed to and helped to pass Jefferson's Statute for Religious Freedom raises the question of the connection between religion and the thought of Thomas Jefferson. In fact, that connection is a contested matter. Jefferson was, of course, militantly heterodox in his religious views, calling himself a Unitarian, and adhering to views close to Deism. He had some very harsh things to say about more conventional Christians, especially Presbyterians, whose doctrine of predestination and other beliefs he gleefully lampooned. This has led some to the conclusion that there is no connection whatsoever, and that Jefferson got all his ideas on subjects like religious freedom from anti-religious Enlightenment sources, especially in France.

This opinion, however, is mistaken. It is abundantly clear that whatever the influence of French thinkers like Voltaire and Diderot, the major part of Jefferson's convictions on religious freedom were directly shaped by John Locke, and while, in turn, Jefferson never seems to have read Williams, "Locke almost certainly did," a fact with important consequences. Locke was able to make Williams's rambling style accessible to people like Jefferson.[35]

There are, to be sure, differences among Williams, Locke, and Jefferson; however, the similarities are striking indeed. The most fundamental, of course, is the belief, as Locke put it, "that liberty of conscience is every man's natural right, equally belonging to dissenters as to themselves; and that nobody ought to be compelled in matters of religion either by law or force."[36] There is also the common emphasis on the distinction between what Locke calls "the outward and inward court," or "the magistrate and conscience," with the magistrate's jurisdiction being confined to the "civil interest," or what the Puritans called, "bodies and goods": "life, liberty, health and indolency of the body [by which Locke meant, freedom from arbitrarily inflicted pain]; and the possession of outward things, such as money, lands, houses, furniture, and the like."[37]

As we saw, similar sentiments are found in the Statute for Religious Freedom, and Jefferson reiterated those sentiments elsewhere with characteristic eloquence: "Our rulers can have no authority over such natural rights, only as we have submitted to them. The rights of conscience we never submitted, we could not submit. We are answerable for them to our God." Accordingly, the "legitimate powers of government extend to such acts only as are injurious to others. But it [should do] me no injury for my neighbor to say there are twenty gods, or no God. It neither picks my pocket nor breaks my leg."[38]

This doctrine of the sovereignty of conscience, so central to Jefferson's thinking, is forcefully supplemented in the writings of James Madison. In his famous "Memorial and Remonstrance," published in 1785 in defense of Jefferson's Statute for Religious Freedom, Madison puts the doctrine with unforgettable clarity: "Man's duty to his Creator is precedent both in order of time and degree of obligation to the claims of civil society." Moreover, in the subsequent debates in 1789 over the proposed Bill of Rights, Madison's suggested draft of the First Amendment included the following wording: "nor shall the full and equal rights of conscience be in any manner, or on any pretext, infringed."[39]

Of interest, too, is Jefferson's allusion, reminiscent of Williams and (with some reservations) of Locke, to a "natural" moral law independent of religious identity or affiliation: "Some have made the love of God the foundation of morality. . . . [But] if we did a good act merely from the love of God and a belief that it is pleasing to him, whence arises the morality of the Atheist[s]? . . . Their virtue must have some other foundation."[40] This idea lies behind Jefferson's famous statement in the Statute on Religious Freedom that "our civil rights have no dependence on our religious opinions."[41]

Locke's view on these questions is somewhat different from Williams and Jefferson. In contrast to them, he tightened the connection between religion and civic virtue by refusing to tolerate atheists because he thought they could not be trusted to keep God's commands, as well as Muslims and Catholics, because, in his opinion, they were inexorably programmed to impose their religion on everyone. Unlike Williams and Jefferson, he thereby suggests that morality is to an important extent not independent of religion, but rather derives directly from it. To hold a certain religious view predetermines how one will perform morally.

At the same time, Locke is not altogether consistent on these matters, and occasionally affirms a view of natural law more in keeping with Williams and Jefferson.[42] It is a view the implications of which might lead to quite different conclusions concerning the tolerability of atheists, Muslims, and Catholics. Rather than starting with official religious doctrine and opinion, one would be obliged to consult the actual conscientious judgments and practices of individuals on a case-by-case basis in order to determine whether or not they "are in their persons," as Williams said, "as civil, courteous and peaceable in nature as any of the subjects in the state they live in."[43] How the connections among religion, morality, and civil order are worked out, and who, accordingly, gets tolerated and who does not, then becomes a matter, not of dogma and declarations, but of individual conscience.

The Eclipse of Conscience: The "Protestant Establishment" of the Nineteenth and Early Twentieth Centuries

Toward the end of the eighteenth century, Timothy Dwight (1752-1817) exhorted the young, struggling American republic "to glory arise" as "queen of the world" and "child of the skies." "Thy genius commands thee; with rapture behold," he continued, "while ages on ages thy splendors unfold." Dwight's encomium epitomized the dominating public image of the new country throughout the nineteenth and well into the twentieth century. Few had either the inclination or the courage to express doubt that "the Star-Spangled Banner waved over the Lord's Chosen Nation." During this period, the idea of "America as a beacon on a hill and an exemplar for the world became a constituent element in historical interpretations of the nation's religious life."[44]

Up to the Civil War, Protestant, and principally Reformed, Christianity became the basis for thinking of America as a "Righteous Empire," in the subtitle of one of historian Martin Marty's best-known books.[45] That wing of Calvinism favoring the civil indispensability of religion and the desirability of governmental regulation gained considerable ground.

> State guarantees of liberty of conscience or the free exercise of religion did not mean that non-Protestants were granted civil rights equal to those enjoyed by Protestants, nor did those guarantees grant license to nonbelievers to cavil against religion. In this largely Protestant society, public expressions of faith, or lack of religious faith, remained subject to the legal order. Several issues highlighting the role of religion in the public order arose in antebellum America: the requirements of oathtaking. [both] to hold public office and to testify in the courtroom; the legitimacy of blasphemy prosecutions; and laws mandating Sunday as a day of rest. All these issues were related to the question whether Christianity was part of the common law.[46]

In 1811, a resident of New York named Ruggles was convicted of uttering in public "these false, feigned, scandalous, malicious, wicked and blasphemous words, to wit, 'Jesus Christ was a bastard and his mother must be a whore.'"[47] The judge in his supporting opinion asserts that the "maliciously reviling" of Christianity is an offense "punishable at common law . . . because it tends to corrupt the morals of the people, and to destroy good order," and because it affects "the essential interests of civil society."

> The people of this State, in common with the people of this country, profess the general doctrines of Christianity, as the rule of their faith and practice; and to scandalize the author of these doctrines is not only, in a religious point of view, extremely impious, but, even in respect to the obligations due to society, is a gross violation of decency and good order. . . . Nor are we bound, by any expressions in the constitution, as some have strangely supposed, either not to

punish at all, or to punish indiscriminately the like attacks upon the religion of
Mahomet or of the Grand Lama; and for this plain reason, that the case assumes
that we are a Christian people, and the morality of the country is ingrafted upon
Christianity. and not upon the doctrines or worship of those imposters.[48]

A similar judgment was reached in a Pennsylvania court in 1824, even
though the defendant, who in the course of a debate had called the Bible "mere
fable," was acquitted on appeal for technical reasons. The judge writes: "While
our own free constitution secures liberty of conscience and freedom of religious
worship to all, it is not necessary to maintain that any man should have the right
publicly to vilify the religion of his neighbors and of the country." "This is
Christianity which is the law of our land. . . . If from a regard to decency and the
good order of society, profane swearing, breach of the Sabbath, and blasphemy,
are punishable by civil magistrates, these are not punished as sins or offences
against God, but crimes injurious to, and having malignant influence on society."[49]

What is perhaps most striking is that this "Protestant establishment," even
though modified in various ways after the Civil War, was not shaken until much
later. In American mythology, the Civil War itself became "a kind of double
holy war." It betokened at once the triumph of righteousness over a divided nation, and the promise of a world about to be "Anglo-Saxonized."[50] In the postwar period,

> this spiritual hegemony was threatened by factories, immigrants, and discon-
> certing modern ideas, but the united evangelical front closed ranks for the tem-
> perance crusade. the Little War of 1898, and the Great War of 1914-1918. Prot-
> estant America, consequently. did not really face its first great moment of truth
> until it marched onto the moral and religious battlefields of the twenties, the
> tumultuous decade of prohibition. immigration. evolution. jazz, the KKK. short
> skirts. the movies. Al Smith. and the Crash.[51]

There were changes during through the second half of the nineteenth century, and into the first part of the twentieth, but they were minor. Blasphemy
prosecutions declined, as did restrictive standards for witness competency based
on religious affiliation. On the other hand, convictions for taking the name of
God in vain continued, despite challenges that such convictions violated rights
of religious liberty. Sunday laws were still enforced, and even expanded, and up
into the 1920s the practice of reading the King James Bible in public schools
was judged constitutional, despite the appeal of Catholics and others to be exempted on conscientious grounds.[52] In a Maine case in 1854, the court denied
damages to one Bridget Donahoe, who was expelled from school for refusing to
read from the King James Bible, and upheld the authority of the school board to
impose such a requirement. "The claim, so far as it may rest on conscience, is a
claim to annul any regulation of the State, made by its constituted authorities. . . .

The right as claimed, undermines the power of the State. It is that the will of
the majority shall bow to the conscience of the minority, or of one. If the several

consciences of the [students] are permitted to contravene, obstruct or annul the action of the State, the power ceases to reside in majorities, and is transferred to minorities."[53]

Perhaps the most famous expressions of majoritarian religious dominance were exemplified in several cases involving Mormons, focusing particularly on their practice of polygamy. In *Reynolds v. United States* (1879) and *Davis v. Beason* (1890), the Supreme Court upheld convictions, respectively, for bigamy and for seeking to register as a voter while knowingly belonging to the Mormon Church. In both cases, the court rejected free-exercise arguments out of hand. In *Davis*, Justice Stephen Field would not even consider Mormon beliefs religious: "To call their advocacy a tenet of religion is to offend the common sense of mankind. . . . The term 'religion' has reference to one's views of his relations to his Creator, and to the obligations they impose of reverence for his being and character, and of obedience to his will. It is often confounded with the cultus or form of worship of a particular sect, but is distinguishable from the latter."[54] The court took similarly dismissive attitudes toward the claims of conscience of pacifists during World War I and after.[55]

These decisions, and many like them, were left unchallenged well into the twentieth century, mainly because the Supreme Court took the position that the First Amendment to the Constitution, prohibiting an establishment of religion and guaranteeing "the free exercise thereof," applied only to federal and not to state law. States, on this reading, were free to interpret the right of religious freedom very narrowly, as they did in the New York and Pennsylvania cases just cited, thereby allowing what looked like a form of majority religious establishment at the state level.

The Fourteenth Amendment, adopted after the Civil War, offered the opportunity of "incorporating" the First Amendment into its provisions, which assured due process and equal legal protection for all citizens. That would have transferred final authority from the states to the Supreme Court, and made possible wider and more robust protection of conscience, particularly in regard to minority beliefs. However, in its wisdom, the Court refrained from taking advantage of that opportunity until 1940, when in a landmark case, *Cantwell v. Connecticut*, a Jehovah's Witness was exempted from a local licensing law regulating public speaking and soliciting because it was held to restrict unduly the free exercise of religion.[56] Unquestionably, *Cantwell* "opened the modern era of free exercise jurisprudence" by providing a vision close to the ideals of Williams, Locke, Jefferson, and Madison,[57] which, as we have seen, gave special priority to the rights of conscience.

This revolutionary decision in favor of an expanded understanding of the rights of religious freedom clearly recovered the "other wing" of the Reformed tradition that we have been examining, and helped to reverse the "eclipse of conscience" so evident throughout most of the nineteenth and early twentieth centuries.

Late Twentieth and Early Twenty-First Centuries

To an important extent, present-day debates over the relation of religion to morality and civil order reflect the same tensions that have existed in the Reformed
tradition from the beginning.

On the one hand, there is widespread concern, loudly expressed in the
1980s by groups like the Moral Majority, but also by President Reagan, then
Secretary of Education William J. Bennett, and by numerous religious leaders,
like Richard J. Neuhaus in his book, *The Naked Public Square*, that "the American experiment . . . is not only derived from religiously grounded belief, it continues to depend on such belief."[58] In order to endure, in order to preserve its
true identity, America must return to its religious roots, must unashamedly es-
pouse and inculcate the fundamental beliefs and values associated with that heritage by means of direct governmental encouragement.

The same ideas have been reaffirmed throughout the nineties and into the
present century by both political and religious leaders. In very prominent ways,
President George W. Bush has cast America's role in the "war on terror" in
highly religious terms: "Our nation is chosen by God and commissioned by history to be a model [of justice] to the world"; "America is the hope of all mankind. . . . That hope still lights our way. And the light shines in the darkness.
And the darkness has not overcome it"; "[America's] responsibility to history is
already clear: to answer these [terrorist] attacks and rid the world of evil."[59]
Elaborating this theme, evangelist Pat Robertson gives voice to the fervent sentiments of many religious Americans: The development of civic virtue, he says,
depends on a return to "ethical systems derived from (and strengthened by)
Judeo-Christian values"; "Common sense tells us that a government should foster the religious values that produce [civic virtue] among its citizens."[60]

Utterances of this kind pose a threat in the minds of many to the protection
of religious freedom. A government identified with a particular set of religious
ideals, and disposed to design and carry out policies in the name of those ideals
would appear to be sharply at odds with the tradition of Roger Williams.

One important reason such a perspective is at odds with that tradition is because it loses sight of a distinction crucial to Williams's thinking, and strongly
operative in the thought of Locke and Jefferson, namely, the distinction between
the internal and external forums, between the "law of the spirit" and the "law of
the sword." As we have seen, the difference presupposes an "outward tribunal"
responsible to enforce within the civil realm a common moral law shared by all
citizens (the law of "bodies and goods" in the language of the Puritans) and distinct from an "inward tribunal" (the conscience, which governs the personal
beliefs and actions of each individual). Of additional importance is the special
priority of the inward over the outward forum (the doctrine, as mentioned, of the
"sovereignty of conscience"). So long as the conscience does not violate, in Williams's words, the "common rights, peace, and safety of all citizens," it ought to
be deferred to by the state.[61]

Conclusion: Contemporary Relevance

The landmark and immensely controversial decision by the Supreme Court, *Employment Division, Department of Human Resources of Oregon v. Smith* (1990), exhibits the "deep tension, if not outright conflict, over attitudes toward religious freedom" in American Protestantism that dates from colonial times. The case is significant for many reasons, not least that it concerns an appeal by members of the Native American community for minority exemption from the laws of the dominant community, against which Native Americans have so long and, for the most part, so futilely struggled.

With Justice Antonin Scalia writing for the majority, the Court denied unemployment compensation to two members of the Native American Church, Alfred Smith and Galen Black, who had been fired from their jobs with a private drug rehabilitation center because they ingested peyote for sacramental purposes in a religious ceremony. Under the free-exercise clause of the First Amendment, Smith and Black claimed a right of exemption from a state law that criminalized all use of "controlled substances" (including peyote) except if prescribed by a physician.

In his widely disputed opinion, Justice Scalia says the Court has "never held that an individual's religious beliefs excuse him from compliance with an otherwise [generally applicable] valid law prohibiting conduct that the State is free to regulate."[62] Cases that appear to come to such a conclusion were "hybrid" cases in which appeals to the free exercise of religion are, in effect, reducible to appeals to free speech or freedom of the press. Scalia obviously suggests that the free-exercise clause of the First Amendment has no independent meaning! Whatever religious exemptions are allowed must be left to the legislatures, who are fully entitled to ignore and override any conscientiously held beliefs of citizens, so long as the laws passed do not specifically single out one individual or group for discriminatory treatment. There is, Scalia implies, absolutely no "constitutionally required" protection from generally applicable laws.[63]

Scalia goes so far as to admit that failing to give constitutional protection to "religious practices that are not widely engaged in"—namely, by minority religions like the Native American Church—"will place them at a relative disadvantage." Nevertheless, that is an "unavoidable consequence," since otherwise "anarchy" would result from a system where "each conscience is a law unto itself or in which judges weigh the social impact of all laws against the centrality of all religious beliefs."[64]

A storm of protest from religious groups, including many Protestants, as well as from other non-governmental organizations and civil libertarians, arose over the *Smith* decision. Opposition forces gathered momentum and eventually coalesced around the Religious Freedom Restoration Act, passed by Congress in 1993. The act declared that the government "may substantially burden a person's exercise of religion only if it demonstrates that application of the burden to the person, (1) is in furtherance of a compelling governmental interest; and (2) is the least restrictive means of furthering that compelling governmental interest."[65] The act held until 1997 when the Court partially overturned it in *City of Boerne v. Flores* for transgressing Congress's authority by trying to tell the Court how to rule on religious freedom issues.

Still, widespread antipathy to the *Smith* decision continues to exist in religious, political, and legal communities, and even the Court itself seems to be moving away from *Smith*. In *Board of Education of Kiryas Joel Village School District v. Grumet* (1994), the Court overruled as an establishment of religion a New York State statute creating a school district that coincided with the boundaries of the religious enclave of the Satmar Hasidim, adherents of a strict form of Judaism. Justice David Souter, a critic of *Smith*, wrote for the majority (with Scalia, along with Clarence Thomas and William Rehnquist, dissenting) that a "state may not delegate its civic authority to a group chosen according to a religious criterion." Souter's opinion clearly has "serious implications for *Smith's* theory that accommodating religion is best left to the legislatures."[66]

The three dissenters in *Smith*—Harry Blackmun, William Brennan, and Thurgood Marshall, were joined in part by Sandra Day O'Connor, in sharply rejecting the heart of Scalia's opinion. They affirmed that previous free-exercise cases as decided by the Court "have all concerned generally applicable laws that had the effect of significantly burdening a religious practice." Justice O'Connor and the dissenters all argue that what amounted to the two-fold test of the Religious Freedom Restoration Act—compelling state interest and least restrictive means of furthering the state interest—effectively epitomize "the First Amendment's command that religious liberty is *an independent liberty* [and not one that is collapsible into other rights such as speech, press, and so forth], *and that it occupies a preferred position.*" Contrary to Scalia, they believe it is the responsibility of the Court "to strike sensible balances between religious liberty and a compelling state interest."[67]

They also add that were we to leave protection of rights to religious freedom purely to the legislative process, that would contradict the clear purpose of the First Amendment, which is "*precisely to protect the rights of those whose religious practices are not shared by the majority, and may be viewed with hostility.*"[68] They go on: "The history of our free exercise doctrine amply demonstrates *the harsh impact majoritarian rule has had on unpopular or emerging religious groups* such as the Jehovah's Witnesses or the Amish," and, we may add, the Native American Church![69]

For our purposes, the *Smith* decision, and the continuing controversy surrounding it, calls attention, as we say, to the conflict in the history of American Protestantism that we have been at pains to illustrate throughout this paper. On the one side, Scalia's opinion lends support to the tendency to reinforce the connection between religion and state by giving the majority the right, through the legislative process, to impose its will, and thereby, should it be so inclined, to ignore and override conscientiously held beliefs, that are, as it happens, frequently the beliefs of an unpopular minority. On the other side, many critics of

Smith exemplify the opposing commitment in the Protestant tradition to a robust and expansive interpretation of the doctrine of sovereignty of conscience.

In particular, two critical assumptions underlying the position of those who favor a robust theory of the sovereignty of conscience (and who generally oppose *Smith*) are worth underscoring.

First, there is postulated an important and vivid distinction between the idea of "compelling state interest," which presumably concerns the shared moral and civil interests of all citizens, regardless of particular identities based on religion, gender, class, race, and so forth, and the interests of individual conscience, which typically concern quite personal and often unpopular beliefs and practices. This is the distinction that is deeply embedded in the Reformed tradition between the "outward" and "inward" tribunal or forum, between civil authority and conscience. While all members of the Reformed tradition would embrace some version of this distinction, those, like Williams, who favor a robust doctrine of sovereignty of conscience, both sharpen the difference and give more prominence and scope to the jurisdiction of the inward forum than do their opponents, like Cotton.

Second, the burden of proof in these matters is on the outward, not the inward tribunal. Individual conscience is assumed to take precedence unless the state is able to demonstrate both that it has a valid overriding interest, and that it intends to satisfy that interest in the way that is least onerous to conscience.

These two assumptions indicate what it means to hold a robust theory of the sovereignty of conscience. The fact that they are so widely held, and that they face so much influential opposition, shows that the inner tensions over religious freedom manifested in the American Protestant tradition are far from dead.

Notes

1. 1 Corinthians 10:29b: "For why should my liberty be determined by another's conscience?" (my translation).

2. John Calvin, *Institutes of the Christian Religion*, ed. John T. McNeill, trans. Ford Lewis Battle (Philadelphia: Westminster Press, 1960), 1:847–48.

3. Calvin, *Institutes*, 1:847–48.

4. Calvin, *Institutes*, 2:1183.

5. Calvin, *Institutes*, 2:1184.

6. Calvin, *Institutes*, 2:1487.

7. Calvin, *Institutes*, 2:1215.

8. Calvin, *Institutes*, 1:272–73.

9. John Calvin, *Calvin's Commentaries: The Epistles of Paul the Apostle to the Romans and Thessalonians* (Grand Rapids, MI: Eerdmans, 1976), 286.

10. A typical expression of this enduring, if grossly fallacious, opinion appeared in the *Economist*: "America has many contradictions, but none greater than the fact that it was founded by Puritans and yet invented tolerance. The tension between the busybodies of 1620 and the free spirits of 1776 has often marked American history," "From There to Intolerance," *The Economist*, July 20, 1991, 9 (U.K. edition).

11. John Cotton, "Massachusetts Does Not Persecute," in *Roger Williams, John Cotton and Religious Freedom*, ed. Irwin H. Polishook (Englewood Cliffs, CA: Prentice-Hall, 1967), 74 (emphasis added).

12. Cotton, "Massachusetts," 73-74.

13. Cotton, "Massachusetts," 72.

14. Cotton, "Massachusetts," 77.

15. Sydney E. Ahlstrom, *A Religious History of the American People* (New Haven, CT: Yale University Press, 1972), 182.

16. He comes very close to saying as much in his study of the ways and language of the Narragansatt Indians, Roger Williams, *A Key into the Language of America* (1643; repr., Bedford, MA: Applewood Books, 1936), 95. Williams points out that the Native Americans are quite exacting and punctilious about their land, "notwithstanding a sinful opinion amongst many that Christians have *a right* to heathen lands" (emphasis added).

17. See Edwin S. Gaustad, *Liberty of Conscience: Roger Williams in America* (Grand Rapids, MI: Eerdmans, 1991), 31-44.

18. It is by now clear that contrary to many mistaken assessments, Williams was, as Perry Miller once said, "a sound, one may even say a conventional, Calvinist," quoted in James Calvin Davis, *The Moral Theology of Roger Williams* (Louisville: Westminster John Knox Press, 2004), 17. See Davis's fine study for further confirmation of this conclusion.

19. Roger Williams, *Complete Writings of Roger Williams* (New York: Russell & Russell, 1963), 3:148.

20. Williams, *Writings of Roger Williams*, 7:154-55.

21. Williams, *Writings of Roger Williams*, 3:66.

22. Williams, *Writings of Roger Williams*, 4:365.

23. Williams, *Writings of Roger Williams*, 3:398.

24. Russell Bourne, *The Red King's Rebellion: Racial Politics in New England, 1675-1678* (New York: Oxford University Press, 1990), 245.

25. Williams, *Writings of Roger Williams*, 7:181.

26. Roger Williams quoted in Davis, *Moral Theology*, 94. It is true that Williams, worryingly, advocates that Catholics should wear some overt identification. Nevertheless, Williams's commitment to an extraordinary degree of tolerance for Catholics should not be overlooked. As Davis says, "besides this method of public identification, Williams rejects any arguments for the restriction of Catholic freedoms that depend on the mistaken belief that they are less capable of civility and moral citizen[ship] than their Protestant counterparts. He even goes so far as to blame the instances of Catholic insurrection in seventeenth-century Britain not on Catholic ignorance of civility, but on the suppression of their consciences and religious practices by the Protestant political authorities," Davis, *Moral Theology*, 159n7.

27. Mark DeWolfe Howe is responsible for serious misunderstanding of Williams's views by advancing the idea that Williams's primary concern was to protect the purity of religion, and was relatively indifferent to civil government, *The Garden and the Wilderness* (Chicago: University of Chicago Press, 1965).

28. Williams, *Writings of Roger Williams*, 4:251.

29. Thomas Jefferson, "An Act for Establishing Religious Freedom," in *The Life and Selected Writings of Thomas Jefferson*, ed. Adrienne Koch and William Peden (New York: Modern Library, 1944), 312-13.

30. Stephen Stanhope Smith quoted in Fred J. Hood, "Presbyterianism and the New American Nation, 1783-1826: A Case Study in Religion and National Life" (PhD diss., Princeton University, 1986).

31. Forrest Church, ed.. "Memorial of the Hanover Presbytery." in *The Separation of Church and State: Writings on a Fundamental Freedom by America's Founders* (Boston: Beacon Press, 2004), 41, 43.

32. "'Preliminary Principles' for 'Form of Government,'" in *Constitution of the Presbyterian Church, U.S.A.* (Philadelphia: Westminster Press, 1955), 239.

33. John Witherspoon, *Sermons* (Edinburgh: n.p., 1804), 5:216.

34. John Witherspoon, *Lectures on Moral Philosophy* (Philadelphia: n.p., 1822), 137.

35. Edwin S. Gaustad, *Sworn on the Altar of God: A Religious Biography of Thomas Jefferson* (Grand Rapids, MI: Eerdmans, 1996), 72. Even Garry Wills, who otherwise (unconvincingly) diminishes Locke's influence on Jefferson, admits a "vivid and traceable influence . . . in the area of religious tolerance," *Inventing America: Jefferson's Declaration of Independence* (New York: Vintage Books, 1979), 171.

36. John Locke, *Letter Concerning Toleration* (New York: Liberal Arts Press, 1950), 52.

37. Locke, *Concerning Toleration*, 17.

38. Thomas Jefferson, "Notes on Virginia." in Koch and Peden, *Selected Writings of Thomas Jefferson*, 275.

39. James Madison, "Proposals to the Congress for the Bill of Rights, 1789," in *Conscience in America: A Documentary History of Conscientious Objection in America, 1757-1967*, ed. Lillian Schlissel (New York: E.P. Dutton, 1968), 47. It is important to note that had the Congress accepted Madison's wording, we would have gone a long way toward avoiding the vexatious constitutional problem produced by the special privileging of religion in respect to the protection of free exercise that is assured in the First Amendment. Substituting the existing wording, "Congress shall make no law respecting the establishment of religion, or prohibiting the free exercise thereof," has arguably led to discrimination in regard to persons "not explicitly motivated by religion," but whose rights to free exercise of (non-religious) conscience have as much right to protection as those of religious believers. See Winnifred Fallers Sullivan, *The Impossibility of Religious Freedom* (Princeton, NJ: Princeton University Press, 2005), 150. In that regard, see also the concurring opinion in *City of Boerne v. Flores*, 521 U.S. 507 (1997) at 536 (which partly overturned the Religious Freedom Restoration Act of 1993) by Justice John Paul Stevens: "The Court does note, however, that the statute, which operates to exempt religious but not secular conduct from compliance with neutral laws of general applicability, evidences a preference for religion which arguably runs afoul of the Establishment Clause of the First Amendment," quoted in Sullivan, *Impossibility of Religious Freedom*, 137. Had Madison's wording been used, the protection of conscience might plausibly have been construed as including conscientious beliefs that are *both* religious *and* secular or nonreligious. (See *United States v. Seeger*, 380 U.S. 163 [1965] for a decision in which the Court expanded the rights of free exercise to people who, though not religious, manifested the same degree of conscientiousness as religious believers.) Consequently, an "establishment of religion," could logically be understood, ala Justice Stevens's suggestion, to prohibit preferential protection of the free exercise only of religious belief and practice.

40. Thomas Jefferson to Thomas Law, June 13, 1814, in Koch and Peden, *Selected Writings of Thomas Jefferson*, 637.

41. Jefferson, like Locke, is not altogether consistent on these matters. On occasion, he can be found adopting the language of the "other side": "Can the liberties of a nation be thought secure when we have removed their only firm basis, a conviction in the minds of the people that these liberties are the gift of God?" Thomas Jefferson, "Notes on Vir-

ginia." in Koch and Peden, *Selected Writings of Jefferson*, 278.

42. See A. John Simmons, *The Lockean Theory of Rights* (Princeton, NJ: Princeton University Press, 1991), 39-41.

43. See footnote 26.

44. Timothy Dwight quoted in Ahlstrom, *Religious History of the American People*, 7.

45. Martin Marty, *Protestantism in the United States: Righteous Empire* (New York: Charles Scribner's Sons, 1986).

46. Michael S. Ariens and Robert A. Destro, *Religious Liberty in a Pluralistic Society* (Durham, NC: Carolina Academic Press, 1996), 99.

47. Ariens and Destro, *Religious Liberty*, 113; *People v. Ruggles* 8 Johns 290 (N.Y. 1811).

48. Ariens and Destro, *Religious Liberty*, 113; *People v. Ruggles* 8 Johns 290 (N.Y. 1811).

49. Ariens and Destro, *Religious Liberty*, 117; *Updegraph v. Commonwealth* 11 Ser. & R. (26 Pa.) 394 (1824).

50. Ahlstrom, *Religious History of the American People*, 8.

51. Ahlstrom, *Religious History of the American People*, 8.

52. Ariens and Destro, *Religious Liberty*, 147-50.

53. Ariens and Destro, *Religious Liberty*, 153-54; *Donahoe v. Richards* 38 Me. 379 (1854).

54. Ariens and Destro, *Religious Liberty*, 194; *Davis v. Beason* 133 U.S. 333 (1890).

55. John Witte, Jr., *Religion and the American Constitutional Experiment*, 2nd ed. (Boulder, CO: Westview Press, 2005), 129-31.

56. See Witte, Jr., *American Constitutional Experiment*, 137.

57. Witte, Jr., *American Constitutional Experiment*, 177.

58. Richard J. Neuhaus, *The Naked Public Square* (Grand Rapids, MI: Eerdmans, 1984), 95.

59. Quotations taken from speeches by President George W. Bush. The first is from a speech quoted in Martin Marty, "The Sin of Pride," *Newsweek*, March 10, 2003, 32. The second is from a speech delivered on September 11, 2002, and the third from a religious service at the National Cathedral, Washington, DC, shortly after September 11, 2001; both are cited in Jim Wallis, "Dangerous Religion: George W. Bush's Theology of Empire," *Sojourners Magazine* (September/October 2003), http://www.sojo.net (accessed March 1, 2007).

60. Pat Robertson quoted in Davis, *Moral Theology*, 134.

61. Williams, *Writings of Roger Williams*, 3:366.

62. Ariens and Destro, *Religious Liberty*, 242.

63. Ariens and Destro, *Religious Liberty*, 244.

64. Ariens and Destro, *Religious Liberty*, 244-45.

65. Ariens and Destro, *Religious Liberty*, 255.

66. Garrett Epps, *To an Unknown God: Religious Freedom on Trial* (New York: St. Martin's Press, 2001), 239, 240.

67. Ariens and Destro, *Religious Liberty*, 245-46 (emphasis added).

68. Ariens and Destro, *Religious Liberty*, 247 (emphasis added).

69. Ariens and Destro, *Religious Liberty*, 247 (emphasis added).

Chapter Four
Putting God into the City: Protestants in France

Sébastien Fath

In contemporary French history, Protestants have constantly been opposed to the idea of a Christian state. Part of the reason for this is rooted in their theology, but their position has been mainly due to their specific history. Their Huguenot past has always reminded them of the danger of an alliance between the Catholic majority and the state. This alliance meant for them discrimination and even persecution, while the Republic and a secular state meant religious freedom. Unlike in the United States, Protestants are a tiny Christian minority in France.[1] They represent today around 2.2 percent of the total French population (62 million). Confronted with the Catholic giant and its rich past of political and societal power, it is no wonder French Protestants have been used to thinking that the further the state is from religions, the better off it is. This idea was widely accepted around 1905. Although not unanimously, the vast majority of French Protestants welcomed the separation between state and church and the principle that guided it, defined by the French as laicity (*laïcité*).[2] The French are quite proud of this concept (wrongly translated as secularism) and like to think of it as their property (however other countries also practice it). *Laïcité* means that the state holds a neutral position in religious matters and offers no support to any religion in particular. This also means that all religions are equal before the law. Freedom of conscience and religion must be total with respect to the rights of individuals. According to specialists such as Jean Baubérot and Claude Nicolet, it attempts to reconcile "freedom of conscience" (everyone has the right to believe what he or she chooses) and "freedom of thought." What does this "freedom of thought" mean exactly? It means that the state, through its public schools, intends to foster emancipation by giving each citizen the opportunity to learn to think freely without being locked into the ideas of his or her native social group. The public school system must allow each individual to be confronted with different systems of thought, different cultural references so that he or she can make choices more freely.

In some ways this "freedom of thought" scares the American public because it seems to give the state too much importance. But it must be understood within a specific historical context. The emphasis on "freedom of thought" can be explained by the fact that France, unlike the United States, was submitted for a very long time to the religious and cultural monopoly of the Catholic Church, the bulwark of the monarchy. When the Republic settled into place durably, it had to fight this Catholic monopoly and educate the population to pluralism and a new democratic culture. Thus, the state chose to take on the role of an emancipator. It is not surprising then if French Protestants, like the Jews, largely agreed with this from the beginning, because it gave them complete equality with Catholic citizens.

How has this attitude evolved in the course of the last century? From 1905 to 2005, three different emphases and contexts can be distinguished: (1) The initial acceptance of an almost complete separation between churches and the state could be typified as a global refusal of the "city of God." (2) A century later, this framework is still present. However, another emphasis emerged in the late twentieth century, the refusal of a "city without God." (3) Finally, the attitude of many French Protestants today would be the will to put "God in the city."

French Protestants in 1905: A Big "No" to the City of God

Many French Protestants did not particularly applaud the 1905 law of separation between churches and state. The majority of them were "far from enthusiastic."[3] However, all of them accepted it, sometimes with gratitude, sometimes with a few concerns. The Lutherans were the most cautious.

The Lutheran Response to 1905: A Cautious Acceptance

With the Reformed church, the Lutherans benefited from the system prevailing before 1905. This system, set up in 1802, felt comfortable to many French Protestants. Throughout the nineteenth century, a controlled religious market where the state played a pivotal role characterized the French religious situation. Until 1905 the French state financed Catholicism, Lutheran and Reformed Protestantism, and Judaism to the exclusion of all other confessions. A French historian has described this situation as the "concordatary game," in which the state regulated the "controlled pluralism" of the recognized religious confessions.[4] The term "concordatary" refers to the Concordat, a special law drawn up in 1801 between the Vatican and the French state, which gave new public privileges to the Catholic Church (priests received state salaries, for example). Later an extension of this system was applied to the Reformed and Lutheran Protestants (1802) and to the Jews (1808); according to this system, which points to a "first stage of laicization,"[5] Protestantism was officially "reintegrated" after over a century of persecution.[6] Until 1905, Protestant ministers were paid by the state (as were Jewish and Catholic priests) and their social role was broadly recognized. At the beginning of the twentieth century, this system was particularly appreciated by the Lutherans, who were considerably weaker than the Reformed Protestants since the French defeat by Germany in 1871, which led to the loss of the eastern provinces (traditional strongholds of French Lutherans). This is why, like the majority of the Jews,[7] they did not push for a law of separation. But unlike the Catholics who refused the consequences of the 1905 law, they abided by it.

The Calvinistic and Evangelical Response to 1905: Overall Support

The Calvinistic and the evangelical responses to 1905 were more enthusiastic. The Reformed churches, proud of their Huguenot past, had more theological reasons than the Lutherans for accepting a clear separation between churches and the state. The influence of Alexandre Vinet (1797-1897) was essential. This Swiss Reformed theologian led a majority of Reformed Protestants to favor a moderate separation. The biggest impact of Vinet was in the evangelical wing of the Reformed churches. At the Anduze Synod, from June 24 to July 4, 1902, this branch of the Reformed churches gave unanimous support to the separation. Vinet's thought has played an essential role. Jean Baubérot describes him as the "first francophone theologian of laicity [*laïcité*]."[8] Reflecting on the fact that the church, the body of Christ, would no longer be supported by the state, Vinet deeply influenced French Reformed Protestants and evangelical Protestants. Among the latter, a small minority did not belong either to the Reformed churches or to the Lutherans.[9] They did not benefit from the Concordat, which built a wall of separation between the "established" (concordatary religion) and the "outsiders" (often described as "non-recognized" or "dissenters").[10] In the same way as the "established" and the "outsiders" studied by Norbert Elias and John L. Scotson in the Winston Parva community, the concordatary Christians and the non-concordatary, or unrecognized religious groups, rapidly became distinct poles, affirming their distinctiveness on each side of a line of separation born of the "concordatary game."

It was among the non-concordatary and the non-recognized Protestants that several new evangelical churches had appeared during the nineteenth century. At the beginning of the century this tendency included a few Quakers,[11] Mora-

vians, and Anabaptists;[12] after the Geneva Revival (1817-20), it was strengthened along with the whole of French Protestantism by reinstating personal conversion and the inspiration of the Bible as central beliefs of what became evangelical Christianity.[13] The growth of international Protestant mission work also
encouraged the development of new churches such as Methodist and Baptist
churches in France during the first third of the nineteenth century.[14] For these
Protestants, the Concordat provided no support. It provided inequality, and gave
arguments to the Catholic Church against new "unrecognized" Protestants.[15] On
the contrary, a full separation between the state and the churches restored equality of status. This is why non-concordatary evangelicals were the most enthusiastic supporters of the law of separation. Religion was no longer state funded,
and the former distinction between "official religions" and "dissident religions"
was no longer valid. For Reuben Saillens, the main leader of French Evangelicals at that time, 1905 was "the best date in French History."[16]

The Protestant Dream: A Neutral Republic Rather than a Clerical City of God

Although French Protestants reacted to 1905 with some diversity, a common feature can be highlighted: almost all of them favored a neutral republic
rather than a clerical city of God. This was a major difference between them and
a large half of French Catholics who had a difficult time accepting the very idea
of a secular republic before 1914. Many Catholic leaders still had some nostal-
gia for an old-fashioned Catholic monarchy. The main reason why all French
Protestants were strong republicans was precisely the fear of a strong Catholic
comeback in French politics.[17] While Catholics, encouraged by a defiant pope,
decided to refuse involvement in the first republican governments, Protestants
rushed to secure ministerial positions. There had been five Protestant ministers
out of nine in the first republican government following the departure of Mac
Mahon in 1879. Along with the Jews, they were resolute in fighting for the Republic against the ghost of an old-fashioned city of God where the crown and the
Catholic Church dictated from above what is right or what is wrong, what is
good religion and what is heresy.[18] While the Holy See and the French government broke diplomatic relations on July 30, 1904, the Protestant elite, on the
contrary, developed closer links with the political power of the time. No wonder
then if one of the major authors of the French law of separation was precisely a
Protestant, Louis Méjean, son and brother of Protestant ministers. Méjean believed that a wise separation would lead to a "spiritual reform,"[19] and that Protestants had nothing to fear in the process. Showing their republican spirit,
French Protestants also handed over all their confessional schools to the state
after the 1905 law, believing that the Republic's education system could continue the educative and moral mission they had promoted.[20]

This common republican emphasis did not mean for the Protestants that the
state should ignore the social or moral role of the churches. The French historian

Patrick Cabanel, who highlights the Protestant roots of a liberal separation that is not supposed to annihilate religion's social role, has particularly emphasized this point. This is why they expressed deep concerns when Emile Combes submitted a first draft of the bill of separation that was perceived as anti-Christian.[21] The solution favored by the French Protestants might have been closer to a kind of American civil religion than to a "laicity without God."[22] To them, the Republic's neutrality was a good thing (even a blessing) as long as it did not become hostility towards religion.

A Century Later: A Growing "No" to a City without God

A century later, the love story between French Protestants and a secular republic is still not over. The commemoration of the centennial anniversary of the 1905 law revealed a wide national consensus, including the Catholic Church and its bishops. However, the global context has changed dramatically in the meantime. In 2005, the threat of a clerical "city of God" has been dead for decades. The war of the two Frances[23]—opposing a conservative, Catholic France and a progressive, republican France—is long forgotten. What French Protestants fear now is no longer a city of God, but a city without God. Three factors explain this new trend.

Christianity as a Foreign Culture

The first factor is the growing absence of Christianity in the French cultural mainstream. After its inception during the French Revolution, the process of dissociating politics and religion reached its climax in 1905, but since then, it seems that a new process has taken place: the gradual eviction of Christianity from French culture as a whole, highlighted by Danièle Hervieu-Léger.[24] Regularly practicing Christians make up only around 10 percent of the population (a little more than four times lower than in the United States), and the younger generation is even less involved in religious practice.[25] The dominant culture of the individual has resulted in the cultural relativization of all religious norms and the triumph of secular leisure over religious observance. In stressing the value of personal appropriation of meaning, it dilutes the notion of any "revealed" truth. Catholic France or Christian France is now defunct, replaced by the new "Pagan France" described by a French bishop, Hippolyte Simon.[26] Ordinary citizens display a growing ignorance of Christian values or culture, leading even Régis Debray, an icon of the French leftist intelligentsia, to plead for a course on religion in state schools.[27] Between 1905 and 2005, Christianity has almost disappeared from the cultural mainstream. To Protestants as to other Christians, the French city appears now as a "city without God."

Christianity under Attack

This perception is strengthened by another fact: Christianity has not only become a foreign culture, it is also more and more visibly under attack.[28] Contrary to the American situation, where Christianity, and particularly evangelical Protestantism, seems sometimes to work like a quasi-de facto religious establishment, religion in general is often disqualified as antimodern. Terrorism from Muslim states like Egypt is regularly linked uniquely to Islam (neglecting the problems of corruption and poverty which also explain terrorism to a large extent). In the same way, Catholicism is often attacked in the public sphere as an old-fashioned and dangerous antimodern superstition.[29] While benefiting from a good "modern" reputation in the media, Protestants are not entirely safe from attack. The Iraq war in 2003 revealed a flourish of articles and publications denouncing the "Bush sect." A widely distributed weekly, *Marianne*, translated George W. Bush's policy in purely religious terms: "Bush's sect attacks."[30] Another left-wing weekly, *Le Nouvel Observateur*, devoted its main report to U.S. evangelicals, "the sect [cult] that wants to conquer the world."[31] Slimane Zeghidour portrays them as "crusaders of the Apocalypse." In the weekly *La Vie*, Jean Mercier described the White House as "taken hostage by a fundamentalist sect."[32] Although one cannot deny that the "theo-conservatives" played a role around President Bush, the French media had a clear tendency to overemphasize the religious factor. While Christianity was also attacked by some secular republicans in 1905, the majority of the population (including many moderate republicans and large sections of the mainstream press) defended it, sometimes very strongly. This is no longer the case and along with Catholics, French Protestants have had to adapt to this new context.

Christianity Challenged and Deregulated

A century after 1905, a third new parameter is the deregulation of the religious marketplace. The 1905 religious landscape was quite simple. On one side, there was republican ideology, supported by the two main religious minorities (Jews and Protestants), on the other side, conservative ideology, supported by a majority of Catholics. Today, while republican ideas have prevailed everywhere, the religious landscape has both weakened and diversified. There are far more than three religious players in contemporary France. Islam has now become the second religion in France while Buddhism is growing steadily and benefits from an extremely positive image in the media. Books devoted to esotericism, Eastern spiritualities, and new religious movements flourish on the shelves of the main Parisian bookshops. The "chain of memory" that is at the heart of inherited religion is challenged by new conversion discourses.[33] Since the 1980s, the mainstream media has discovered that "sects" seem to be developing everywhere, while all organized religions have been undergoing not only decline, but also internal reshaping. Vertical authority and institutional discipline are more and more challenged (even in Catholicism), while personal charisma, conversion and voluntary associations are promoted,[34] creating many new movements. In Protestant circles, this tendency nurtured the growth of the evangelical movement. Still weak in 1945, with about fifty thousand believers, the evangelical constituency has vastly multiplied in size, so that there are today two hundred thousand Pentecostals, forty thousand Baptists, not to mention charismatics,[35] members of Brethren Assemblies, independent evangelicals, Mennonites, Methodists, and many others. In 2005, evangelical Protestants amounted to almost four hundred thousand believers if we include all ethnic churches,[36] and they have generated an important internal recomposition of Protestantism.[37] This process of fragmentation, restructuring, and deregulation has created identity problems. On the one hand, republican ideology is less vocal now, opening the way to other discourses. On the other hand, more and more distinct communities express their need to exist as specific identities. Marcel Gauchet has typified this trend as a "Republic of identities" (*République des identités*),[38] while political scientist Philippe Portier emphasizes the republican will to articulate "differences with democracy."[39] In this new context, identities, including the Protestant identity, have to compete if they want to exist in the public space.

French Protestants and Politics Today: God in the City

In the political arena, French Protestants today have no intention of restoring a so-called "city of God." But they do not want either a "city without God." What they are fighting for in 2005 is different. As Christians, they are unwilling to be reduced to the private sphere. They intend to witness "God in the city" in a pluralistic context in which their distinct identity needs to be heard. This has been very clearly stated by several Protestant leaders, including Jean-Arnold de Clermont, president of the French Protestant Federation. In April 2004, he wrote: "French Protestantism and laicity [*laïcité*] have long been like a 'fish in water,' but today, the fish lacks oxygen." Explaining what he meant by that, he denounced the "privatization of religion" in the name of laicity, insisting that the public sphere needs religious voices.[40]

Protestants More Vocal in Politics?

The first sign of this new Protestant boldness might be seen in a slightly more direct involvement in politics. Protestants have always been engaged in republican politics. In the 1980s and the 1990s, Protestants held several major ministerial posts, including the post of prime minister (Michel Rocard, from 1988 to 1991, and Lionel Jospin, from 1997 to 2002). However, this political involvement was not dictated by denominational interest. Jospin and Rocard did not influence French politics as representatives of Protestant options, but as Socialist leaders. One could argue that fifteen years before, a very famous political statement from the Protestant Federation, the document *Eglise et pouvoir* (1971), had a big impact. Heavily influenced by the Marxist mood of the moment, *Eglise et pouvoir* described capitalist society as "unacceptable." However, if this document had indeed some political impact, it was not presented as a political proposition, but in a prophetic mode. It was less a Protestant contribution than a universal and transconfessional statement. Following this document, which created an intense debate in Protestant ranks,[41] the political involvement of Protestants has remained cautious and careful. This kind of discreet involvement in the political elite is still visible today. The traditional affinity of a majority of Protestants with left-wing parties, which can be explained by the historic link between left-wing parties and republican ideology, still works as well. A survey conducted between 2003 and 2004 reveals that 42.5 percent of French Protestants included in the panel said they preferred the Left, while only 30 percent said they preferred right-wing parties.[42]

But along with these continuities, one cannot help but see that French Protestants have recently engaged in new paths. First, the strong evangelical minority that emerged after 1945 seems to have disturbed the traditional discretion of the Protestant voice in the public arena. The main example of this is the Comité Protestant Evangélique pour la Dignité Humaine (CPDH [Evangelical Protestant Committee for Human Dignity]),[43] a new network created in 1999. Linking various evangelical networks, the intent of the CPDH is to promote a Bible-based ethic and fundamental Judeo-Christian values, and to take a stand in the media and vis-à-vis the administration on key social issues.[44] Although far less influential than its U.S. evangelical counterparts, the CPDH works on a similar basis: active lobbying in the public place. Another sign of change is the increasing will of the French Protestant Federation and many Protestant representatives to have regular access to the government, copying in this way the Catholics and the Jews. The new "Reformation dinners," bringing together the Protestant elite and actors from the political arena is an example of this trend. The first one was organized October 14, 2004, at the French Senate, and invited as a guest speaker Régis Debray, former adviser to French President François Mitterrand.[45] During his meeting with Jean-Pierre Raffarin, the French prime minister, one of the main requests expressed by Jean-Arnold de Clermont, president of the French Protestant Federation, was an annual meeting with the government.[46] It seems that the Reformation dinner may have provided a springboard for this: several major political figures, including Finance Minister Thierry Breton (the main speaker) were present at the second Reformation dinner, held on October 13, 2005. Although French elites likes to present themselves as egalitarian and against *communautarisme* (ethnic or religious factionalism), the reality of today's France is characterized by the growing role of religious communities per se, each one competing for access to the republican state. Once again, the French situation is still far from the American scene, but some converging trends are obvious.

A Vital New Front: The Media

Gaining access to state elites is only part of the new Protestant attitude towards politics. Even if the media are not supposed to play a role in politics, they obviously get involved in the game as a "fourth power." Therefore, French Protestants know that if they want fair treatment, even in local situations, they need to be known by the media. In a context of severe decline of religious culture in the younger generation, Protestants could easily be put on a par with cults, compromising the religious life of several communities, particularly in evangelical circles and ethnic churches. They also face another risk: their "modern" image of an individualistic Christianity open to reform and debate could tend to dissolve their specific religious identity. In this context of "Protestant precariousness" in contemporary France,[47] the Protestant Federation and the Reformed and Lutheran churches have developed new media strategies in the last twenty years, particularly through the Internet,[48] but also through French television (through religious services broadcast on Sunday mornings). But the most active Protestants in this area have probably been French evangelical churches. As newcomers, characterized by a strong emphasis on conversion and religious advertising, they suffer from an image deficit. But they use many strategies to counter this deficit. In addition to a huge investment in the internet,[49] they have developed many media-friendly events (like their invitation to Billy Graham in 1986) emphasizing contact with political representatives where possible. For example, Billy Graham had a personal interview with President François Mitterrand in 1986, and generated comparisons with Pope John Paul II, who visited France the same year.[50] Eighteen years later, Nicolas Sarkozy, interior minister in the Raffarin government, was invited to the general assembly of the French Evangelical Federation.[51]

The Fight for Institutional Weight

Last but not least, French Protestants tend today to invest in their most neglected field: their own institutions. Traditionally, Protestants do not really like institutions, and they certainly do not sanctify them. Opposed to the church model defended by Catholic Rome, they favor voluntary societies in which central institutions play a minimal role. This remains globally true in the contemporary French Protestant scene. However, the refusal of a rigid institutional "church" structure does not imply that religious socialization is narrowly situated in this or that association or autonomous community, as Nancy Ammerman, among others, has suggested.[52] The number and effectiveness of supralocal French Protestant networks is proof enough. Among them, two have been gaining significant institutional weight.

The bigger and the most important one by far is the French Protestant Federation (FPF). Created in 1905 to defend Protestant interests in French society, the FPF has gradually developed into a representative body of almost all French

Protestant families including evangelicals. Pastor Jean-Arnold de Clermont, current president of the FPF, is obviously convinced of this representative role in the political arena. During the 2001 debate on the so-called anti-cult legislation passed by the French Parliament, he repeatedly gained the attention of the main media through his criticisms and comments. In the name of the FPF, he also expressed several concerns about the 1905 law and the need to adapt it to the new context. When an African evangelical community in Paris seemed to be discriminated against early in 2004, de Clermont and the FPF played a prominent role in the public debate about religious freedom. In a confrontation with Jean-Pierre Brard, a Communist mayor suspected of discrimination, the FPF took him to court.[53] The impact of the FPF's actions such as these is heightened to the extent that the federation's weight is seen to be significant. In that respect, the pursuit of the enlargement of the FPF can be seen, not only as a purely ecumenical affair between Protestants, but also as an effective way to gain more influence in the public arena.[54]

Among French evangelical Protestants, the need for a more significant institutional weight can also be noticed, albeit to a lesser extent. The French section of the Evangelical Alliance (AEF) plays a coordinating role. It was relaunched in 1953 under the leadership of Pastor Jean-Paul Benoît. The creation of the Fédération Evangélique de France (French Evangelical Federation [FEF]) on March 22, 1969, also participated in the networking dynamic.[55] Its starting position was clearly fundamentalist, countercultural, and eager to build a rampart against "bad" influences. However the federative logic (necessarily integrating a certain amount of internal diversity) brought more flexibility to its official discourse. By evolving gradually toward more dialogue and more multilateral orientation, the FEF has strengthened its ties with the French Evangelical Alliance. Today these two main evangelical networks have defined a common "platform." This has led to the creation on January 7, 2002, of the Conseil National des Evangéliques en France (National Council of French Evangelicals [a temporary name]). It is too early to evaluate the public impact of this new structure, but what is already clear is that in spite of their decentralized culture, French Protestants have learned that in the more and more pluralistic and secular arena in which they live, they need to regroup their forces if they want to be heard by politicians and the media.

Conclusion

If the hard statistical data seems to suggest that "God is dead" in contemporary Europe,[56] the French case leads us to realize that after all, religions and politicians alike still need to find a place for "God in the city." The example of French Protestant activism today, fuelled by a less rigid republican attitude towards identities and by the growth of evangelical churches, seems to show that a moderate interaction between a monotheistic God and the Republic is not purely an American thing. Along with Catholics and Jews (and to a certain extent Muslims), French Protestants want to choose neither an aggressive Pat Robertson way, nor a purely secular society reducing God to a private matter. Unabashed by hard-line secularist opponents, they believe that a respectful Christian involvement in the public place can strengthen the Republic instead of defeating it, and bring social and political benefits for society as a whole.

Might their influence contribute to a movement going beyond the founding myths of French *laïcité*,[57] towards a kind of new French civil religion? Historically, American civil religion was created in order to deal with a very broad and diverse religious landscape more or less infused by a democratic spirit.[58] A generic God and shared beliefs had a vital function to unite the U.S. melting pot and create an "imagined community."[59] On the contrary, the different way chosen by French laicity (*laïcité*) can be explained by a situation of a relatively undiversified religious landscape, where the Catholic majority faced the republicans. These conditions have changed dramatically today. In spite of the impact of secularization, France's religious landscape is far more diversified, including a wide range of Protestant churches, denominations, and sects, while the war of the two Frances is over. Even if many people in France might have a hard time admitting it, these changes could create a social and religious situation closer to what Americans experienced through their civil religion.

Notes

1. The French Protestant Federation (FPF) estimated the total number of Protestants to be around 1.1 million in 2005: nine hundred thousand in the FPF and two hundred thousand outside. A survey conducted by the IFOP polling company for the Protestant weekly *Réforme* in 2003-4 was more generous, with an estimate of 1.3 million. See "Éléments d'analyse sur la sociologie et le positionnement politique des protestants en France," *Réforme*, January 2005.

2. There is no accepted convention for transcribing this term in English. One can find "laïcity," "laicism," or "laicite." By far the worst option is "secularism." "Laicity" is *not* a synonym of secularization. It is a *specific way* to organize a secular and pluralistic society.

3. André Encrevé, *Les protestants en France de 1800 à nos jours, histoire d'une réintegration* (Paris: Stock, 1985), 227.

4. Brigitte Basdevant-Gaudemet, *Le jeu concordataire dans la France du XIXe siècle* (Paris: PUF, 1988).

5. Jean Baubérot, *La laïcité, quel héritage? De 1789 à nos jours* (Geneva: Labor & Fides, 1990).

6. Encrevé, *Les protestants*.

7. Sébastien Fath, "Juifs et protestants face à la loi de 1905 sur la séparation des Églises et de l'Etat," *Les Cahiers du Judaïsme* 9 (Winter-Spring 2001): 104-20.

8. Jean Baubérot, "Les évangéliques et la séparation française des Églises et de l'Etat," in *Le protestantisme évangélique. Un christianisme de conversion*, ed. Sebastien Fath (Turnhout, Belgium: Brépols, 2004), 236.

9. In the U.S., many Reformed churches would be regarded as "evangelical." In

France, however, even if there is an evangelical tendency within the Reformed Church. Reformed Protestants are usually not considered as full evangelicals, because their local communities do not select their members solely on the basis of individual conversion.

10. See Sébastien Fath, *Une autre manière d'être chrétien en France. Socio-histoire de l'implantation baptiste, 1810-1950* (Geneva: Labor & Fides, 2001), 1043-61.

11. Henri Van Etten, *Chronique de la vie quaker française, 1745-1945* (Paris: Société Religieuse des Amis, 1947).

12. Jean Séguy, *Les assemblées anabaptistes de France* (The Hague, Netherlands: Mouton, 1977).

13. Alice Wemyss, *Histoire du Réveil, 1790-1849* (Paris: Les Bergers et les Mages, 1977).

14. Fath, *Une autre manière*.

15. Michèle Sacquin, *Entre Bossuet et Maurras. L'antiprotestantisme en France de 1814 à 1870* (PhD diss., University of Caen, 1997).

16. Reuben Saillens quoted in Fath, *Une autre manière*, 911.

17. Patrick Cabanel, *Les protestants et la République de 1870 à nos jours* (Paris: Complexe, 2000).

18. Patrick Cabanel, *Juifs et protestants en France. Les affinités electives, XVI-XXIe siècle* (Paris: Fayard, 2004).

19. L.V.Méjean, *La Séparation des Églises et de l'Etat, L'oeuvre de Louis Méjean, dernier directeur de l'administration autonome des cultes* (Paris: PUF, 1959), 207.

20. In 1905, there were 1,608 French Protestant schools that were working according to the Falloux law. Protestants gave up this confessional network in the name of French laicity (*laïcité*). See Cabanel, *Les protestants*, 63.

21. This draft forbade national religious organizations. This measure was a threat for Catholics, but even more for small religious minorities like the Protestants. "The innocent [Protestants] get worse treatment than the culprits" (*Les innocents plus maltraités que les coupables*), Louis Pédézert, *Le Christianisme au XXe siècle*, December 1, 1904, quoted in Jean Baubérot, *Le retour des Huguenots. La vitalité protestante, XIX-XXe siècle* (Paris and Geneva: Cerf-Labor et Fides, 1985), 89.

22. Patrick Cabanel, *Le Dieu de la République. Aux sources protestantes de la laïcité, 1860-1900* (Rennes: Presses Universitaires de Rennes, 2003).

23. Emile Poulat, *Liberté, laïcité. La guerre des deux France et le principe de la modernité* (Paris: Cerf-Cujas, 1987).

24. Danièle Hervieu-Léger, *Catholicisme. La fin d'un monde* (Paris: Bayard, 2003).

25. Among the fifteen- to twenty-four-year age group, only 7.6 percent of women and 9.2 percent of men practice a religion, according to the INSEE (Institut National de la Statistique et des Etudes Economiques). See *Enquête Permanente sur les Conditions de Vie des ménages* (Paris: Institut National de la Statistique et des Etudes Economiques, 2004).

26. Hippolyte Simon, *Vers une France païenne?* (Paris: Cana, 1999).

27. See Régis Debray, *L'enseignement du fait religieux dans l'École laïque* (Paris: Odile Jacob, 2002).

28. René Rémond, *Le christianisme en accusation* (Paris: Desclée de Brouwer, 2000).

29. See the huge success of Michel Onfray's books; this atheist philosopher would have a very narrow audience in the United States. In France, he is widely published and read. Raised in a Catholic school, Onfray pleads for the complete eviction of religion and its replacement by an atheistic ethic. In Michel Onfray, *Traité d'athéologie* (Paris: Grasset, 2005), the author compares Pope Pius XII to Adolf Hitler.

30. "La secte Bush attaque," *Marianne*, March 24, 2003.

31. "Les évangéliques, la secte qui veut conquérir le monde," *Le Nouvel Observateur*, February 26, 2004.

32. Jean Mercier, "Sur les terres du Président," *La Vie*, March 13, 2003, 44.

33. Danièle Hervieu-Léger, *Religion as a Chain of Memory* (Cambridge: Polity Press, 2000).

34. Danièle Hervieu-Léger, *Le pèlerin et le converti. La religion en mouvement* (Paris: Flammarion, 1999).

35. Evert Veldhuizen, *Le renouveau charismatique protestant en France, 1968-88* (PhD diss., University of Paris IV Sorbonne, 1995).

36. Sebastien Fath, *Du ghetto au réseau. Les protestants évangéliques en France, 1800-2005* (Geneva: Labor et Fides, 2005); and Sebastien Fath, "Evangelical Protestantism in France: An Example of Denominational Recomposition?" *Sociology of Religion* 66, no. 4 (2005): 399-418.

37. Jean-Paul Willaime, "Les recompositions internes au monde protestant: protestantisme 'établi' et protestantisme 'évangélique,'" in *La globalisation du religieux*, ed. Jean-Pierre Bastian, Françoise Champion, and Kathy Rouselet (Paris: L'Harmattan, 2001).

38. Marcel Gauchet, *La religion dans la démocratie. Parcours de la laïcité* (Paris: Gallimard, 1998).

39. Philippe Portier, "De la séparation à la reconnaissance. L'évolution du régime français de laïcité," in *Les mutations contemporaines du religieux*, ed. Jean-Pierre Willaime and J.R. Armogathe (Turnhout, Belgium: Brépols, 2003), 7.

40. Jean-Arnold de Clermont, "Le protestantisme français a longtemps été comme 'un poisson dans l'eau' en ce qui concerne la laïcité, mais il vient à manquer d'oxygène," http://www.protestants.org (accessed April 30, 2004); Jean-Arnold de Clermont "Protestantisme et laïcité," http://www.protestants.org (accessed April 30, 2004).

41. It has also been analyzed form a sociological point of view by Jean Baubérot, *Le pouvoir de contester: contestations politico-religieuses autour de Mai 68 et le document Eglise et pouvoirs* (Geneva: Labor et Fides, 1983).

42. Data taken from IFOP poll, "Éléments d'analyse sur la sociologie et le positionnement politique des protestants en France," *Réforme*, January 2005. French evangelicals, however, seem far more balanced. They even tend to favor the Right, according to Solange Wydmusch, *Les attitudes religieuses et politiques des protestants français* (PhD diss., EPHE Sorbonne University, 1995). This evangelical influence weakens the traditional left-wing leaning of the majority of French Protestants.

43. The French for "Evangelical Protestant Committee for Human Dignity" is *Comité Protestant Evangélique pour la Dignité Humaine* (CPDH).

44. The CPDH statement in French reads: "rappeler et de promouvoir une éthique basée sur la Bible et les valeurs judéo-chrétiennes fondamentales, de prendre position auprès des médias et des pouvoirs publics sur les grands thèmes de société," *Annuaire évangélique (FEF) 2005* (Dozulé: Barnabas, 2004), 501.

45. Excerpts from Regis Debray's lecture were published in *Réforme* (the main French Protestant weekly), "Les protestants selon Régis Debray," *Réforme*, October 21, 2004, 2.

46. This meeting, widely reported in the secular press, occurred on January 11, 2005. In the weekly *L'Express*, Christian Makarian wrote: "Against a new excess of Republican zeal, Protestants ask for a revision of the 1905 law" (Contre un nouvel excès de zèle républicain, les protestants demandent la révision de la loi de 1905), *L'Express*, January 17, 2005.

47. Jean-Paul Willaime, *La précarité protestante. Sociologie du protestantisme contemporain* (Paris-Genève: Labor & Fides, 1992).

48. See http://www.protestants.org, the main portal of French Protestants.

49. See http://www.topchretien.com, the main portal of francophone evangelical Protestants.

50. Jean Baubérot, Françoise Champion, and Agnès Rochefort-Turquin, "Deux leaders religieux: Billy Graham et Jean-Paul II," in *Voyage de Jean-Paul II en France*, ed. Jean Séguy, et al. (Paris: Cerf, 1988), 161-83.

51. "Sarkozy en visite chez les évangélistes," *Le Parisien*, February 2, 2004.

52. Nancy T. Ammerman, *Congregation and Community* (New Brunswick, N.J., Rutgers University Press, 1997).

53. See Bernadette Sauvaget, "L'affaire de Montreuil en procès," *Réforme*, March 10, 2005.

54. Important negotiations have started with the Assemblies of God (ADD), the main French Pentecostal denomination. If the ADD joined the FPF, around seventy thousand new French Protestants would be represented in this network.

55. The FEF was originally called L'union des Eglises et Assemblées Evangéliques Françaises. It took its new title in November 1969, *Notre position face à certains problèmes actuels* (Paris: French Evangelical Federation, n.d.).

56. Steve Bruce, *God is Dead: Secularization in the West* (Oxford: Blackwell, 2002).

57. Blandine Chélini-Pont and Jeremy Gunn, *Dieu en France et aux États-Unis: quand les mythes font la loi* (Paris: Berg International, 2005).

58. Robert Bellah, "Civil Religion in America," *Daedalus* 96, no. 1 (1967): 1-18.

59. Benedict Anderson, *Imagined Communities: Reflections on the Origin and Spread of Nationalism* (London: Verso, 1983).

Part III: Catholicism

Chapter Five

The Catholic Story: The Political Consequences of Internal Pluralism

R. Scott Appleby

Voting Patterns[1]

In the May 1996 issue of *Rising Tide*, a magazine published by the Republican National Committee, a third-generation American Catholic and first-generation Republican, Ed Gillespie, boasted that "we Catholics provided the margin of victory [in 1994] needed to create the first Republican Congress in 40 years." Republican-voting Catholics made the same claim regarding the presidential election of 2004: we are the voting bloc, they boasted, that made the difference in nudging the Republican incumbent, the Methodist George W. Bush, over the finish line first, ahead of his Democratic opponent John Kerry, a Roman Catholic.[2]

The Democratic Party's abandonment of "the values many of us hold dear," Gillespie claimed, was prompting a widespread defection from the Democratic coalition built during the New Deal era. And what values were those? Contemporary Democrats, Gillespie charged, were gutting defense to pay for social spending, opposing tax cuts for working Americans, and mandating discrimination in the form of quotas. Just as high taxes, stifling business regulations, and forced busing drove Catholic families from the cities to the suburbs, so "the national Democrat Party grew so liberal it drove ethnic Catholics from our once natural political home."[3]

In 1996, 2000, and 2004, as well as in off-year congressional elections, the Republican Party vigorously courted the support of American Catholics like Mr.

Gillespie. The recent history of national voting patterns gave rise to such hopes: the Catholic vote had been swinging since 1976, and the direction of the swing has correlated with victory at the polls. In 1980, 1984, and 1988 Catholics made up the core of "Reagan Democrats" who helped traditional Republicans win the White House. In 1976 and 1992, winners Jimmy Carter and Bill Clinton carried a plurality of the Catholic vote, but the majority of Catholics had not voted for a Democratic presidential candidate since they supported Carter in 1976. (In 1992 George H. W. Bush and Ross Perot together attracted more Catholic voters than Clinton.) In 1994, deepening the trend, 52 percent of Catholics voted Republican, the first time the majority of Catholics had done so in a mid-term election. In 1996 Clinton carried the Catholic vote: Bob Dole was a lackluster pro-life candidate, and he seemed harshly anti-immigrant. But President Clinton's landslide victory did not reverse the trend of Catholics toward the Republican Party, as the 2000 and 2004 elections demonstrated.

Indeed, the importance of the Catholic vote is a matter of public record: while the 70 million American Catholics constitute approximately one-fourth of the U.S. population in 2006, the 35 million voters among them account for 30 percent of the actual electorate. Furthermore, the Catholic population is concentrated in the ten largest electoral college states, including California, New York, Texas, and Florida (all of which contain sizeable populations of Latino Catholics, who continued in the 1990s to vote overwhelmingly Democratic, except for the Cuban Americans in Florida). In battleground states such as Michigan, Ohio, Illinois, Wisconsin, Pennsylvania, New Jersey, and Connecticut, Catholics account for up to 41 percent of the overall vote.

In order to explain Catholic voting patterns and political tendencies, one must take into account the political birth, aging, and death of twentieth-century generational cohorts; the achievement of upper middle class affluence by a significant subset of white, "post-ethnic" Catholics in the United States whose forebears hailed from Ireland, Italy, Germany, Poland, and elsewhere in Europe; and the fragmentation of Catholic religious culture following the Second Vatican Council (1962-65).

The political scientist David Leege is the authority on Catholic voting patterns during the twentieth century. He has demonstrated that political divide among ethnic Catholics set the stage for the volatility of partisan affiliation and presidential vote choices that characterized Catholic politics in the twentieth century.[4] Ethnic history and assimilation patterns determined Catholic partisanship: general patterns over the course of the century indicate that English, Scandinavians, and Germans were solidly Republican; Eastern European, Polish, Irish, and Italian Catholics were evenly split, especially in the most recent period; while French, Hispanic, and African American Catholics remained solidly Democratic.

Trends within and across these various ethnic blocs developed at different times and under various circumstances. With the 1928 presidential campaign of Al Smith, the rise of the Ku Klux Klan, and a new wave of nativism associated with the GOP, Catholics began moving en masse to the Democratic Party, and swelled its ranks during the presidency of Franklin D. Roosevelt. The New Deal coalition endured throughout the first two postwar decades and coincided with the assimilation of European Catholic ethnics into the American mainstream, the ascendancy of greater and greater numbers of Catholics into the middle class, and the suburbanization of the Catholic population.

In many ways the postwar decades were the golden age of American Catholicism.[5] Catholic institutions such as the parochial school provided a strong sense of identity and solidarity for generations of immigrants, and served as way stations on the road to Americanization. Under the theological-philosophical canopy of Neo-Thomism a revival in spirituality and associational life led to a parallel renewal of Catholic literature, art, and history. The 1940s and 1950s saw the popular culture's celebration of Catholic "innocence," patriotism, sports, and even religious life (with movies about attractive priests and nuns who would break out into song on a moment's notice). One historian, citing Flannery O'Connor, described the corresponding attitude of "Catholic smugness."[6]

During the 1940s and 1950s the theological system known as Neo-Thomism, versions of which informed the curricula of the parochial school system and Catholic colleges and universities, inculcated subtle and not-so-subtle political lessons. Ideologically, Catholic voters came closest in this period to forming a viable bloc: fervid patriotism, virulent anti-communism, and strong identification with the working class and labor unions were the staples of the Catholic political identity. A majority of Catholics tended to vote Democratic with the exception of the presidential races of the 1950s, when they backed Dwight D. Eisenhower. In 1960, with an overwhelming confidence that they had arrived fully and permanently on the American political and cultural scene, 83 percent of Catholic voters helped to ensure the election of the first Roman Catholic president, John F. Kennedy.

Kennedy's election definitively removed the political stigma marking Catholics; ironically, the Catholic Democrat Kennedy's election thus made it possible for the Republican Party to court the Catholic vote and promote Catholic politicians within its ranks. Social trends during the 1960s also contributed mightily to the unraveling of the New Deal Catholic coalition: the breakup of ethnic neighborhoods, the consolidation of suburbia, the divisive crisis of the Vietnam war, the violent controversy over civil rights and race relations in general and busing in particular—each of these developments alienated Catholics from one another and from the Democratic Party. Whereas 64 percent of New Deal generation Catholics (those born between 1910 and 1940) voted for Kennedy in 1960, only 21 percent of these Catholics voted for George McGovern in 1972, and only 44 percent voted for Michael Dukakis in 1988.

When the Catholic boomers began to move into the economy in the 1970s, they ended any hope of reconstituting the old-Catholic vote, for they formed a new generational cohort of voters with tendencies quite different than the New Dealers. For all their disgruntlement with the Democrats, no more than 35 percent of New Deal Catholics ever joined the Republican Party. Yet boomers have always been less Democratic than their New Deal-era parents; the youngest part of this generation, which entered the electorate in 1980, was 20 percent less Democratic than their parents. Among this youngest cohort, Republican Catholics outnumber Democratic Catholics, and they are more loyal to their party. The Catholic boomers are disproportionately Southern, and as fully Republican as are Southern evangelical Protestants. (The experience of assimilation and their extraordinary rise in socio-economic status leads to the expectation that the Irish would be even more Republican than they are, but their history of discrimination keeps their loyalty to the Democrats alive.) The youngest boomers provided the Catholic margin for Ronald Reagan and George H. W. Bush, and they are part of the core of the Republican Party today.[7]

By the 1990s the three generations of laypeople in the church included pre-Vatican II Catholics, born in the 1910s, 1920s, and 1930s; Vatican II Catholics, born in the 1940s and 1950s; and post-Vatican II Catholics, born in the 1960s and 1970s. The "New Deal Catholics" include the preconciliar generation as well the older Catholics who came of age during Vatican II. The older boomers are also Vatican II Catholics, but the younger ones came of age in the postconciliar period.

On any number of religious and sociomoral issues, from a yearning for democracy in the church to a belief in the supremacy of the individual in moral decisions, each succeeding generation has been increasingly more "liberal." (The term is employed in this context as an ecclesial, not a secular-political marker.) On economic questions, however, lay Catholics have become increasingly conservative, with the younger boomers constituting by far the most conservative cohort.

According to a team of sociologists who published their findings in 1996, more than 50 percent of post-Vatican II Catholic laity believe that the individual (rather than the magisterium) is the supreme moral judge in matters of birth control, abortion, homosexuality, and sex outside of marriage. And levels of religious commitment have declined over the generations: whereas 59 percent of pre-Vatican II Catholics think that "the Church is important," only 29 percent of the postconciliar Catholics agree with the statement. Mass attendance and daily prayer have fallen off in the same proportions, as have general levels of familiarity with church teaching. Whereas 26 percent of the pre-Vatican II Catholics and 24 percent of the Vatican II Catholics are aware of the U. S. bishops' 1986 pastoral letter on the economy, only 11 percent of the post-Vatican II Catholics say they know of its existence.[8]

Post-Vatican II Catholic boomers place a higher priority on being a good "Christian" than being a good "Catholic"; they have a deinstitutionalized and democratic view of the church; they reserve the right to make up their own minds on religious and moral as well as political and economic issues; they believe they have direct access to the Creator's love apart from the institutional church; they are more likely to disagree with the church's teachings; they are almost entirely uninformed about church teachings; they lack a vocabulary that would help them to form a Catholic identity or interpret their Catholic experiences; and they are situational in their ethical thinking. Young Catholic boomers who are Republican say they are attracted to the party on economic rather than sociomoral grounds. Survey data indicate that the more deeply religious Catholics—those who pray and attend Mass regularly—are less likely to be Republican, despite the party's anti-abortion platform. Indeed, among both New Deal and baby boom Catholics, "those for whom religion is *less* salient in both groups are more likely to vote Republican." New Deal Catholics, the data indicate, are more religiously involved and socially compassionate on welfare issues.[9]

What do those shifts mean? This is difficult to determine—harder, certainly, than the days when the adage "vote your conscience" meant something fairly definite for Catholics. It is not the case that Catholics have no conscience these days; rather, they have many consciences. After a generation of experimentation in forming Catholic identity, the survey data indicate that there are many kinds of individual Catholics (emphasis on the word *individual*) and thus many certifiably Catholic consciences.

From the 1980s to the present, however, the boomers have been in the ascendancy. By 1988 only 39 percent of the Catholic electorate hailed from the New Deal/Democratic generation. Strikingly, 30 percent of those who described themselves as Catholic in recent surveys never attend Mass and are not religious; they are disproportionately under age forty-five. When economic issues predominate, they vote Republican; when social issues are paramount, they vote Democratic. They most resemble "seculars," those with no religious affiliation, in their voting patterns, but often they do not vote at all. At the other end of the spectrum are the evangelical Catholics: the sacramentally active, Bible-reading, evangelizing true believers who are most likely to promote the Catholic Social Tradition. This group is the opposite of the seculars; when economic issues are paramount, they vote Democratic, when social issues are front-burner, they vote Republican.

The Catholic electorate, of course, is by no means monolithic: the mix includes urban Catholics, suburban Catholics, rural Catholics, Hispanic Catholics, Asian Catholics, and African American Catholics. And then there are conservative or "orthodox" Catholics.

The two most important changes within the American Catholic community in the last thirty years—a shift in voting patterns that has increased the Republican Party's share of the Catholic vote, and the community's increasingly lax adherence to Catholic teaching on everything from artificial birth control to social and economic teachings (particularly among the young and affluent)—are related. Ironies abound, of course. With the intention of promoting a more liberal, social-justice-oriented style of Catholicism, the progressives of the 1960s and 1970s ended up diluting the devotional tradition, altered the process of forming consciences, and encouraged conscientious dissent from official church teaching—all of which had the paradoxical effect of laying the foundation for the current swing to the political Right.

Like most major historical events, Vatican II had unintended consequences. The theological and religious pluralism it fostered, coupled with the uneven quality of Catholic catechesis in general and the teaching of Catholic social doctrine in particular, effectively put an end to the Catholic bloc as a political entity. Plural religious cultures within "big-tent Catholicism" led to plural Catholic political cultures.

The Catholic electorate is different today, in short, because the Catholic Church is different than it was before the recent voting shift began approximately thirty years ago. If one admits even a degree of correlation between religious culture and political affiliation, it is clear that the postconciliar changes in American Catholic religious culture stand behind the shifts in the Catholic electorate.

While U.S. Catholic bishops have attempted to exercise influence over the voting patterns of U.S. Catholics at key moments in this long history, the extent and depth of that influence is highly contested. During the period of ethnic bloc politics in the inter-World War and post-World War decades, bishops and priests led their flock in affiliating with the Democratic Party. The bishops have been politically active during the recent shift as well, in response to the fragmentation of the Catholic religious—and religio-political—community. They take the word "Catholic" to be their institutional trademark, and they tend to resist any attempt by outsiders to infringe upon the copyright. (The bishops are particularly concerned about the diffusion of the Catholic voice when movements and groups claiming the name "Catholic" issue political statements at odds with their own positions.) In their 1995 "Statement of Political Responsibility," the bishops advocated many of the same positions taken by the New Christian Right, including strong opposition to abortion; the return of power to state and local governments; and a stand against a creeping secularism, advanced by many policymakers who operate as if the Constitution's guarantee of religious freedom means freedom *from* religion's influence. In the run-up to the 2004 presidential election, a minority of the U.S. bishops—no more than twelve or thirteen from a population of more than three hundred bishops—suggested that any Catholic political candidate who was pro-choice on the abortion issue, should be denied Holy Communion at Mass and perhaps be formally excommunicated. Some observers believe that the controversy and public attention given to this issue seriously wounded the presidential candidacy of the Roman Catholic pro-choice Democratic nominee John Kerry. If this is true, the bishops have retained at least a measure of their historic influence, despite their weakened status in a fragmented Catholic population scandalized by the public scandal around the sexual abuse of children and young adults committed by some priests over a forty-year period, and covered up by a significant percentage of the bishops during this period.

Explanations

Secularization by Way of Indifferentism

Have Catholic voting patterns become detached, or uncoupled, from Catholic religious identity? The question is complex, in that the relationship between the two was never straightforward: Catholics, that is, have always included "non-religious" factors, such as economic self-interest, in their voting calculations. But the church once provided a theological, sacramental, and ethical lens through which the "extra-religious" factors were perceived and interpreted. Has this role diminished during the recent shift in Catholic voting patterns?

Certainly there is no dearth of anxious voices claiming that the influence of the hierarchy and the institutional church has suffered decline. The anxiety can be traced to the post-World War II period, when Catholic assimilation into mainstream American society began to accelerate. Two centrally positioned priests, Joseph Clifford Fenton (1906-69) and Francis Jeremiah Connell (1888-1967), raised the first alarm. Fenton, ordained in 1930, began his teaching career in 1934, arrived at the Catholic University of America in 1938, and became editor of the *American Ecclesiastical Review* (*AER*) in 1944, serving in that capacity until he suffered a heart attack in 1963. He published 189 articles in the *AER* alone. Connell, a Redemptorist priest ordained in 1913, taught theology for twenty-five years before moving to Catholic University in 1940, where he authored an astounding 641 pieces, over five hundred of which were answers to questions sent by the many priests who subscribed to the journal.[10]

Fenton and Connell argued that an undiscriminating religious environment had been created in the United States as a consequence of the nation's experience in the Second World War. Coinciding with the first generation of American Catholics to come of age after immigration restriction, the war and its aftermath led to a new social mobility, economic prosperity, and a reinvigorated nationalist ideology, trends which Catholics experienced or embraced as readily as did other Americans.

During the war Catholics and Protestants alike seized upon the rise of Nazism and the dramatic collapse of France before the German onslaught as illustrations of the moral and military decrepitude of an increasingly secular West. In a deft blending of traditional jeremiad and institutional special pleading, Protestants urged the citizenry to return to religion, and thereby strengthen the Republic. The personal liberties and democratic polities of the West, it was argued, had been derived from a biblical anthropology that nurtured respect for the inalienable dignity of the human person. The fragility of the democratic experiments—amply illustrated in their ineffective response to totalitarian aggression—had to be countered with a strengthening of their spiritual and moral foundations. Catholic apologists, meanwhile, had been using socialism and communism as examples of human autonomy gone awry since the nineteenth century, and it was not difficult to incorporate Nazism into the litany of ills with which to flay liberalism. Fenton momentarily grabbed this opportunity, arguing that the perennial philosophy is the "great weapon of civilization" for it provides "the fundamentals upon which an enduring civilization can be based."[11]

In wartime relief efforts and pastoral work no less than in sociocultural criticism, the menacing power of a revitalized paganism required a coordinated Christian response. Intercreedal collaboration during the war led to a makeshift ecumenism, the justifications for which were left to theologians of the several cooperating Christian denominations. The exigencies of this international crisis raised a "strictly theological issue" for Catholics, which the Jesuit public philosopher John Courtney Murray posed as follows: "Can Catholics and non-Catholics form a unity by the fact of co-operation without thereby compromising the Catholic Unity of the Church?"[12]

What would count as compromise became the crux of a bitter controversy in the postwar years leading up to Vatican II. Fenton and Connell fought doggedly for well over a decade against what they perceived as a rising tide of *Catholic indifferentism* that threatened distinctive Roman Catholic identity in the United States. The wartime mobilization of millions of Americans hailing from diverse religious backgrounds had strengthened that troublesome spirit, Connell explained, and the principles of latitudinarianism were becoming powerful as a result of "above all, the governmental attitude so consistently practiced in all matters pertaining to religion, that all forms of religious belief are equally good."[13] By "indifferentism" they meant the idea that religious differences are, or ought to be, of little or no importance in the public arena. Occasioned by postwar ecumenism and liberalism, indifferentism was a threat to the priority of the supernatural over the natural elements in religion; Fenton and Connell responded by emphasizing the exclusive and absolute truth-claims of Roman Catholicism. They were reluctant to endorse further Catholic assimilation into the American mainstream, for fear that economic prosperity tied to social integration required unacceptable compromises.

Connell, citing Pope Pius XII's 1950 encyclical *Humani generis*, reminded Father Murray that knowledge of the moral (natural) law in all its details depends upon a prior apprehension of divine revelation. "How, then, can civil rulers know their duties of natural law unless they have recourse to revelation, as interpreted by the one authentic teacher of revealed truth, the Catholic Church?" he asked. "If a person tries to solve the moral problems connected with sterilization, euthanasia, contraception, etc., he will very easily go astray unless he relies on Christian revelation as proposed by the teaching authority of the Church." Connell sharply "reminded" Murray of "the Catholic doctrine regarding the obligation of the state to acknowledge and obey the law of Jesus Christ, and to recognize in His Church certain rights and privileges granted by divine positive legislation."[14]

Secularization by Way of Internal Pluralism

Fenton and Connell believed that their fears had been realized by 1960. By the time of Kennedy's election to the presidency Catholic insularity and autonomy in the political sphere was already giving way to lay Catholic conformity with the norms of the mainstream culture. Vanishing were the triumphant, massive public rituals that had been common in the pre-suburban world of American Catholicism. The meanings and relationships symbolized in these rituals, originally developed in the context of a hierarchically controlled, deferential and devotional insular church, no longer expressed the values of Catholics yearning for the suburbs. The suburbs fostered family-centered activities and pushed people away from commitments to participation in larger social networks.

The waning of the comprehensive authority of the parish priest over his once-immigrant flock was also well advanced. By establishing his political independence from the pope and the bishops without losing his Catholic identity, Kennedy became an icon for the new postwar generation of upwardly mobile Catholics. These university-educated Catholic scientists, lawyers, politicians, and business executives—the parents of the baby boomers—were more likely than their immigrant grandparents to compartmentalize their religious identity and take their political and economic signals from the secular order rather than from their priests and bishops. Vatican's II's emphasis on lay autonomy and leadership, coupled with its ringing endorsement of religious freedom, the priority of conscience, and the separation of church and state, inadvertently reinforced the new sense of political independence and contributed to the fragmentation of the Catholic vote.

Among the most far-reaching consequences of Vatican II was the rise of theological pluralism within Roman Catholicism; almost overnight, it seemed, biblical theology, early versions of liberation theology, and other experiential theologies displaced Neo-Thomism at the center of the Catholic intellectual world. By the 1970s the new theologies had reinforced a postconciliar paradigm for the relationship between church and world: the image of the church as a pilgrim on earth, a sinner on the road to salvation, in marked contrast to the preconciliar, Tridentine notion of the church as the spotless Bride of Christ, the "perfect, eternal society."

The "new" content of Catholic identity included the tenets of Catholic social teaching, an unfolding tradition inaugurated by Pope Leo XIII in 1891 with the promulgation of his encyclical letter *Rerum Novarum* (The Condition of Labor). Based on natural law, *Rerum Novarum* defended the right of workers to organize, asserted the inviolable and sacred right of the individual to own private property, and condemned atheistic socialism as well as the excesses of laissez-faire capitalism. From the time of Leo XIII the Catholic Social Tradition (CST) has been a specifiable body of doctrines and principles governing Catholic participation in the social order. As such, it forms the foundation of American Catholic political philosophy; it constitutes, in other words, the official frame of reference for every Catholic exercising his or her civic rights in the political order. Certain documents of Vatican II—especially *Gaudium et Spes*, (Pastoral Constitution on the Church in the Modern World)—can be read as positioning the CST in the very center of Roman Catholic self-understanding, doctrinal teaching, and pastoral practice.

In 1971 a synod of Catholic bishops meeting in Rome to reflect on this legacy of Vatican II issued the document *Justice in the World*, which proclaimed a principle held dear by a generation of Catholic social activists and educators: "Action on behalf of justice and participation in the transformation of the world fully appear to us as a constitutive dimension of the proclamation of the Gospel, or, in other words, of the Church's mission for the redemption of the human race and its liberation from every oppressive situation."[15]

The basic principles of the CST include: (1) *the common good*, the notion that Catholics ought to pursue policies and programs that serve the best interests of the public at large rather than a particular sub-group within society; (2) *solidarity*, the affirmation that all people at every level of society should participate together in building a just society; (3) *subsidiarity*, the dictum that greater and higher associations or governing bodies ought not to do what lesser and lower (more local) associations can do themselves (a sort of Catholic federalism); (4) *a preferential option for the poor*, a principle with concrete implications for a host of social programs, beginning with welfare; (5) *the priority and inviolablilty of human rights*, especially the cornerstone right to life, but also the economic rights to own private property, to work for a just wage, and so forth; and (6) *preferential option for the family* as the basic social unit.

A monumental case of bad timing hurt Catholics in the postconciliar years: just when these principles were being articulated and discussed at the highest levels, most American Catholics—clergy, laity, and women religious alike—had neither the necessary preparation nor the specialized knowledge necessary to disseminate the CST at every educational level. Prior to Vatican II a small elite company of diocesan and religious order priests had been studying the new theology from Europe and the growing tradition of Catholic social doctrine. In the 1960s they crafted their own programs of social action in urban and rural areas. When Vatican II seemed to give an official blessing to these efforts, these pioneers began to promote the teaching of the CST in the parishes as well as the Catholic colleges and universities. Their impact was limited, however, by other crises such as the growing number of defections from the priesthood and sisterhood, which diverted pastoral attention and energies elsewhere.[16]

In short, the new pluralism had its dizzying downside. The debate about the proper relation of education and formation led to a general confusion in catechetical circles, exacerbated by the tendency of some educators to adopt what amounted to a pastiche approach to curricular reform—a dash of scripture here, a touch of pop psychology there. A stultifying randomness characterized methods of religious instruction and textbook content in the late 1960s and throughout the 1970s; in most cases, regrettably, the coherent principles and teachings of the CST did not form the foundation of the new catechetical approach.

Sociologist William Dinges has aptly characterized the period as a time of "severe disorientation." By the mid-1970s the American church had become almost paralyzed by the variety of seemingly conflicting teachings attributed to Vatican II, and by searching questions about the appropriate roles of clergy, laity, and women religious. Disarray and confusion in Catholic education was perhaps the strongest symptom of the identity crisis.

As a result boomer Catholics, especially the younger members of the generation, either were not sufficiently exposed to the CST, or rejected it, along with other forms of authoritative teaching. Many boomers did not understand, much less experience, the intimate relationship between the new vernacular Mass and the call to greater engagement in the works of social justice. The liturgical reforms, properly practiced and interpreted, were intended to reinforce the church's turn to the world; often they served merely to confuse or bore untutored Catholics. A golden opportunity was therefore missed. What could have been a stable and comprehensive foundation for a new Catholic solidarity on public and political issues became, instead, the province of what historian David O'Brien calls the "evangelical Catholics," the sub-group of aging Catholic New Dealers and fresh-faced boomers who did accept and internalize the CST.

Evangelical Catholics embraced the CST with a passionate sense of commitment, but they were not altogether suited to be the bearers of traditional teaching. Some sympathized with or joined the outspoken opponents of Pope Paul VI's 1968 encyclical, *Humanae Vitae*, that restated the traditional Catholic ban on artificial birth control. Thus they were in the front ranks of those who popularized the notion of dissent from the teaching of the magisterium. In their efforts to promote the CST, the classic dilemma of the Catholic liberal haunted them: how to avoid authoritarianism while inculcating principles and norms deemed to be essential to the formation of (the new) Catholic religious identity?

The explosion of theological pluralism also contributed to the vague sense that much of Catholic teaching was offered on a consumerist model (that is, take what you want and ignore the rest).

In the most debilitating of ironies, the very American bishops who railed against pick-and-choose Catholicism, contributed inadvertently to the ethos informing it. In their widely publicized pastoral letters on the economy and the arms race in the 1980s, the bishops acknowledged that people of good will, including Catholics who share their basic theological assumptions and moral principles, have a right to disagree on the prudential application of those principles in formulating specific public policies.

Such a right came in handy for doctrinaire capitalist commentators on the Catholic Right who were quick to reject the specific recommendations of the pastoral letter on the U.S. economy (*Economic Justice for All* [1986])—which was informed, they thought, by a kind of vague socialism termed "distributive justice." In the 1980s high profile Catholic laymen (including cabinet members in the administrations of Richard Nixon and Ronald Reagan) also seized the opportunity of "prudential judgment" to oppose central elements of the social teaching of the bishops.[17]

Conclusion

Sociologists employ the concept of "elective affinity" to explain a pattern of social grouping by which individuals shape or accept ideas that underwrite and reinforce economic or institutional self-interests. For roughly the first half of the twentieth century, the immigrant parish protected Catholic economic and political self-interests. A "sacred canopy" of beliefs and practices encompassed Catholic participation in the public square, including voting patterns. The postwar move to the suburbs and the steady assimilation of white post-European Catholics into the American mainstream sundered their bonds to the thought-world of the immigrant church and to a devotional culture that emphasized hierarchy, authority, and theological conformity. The Catholic-Democratic voting bloc began to disintegrate as newly middle class Catholics increasingly took their social cues not from the pastor or bishop but from professional colleagues, including Protestants.

Not long after these trends took hold, the Catholic civic and political presence in U.S. society became more professionalized, specialized, and "elitist" in an era of "public Catholicism" that saw the rise of sophisticated lobbying on Capitol Hill (by the U.S. Catholic Conference of Bishops) and before state legislatures (by state Catholic conferences). This public presence incited complaint from some quarters against the "promiscuity" of the U.S. Catholic Conference: Did Jesus come to save campaign finance reform, or souls? And whose "interests" did the lobbying group represent?

The new generation of "professional Catholics" did not confine their efforts to the national and state Catholic conferences; they also worked in education at all levels, engaged in local advocacy for the poor and dispossessed, and led community based organizing efforts. They volunteered to assist in refugee relocation, created and staffed local programs for the disabled, and became involved in countless charitable and social justice initiatives.

This postconciliar professionalized outreach beyond the Catholic community was not designed to build or reinforce a voting bloc, garner votes, or even influence elections. "If we did nothing but legislative advocacy, we would still be relatively unique," notes John Huebscher, the director of the Wisconsin Catholic Conference "*because most of our advocacy is for someone else*—the unborn, poor children, and others without a voice."[18]

Yet leaders of the national and state Catholic conferences are acutely aware that the right kind of political leadership is critical to sound and generous social policy; and they have worked assiduously for a generation to inculcate the fundamental principles of Catholic social teaching in Catholic youth and young adults. A vital, conscientious, and politically informed cadre of high school and college students and young adults owe their existence in part to these educators and social justice advocates. Reconstituting a Catholic voting bloc nonetheless seems beyond their purview; and the precise political payoff, in terms of voting patterns of "enlightened" Catholics formed in the CST, remains unclear. For various reasons the educational effort has not overcome the fragmentation of the Catholic electorate described in this essay.

Notes

1. The first part of this chapter—the discussion of Catholic voting patterns in the twentieth century—is adapted from a previously published essay: R. Scott Appleby, "Roll Call: The Vanishing Catholic Vote." *Notre Dame Magazine* 25, no. 4 (Winter 1997): 17-21.

2. *Rising Tide* (May 1996): 6-11.

3. *Rising Tide* (May 1996): 6-11.

4. David C. Leege, *Rediscovering the Religious Factor in American Politics* (Armonk, N.Y.: M.E. Sharpe, 1993); David C. Leege, "Divining the Electorate: Is There a Religious Vote?—Political Campaigning to Obtain Support by Religious Groups," *Commonweal* 127, no. 18 (2000): 16-19; David C. Leege and Michael R. Welch, "Religious Roots of Political Orientations: Variations among American Catholic Parishioners," *Journal of Politics* 51, no. 11 (1989): 137-62.

5. Jay P. Dolan, *The American Catholic Experience: A History from Colonial Times to the Present* (Notre Dame, IN: University of Notre Dame Press. 1992), 350.

6. Dolan, *American Catholic Experience*, 352.

7. William V. D'Antonio, James D. Davidson, Dean Hoge, and Ruth Wallace, *Laity: American and Catholic, Transforming the Church* (Kansas City: Sheed and Ward, 1996), 69.

8. D'Antonio et al., *Laity*, 76.

9. D'Antonio et al., *Laity*, 79.

10. *The American Catholic Who's Who 1964-65* (Grosse Point, MI: Walter Romig, n.d.), 75, 135. Joseph M. White reports on the priests' output in *The Diocesan Seminary in the United States: A History from the 1780s to the Present* (Notre Dame, IN: University of Notre Dame Press, 1989), 333. Also see Joseph J. Farragher, S.J., review of *Father Connell Answers Moral Questions*, by Francis J. Connell, C.SS.R., *Theological Studies* 21 (1960): 312. See R. Scott Appleby and John Haas, "The Last Supernaturalists: Fenton, Connell, and the Threat of Catholic Indifferentism," *U.S. Catholic Historian* 13 (Winter 1995): 23-48.

11. Joseph C. Fenton, "The Perils of Consistency," *Commonweal* 21 (1935): 733-34.

12. John Courtney Murray, S.J., "Intercreedal Co-Operation: Its Theory and Its Organization," *Theological Studies* 4 (1943): 257.

13. Francis J. Connell, "Pope Leo XIII's Message to America," *American Ecclesiastical Review* 109 (October 1943): 254.

14. Connell, "Pope Leo XIII's Message," 254.

15. "Justice in the World," in *The Gospel of Peace and Justice*, ed. J. B. Gremillion (Maryknoll, NY: Orbis, 1976), 514.

16. Paul Wilkes, *A Good Enough Catholic: A Guide for the Perplexed* (New York: Balantine Books, 1996); Jim Naughton, *Catholics in Crisis: An American Parish Fights for its Soul* (New York: Addison-Wesley, 1996); Ivor Shaprio, *What God Allows: The Crisis of Faith and Conscience in One Catholic Church* (New York: Doubleday, 1996); Michael Warner, *Changing Witness: Catholic Bishops and Public Policy, 1917-1994* (Washington, D. C. and Grand Rapids, MI: Ethics and Public Policy Center and Eerdmans, 1995); R. Scott Appleby, "Crunch Time for American Catholicism," *The Christian*

Century 113, no. 11 (1996): 370-76; "Catholics in Turmoil," *Chicago Tribune*, a twelve part series, December 8-20, 1996.

17. "Catholics in the Public Square," unpublished working group manuscript (2002). The question of the practical application of Catholic social doctrine is discussed in the volume that issued forth from the conference and draft manuscript cited here. In Margaret O'Brien Steinfels. ed. *American Catholics & Civic Engagement: A Distinctive Voice* (Lanham. MD: Rowman & Littlefield, 2004), see the following chapters: John A. Coleman, "The Common Good and Catholic Social Thought," 3-18; William A. Galston, "Contending with Liberalism," 42-57; Michael Lavey and William M. Shea, "Catholics and the Liberal Tradition," 58-68.

18. "Catholics in the Public Square," unpublished working group manuscript (2002). See also John Huebscher's published comments in William Bole. "What Do State Catholic Conferences Do?" in Steinfels, *American Catholics & Civic Engagement*. 92-109.

Chapter Six
French Catholics, Secularization, and Politics

Blandine Chélini-Pont

A New Turn

A Turn of the Century Religious Revival

In 1985, Marcel Gauchet published *Le désenchantement du monde* (The disenchantment of the world).[1] In the wake of his analysis, two generations of political and social scientists working in the field of religion have added their weight to the theory of the inexorable "secularization" of contemporary societies, according to which modernization "negatively" entails a decline in religion as a cultural source for society and as a structuring framework for behavior and "positively" allows for the deployment of critical thinking, concerted democratic choices, and individualized lifestyles. Today, these same political and social scientists of religion seem to be backpedaling. To give an example of this, in 2002 the French edition of a book edited by the American scholar Peter Berger bore a symptomatic title: *Le réenchantement du monde* (The reenchantment of the world), a retrospective allusion to the work of Marcel Gauchet.[2] The underlying argument of the book, the fruit of numerous investigations, some of them French, is that our epoch has become "furiously" religious (this is the term that Berger uses), and that the predictions linked to the inexorability of secularization have been shown to be erroneous. Accelerated modernization has, on the contrary, engendered a movement of extremely acute counter-secularization—a movement that has propagated itself rapidly given the speed of media interconnections, their technological power, the increasing intermingling/cross-fertilization of populations, their deterritorialization, which, in some ways, has provoked the birth of a postmodern spiritual nomadism, in part due to economic migrations in which over ten years more than 50 million people have migrated across the world—a figure that is truly staggering.

European Secularization

What has become of the movement towards secularization? Researchers tell us that it is continuing but that it is neither inevitable nor universal in scope. It is concentrated in continental Europe, which now appears to be the only region in which secularization is a deeply rooted cultural phenomenon. There it appears all the more entrenched because it is the fruit of a long process of internal maturation characterized by dwindling rates of religious observance, a numerical and normative decline in traditional religious institutions, and a marked tendency to engage in purely political debates. This type of argument is behind the latest book by Jean-Paul Willaime, *Europe et religions, les enjeux du XXIè siècle.*[3] It is acknowledged that Europe has seen the arrival of a growing number of "sects" as well as the growth of forms of Christianity rooted in Anglo-Saxon or third-world countries that are at home amid today's competitive fragmentation of religious denominations, the penetration of Westernized forms of Buddhism, and the settlement of many variants of Islam, some of them very radical in nature. Yet these developments pale into insignificance when compared with the upsurge of evangelicalism in Latin America, the exponential growth of atomized religious movements in Africa, and the growing power of Salafist Islamic movements in Central Asia, Africa, and Southeast Asia. Europe is exceptional by virtue of the depth its secularization, of which France is without doubt the clearest example.

French Catholics and Secularization

French Catholics are certainly aware that religion is making a comeback. An opinion survey conducted by the CSA polling company for *Le Monde des religions* in June 2005 found that 56 percent of those questioned felt religion occupied a more important position than ten years earlier.[4] A similar proportion (59 percent) felt too much importance was given to religion in the world as a whole and 47 percent said the same of France; 57 percent said religions were unimportant for a successful personal life, while 41 percent disagreed. Some 48 percent were less interested in religions than ten years earlier; only 26 percent said their interest in the subject had grown during that period. Only 14 percent felt religions were progressive forces; 38 percent felt they were retrograde forces while 40 percent were undecided. This survey shows that most people in France are very wary about religion and the effects of secularization seem to have deeply impregnated Catholics themselves. The sociologist Danielle Hervieu-Léger argued in 2003 that Catholicism is quite simply no longer part of the shared system of references in the French cultural universe.[5] Its values, ideas, and human representatives are disappearing from everyday social life. Despite the Catholic funeral of former President François Mitterrand, the weekly act of worship of President Jacques Chirac, and the unexpectedly large gathering of a million young people in Paris during the Catholic Church's Journée Mondiale de la Jeunesse (World Youth Day) in 1997, there is no sign of a religious revival among the French in general or in favor of French Catholicism in particular. Opinion surveys consistently suggest that Catholicism is continuing to lose ground in French society. A survey carried out for *La Croix* in December 2004 found not only that the Catholic population was predominantly female (55 percent of those declaring themselves to be Catholics were women), but also that it was concentrated among older generations. Some 50.3 percent of those declaring themselves to be Catholics were over fifty years old; 12.2 percent were over seventy-five.[6]

Researchers such as Jean-Marie Donegani specializing in the relationship between Catholicism and politics have tended increasingly to argue that Catholics no longer constitute a distinctive political strand.[7] For the history of Catholicism in France, this really does look like the end of an era if not of the world. The political history of France cannot be understood without giving due weight to Catholicism, its role under the Ancien Régime, the importance held by its totalizing political ideas until the end of the nineteenth century, and the fierce resistance of its leaders against the liberal, democratic ideas of the other France which emerged from the Revolution of 1789. Neither can we understand the history of twentieth-century France without acknowledging the importance of the pro-Catholic Action Française movement up until the Second World War and then its inversion and replacement by its political opposite, the Christian Democratic movement, after 1945.

The broad picture sketched above nevertheless needs to be nuanced. Researchers such as Guy Michelat have on the one hand highlighted the strong dilution of Catholic identity in France,[8] including that pertaining to political influence, while at the same time noting the paradox of a phenomenon of impregnation which makes it impossible to conclude that there is no real Catholic perspective, either in general or with reference to political questions in particular. In a sense, Catholics are now nowhere and everywhere. The Catholic religion is still dominant in terms of the identity to which people in France say they "belong"—64 percent of French people referred to themselves as Catholics in the December 2004 CSA survey, and 78 percent of those questioned in the June 2005 *Le Monde des Religions* poll said they believe human beings have an essential need for religions. This religious affiliation still affects electoral behavior and plays a part in major social debates. Also, it turns out that a minority characterized by Guy Michelat as "undiluted" Catholics retains a strong internal religious cohesion (through faith, religious observance, and the transmission of these properties) simultaneously with strong political and social orientations that they are determined to defend.[9] In the final analysis, therefore, a Catholic presence in contemporary political debates is still perceptible. As Italian historian Giancarlo Zizola writes, that presence is no longer such as to give "power a conscience" but continues, in a toned-down form, to ensure that "conscience has a degree of power."[10]

The "Solubility" of Catholics in French Politics

Lower Numbers and Thinner Beliefs

If we return to the general idea of an absence of Catholic specificity in contemporary political debates, a primary cause of this would no doubt be the substantial numerical weakening of Catholics, accompanied by a transformation in their sense of belonging that means that, when they see themselves as Catholics, they do so only in an extremely diluted fashion.[11] Numerical weakening may be illustrated by reference to statistical research on beliefs published in the social data collected by the state statistical agency INSEE in 2002, together with a commentary by the researcher Yves Lambert.[12] Other sources are also available for this period, such as the 1999 European Values Survey highlighted in a special edition of the review *Futuribles* in 2002.[13] The data presented by Lambert showed that in the year 2000, when the population of France stood at 60.7 million, 44 percent said they had no religion; among teenagers and the eighteen- to twenty-nine-year-old age group, the proportion saying they had no religion was 53 percent. In 1981, the proportion of the national population professing no religion was 29 percent. Catholicism has been the main victim of this sharp decline in religious belief. Among those professing religious beliefs in 2000, some 52 percent were Catholics compared with 71 percent in 1981 and 86 percent in 1966, when 2 percent had declared themselves to be Protestants while the combined total of Jews, Muslims, Buddhists, and adherents of other faiths had accounted for only 1 percent of all religious believers.

Two more recent surveys are slightly less bleak for Catholics. In a poll conducted in March 2003 for *La Vie-Le Monde*, 62 percent said they were Catholics, 5 percent were Muslims, 3 percent were of other religious faiths, and 30 percent had no religious beliefs.[14] The results of CSA's December 2004 survey for *La Croix* were similar: 73 percent said they had a religion, among whom 64 percent were Catholics and 9 percent were of other faiths (half of the latter were Muslims, with Protestants and Jews accounting for most of the rest); 27 percent said they had no religion. Some 42 percent of children had been taught the catechism.[15] Despite the variations in some of these data, they clearly suggest that there has been a twenty point fall in the percentage of the population professing the Catholic religion, notwithstanding the fact that about 60 percent still say they are Catholics.

But what kind of Catholicism is this? The 2004 CSA-*La Croix* survey found that only 8 percent of the French could be regarded as fully practicing Catholics (with regular weekly acts of worship, a wider understanding of their faith, and social behavior influenced by it). Some 41 percent of those declaring themselves to be Catholics said they never practiced the religion and 10 percent never "used" the religion, except for special occasions or rites of passage. On the question of major life events, according to a report in the Catholic newspaper *La Croix*, June 19, 2003, 60 percent of the French population as a whole still had recourse to the church in connection with births, 50 percent for marriages, and 80 percent for funerals.[16] Michelat has underscored the paradoxical situation that now exists.[17] While Catholicism remains the dominant religion in terms of the numbers professing it, it is now in a minority situation in terms of real religious practices. Moreover, the fragmentation of the Catholic religion is such that those who say they adhere to it have in many cases shifted towards a culture in which religion no longer serves as the principal reference point and explanatory framework for the world. The vast majority of French Catholics are "heirs with no inheritance,"[18] lacking the explanatory beliefs and symbols that were transmitted in the past. Even more striking than the decline in religious observance is the fact that Catholic beliefs are no longer known, understood, or accepted, by those who consider themselves to have inherited the religion.[19]

Widespread Rejection of Catholic Norms on Sexual and Family Matters

In this minority situation, what sort of measurable difference can Catholicism make in political debates on domestic or international matters? On a great many points, Catholic specificity has disappeared, and Catholics today are hardly distinguishable from the rest of the French population.

For example, in a survey on "The French and laïcité" carried out in December 2003 by the BVA polling company,[20] 46 percent of those questioned felt that the Catholic Church was acting within its role when intervening in cultural questions, while 45 percent were of the opposite view. Some 44 percent felt the church was entitled to intervene on economic and social questions, while 44 percent were of a contrary opinion. However, 60 percent considered that the church was overstepping its role when taking positions on moral questions (such as abortion, sexuality, and procreation). Some 73 percent felt that homosexuality was an acceptable way of living one's sexuality, and 67 percent felt that the adoption of the PACS (Pacte civil de solidarité [civil unions open to homosexuals]) did not endanger the family as an institution. These responses to questions, which might at first sight appear out of place in an opinion survey on *laïcité*, suggest that sexuality and procreation are considered as falling within the domain of *laïcité* in France, that is to say, they are seen as quite separate from religion, indeed one might say that they are regarded as purely "political."

This general view among the French population has to be related in turn to the opinions of Catholics on questions of personal morality. In his analysis of a 1994 survey on the French and Christian beliefs,[21] Jacques Sutter noted that 83 percent of those questioned said they listened to their own conscience rather than to the official position of their church when taking major decisions in their lives.[22] Observing that the low rate of orthodox conformity (9 percent) stood at a similar level to the low rate of regular religious observance (7 percent), Sutter found that this confirmed an earlier analysis he had carried out in 1986:

> If a person declares himself or herself to be deeply Catholic, it is virtually in-conceivable for that person not to have recourse to his or her conscience, which one would ordinarily expect to be situated, informed and guided by the positions of the Church. This is very different from the conscience of Catholics who are less deeply committed to their religion, a conscience that is emancipated, independent, autonomous, bathed in the spirit of modernity. The conflict between these two approaches is very obvious.[23]

For this new type of Catholic, what Sutter calls the "extra-territoriality of human behavior vis-à-vis the field of religion" is almost complete. The "disinheritance of sin" is part of what Danielle Hervieu-Léger calls the ex-culturation of French Catholics. The importance attributed by Catholic doctrine to sin in the regulation of human behavior has almost vanished. In his analysis of attitudes towards a spectrum of notions embracing personal behavior, circumstances, wrongdoing, moral culpability, and sin, Sutter concludes that the traditionally close relationship between behavior and faith has now been lost by French Catholicism. Thus today, 75 percent of professed Catholics say that cohabitation outside marriage is a personal matter and 13 percent say it depends on circumstances; 60 percent say homosexuality is a personal matter and only 11 percent say it is wrong. Similarly, 55 percent say abortion is a personal matter and 13 percent say it depends on circumstances; in other words, 68 percent do not consider abortion to be a sin. Neither has there been any large-scale Catholic mobilization against contraceptives since their legalization in 1967. The prohibition on artificial contraceptives was never really accepted in France, where historians have shown the birth rate to have been kept low since the eighteenth century. This perhaps explains the paradoxical silence in France which followed the 1968 papal encyclical *Humanae Vitae*. Martine Sévegrand has argued that if French Catholics protested less than their American, German, and Belgian counterparts, it was because they were quietly continuing to "compromise" as they had already done for decades.[24] Similarly, when divorce was made easier in 1975, this generated no great shock and quickly became widely used, while simultaneously the rate of cohabitation and childbearing outside marriage steadily rose.

It is clear from all this that where family relationships are concerned, legislation responding to demands for personal freedom and an end to institutional norms has been accepted and acted upon by the French population with a rapidity that may well have surprised those who introduced the new laws and that has certainly decimated the ranks of Catholics. As Danielle Hervieu-Léger has shown, the traditional ideal of Catholic transmission and reproduction through a hierarchical family model based on the institutional structure of the church itself has collapsed and given way, like a breached dike, faced with the rising tide of "relationally based families" characterized by instability, recomposition, and contractual logic.[25] The vertical family of old has given way to the horizontal family in which the individual and the "secular religion of love" have replaced the traditional norms of the church.[26]

Secular Integration and Softer Secularism

No less remarkably, French Catholics appear well integrated in the general structure of French society, and recognize as their own that which for over a century was the bête noire of their religious leaders, that is, the Republic and its secular foundations, reflected in the functioning of its institutions and the content of what may be regarded as a kind of civil religion.[27] *Laïcité* has become the cultural norm for French Catholics. In her analysis of data collected in a 2003 BVA survey, Martine Barthélémy has shown that the attachment of Catholics to *laïcité* is broadly as strong as among the rest of the population.[28] In the same way that Catholics have "blended into" the values of the Republic, French people in general—87 percent of whom feel that *laïcité* is a fundamental value—have ceased being distrustful or resentful towards Catholicism. The great conflicts of old now seem gone. Anti-clericalism, the cement of secular thinking, has diminished from French consciousness in parallel with the disappearance of religious culture. To offer one example from the December 2003 BVA survey: while 38 percent of the general population still consider that the Catholic Church may be to some extent a danger to *laïcité*, 57 percent feel that it is no threat at all or virtually no threat to *laïcité*.

From indicators such as these we can derive a clearer understanding of the "lost frames of reference" frequently lamented by French intellectuals and the media. A country that used to be clearly divided into two camps that knew each other well and based their existence partly on their reciprocal hatred has now become a country in which each camp is infused by the ideas of its old enemy, constructing a vague consensus that fills politicians with despair. This Catholic-secular consensus has now become the cultural identity of the nation.

The Disappearance of Catholic and Christian-Democratic Political Culture

In this confusing debacle the responsibility of French Catholics is considerable. Along with the march of secularization, the evolution of the church itself and the political circumstances of the postwar period have all contributed to the "political absorption" of Catholics.

With the end of the war in 1945, the head of the Catholic Church in Rome moved away from the traditional idea of the "city of God" as a place in which the spiritual and the temporal were to work jointly for the salvation of humanity and replaced this with the idea that the morality of the temporal order was to be judged by its respect for justice and the common good. The movement in this direction had already begun under Pope Leo XIII, who in 1892 had urged French Catholics to accept the Republic. It gathered strength under the papacy of Pope Pius XII in the face of totalitarian regimes. In his Christmas message of 1944, Pius XII in effect integrated the principles of democracy and universal suffrage into Catholic doctrine by no longer allowing democracy simply as a possibility but by recognizing it as inherently legitimate because of its capacity for fulfilling fundamental rights such as the right to express personal opinions, the right to have one's opinion heard, and the political participation of the largest possible number. An important contribution to this current of thought was made by Jacques Maritain in *Christianisme et Démocratie* and *L'Homme et l'Etat*,[29] where democracy is no longer regarded as one legitimate form of governance among others on condition they ensure the common good but as the only full embodiment of the spirit of the Gospels. With Vatican II, the pastoral constitution *Gaudium et Spes* gave a central position in Catholic doctrine to the basic principles of democracy: respect for human rights, moderation in the exercise of power, the rejection of authoritarianism, and the importance of political checks and balances. Nourished by the work of Jacques Maritain and other thinkers like him, together with the official clarification of Catholic doctrine on the political order, French Christian Democracy took shape. French Christian Democrats received their political baptism in the Resistance movement during the war.[30] Their courage gave them a position of political preeminence during the Liberation already prefigured in Charles de Gaulle's appointment in 1943 of Georges Bidault, leader of the prewar Parti Démocrate Populaire, as president of the National Resistance Committee.

The Second World War brought the disintegration of the conservative parties towards which Catholics had traditionally gravitated, the discrediting of Third Republic politicians who had voted for the death of the Republic in 1940, paving the way for the Vichy regime, the disgrace of Charles Maurras and of Action Française nationalists who collaborated with the Nazis, and the de facto legitimacy of General de Gaulle. Together with American support, these all help to explain the very considerable success of Bidault's Christian Democratic Mouvement Républicain Populaire (MRP) among French voters from 1945 onwards, and the accession of its members to the highest positions of state. Following the Liberation it was the MRP that brought together the dispersed groups of Christian-Democratic inspiration from the prewar period.

Pierre Letamendia's 1995 study of the MRP explains very clearly the eventual disappearance of this party due the realization of its goals.[31] It was thanks to the MRP that Catholicism regained acceptance in French political life. The leaders of this party, which in varying degrees participated in government throughout the Fourth Republic, achieved an impressive feat in rallying to democratic and republican values large numbers of Catholics who had up to this point been distrustful towards a Republic that they had seen as a force of "persecution." MRP leaders forced the other political players of this period—radicals, Socialists, and Communists—to give due weight to the Catholic vote within electoral politics under a constitution which all sides understood, from the outset, as secular in nature. In this way the MRP, during its most influential phase, infused into French *laïcité* the spirit of the party's economic ideals, notably in terms of the worth attached to individual human beings through the legal redistribution of wealth. Amid the need to reconstruct an economy that had been devastated through war, it supported social reforms that were directly compatible with the social doctrine of the church, such as the organization of social security, improvements in labor legislation, the introduction of a minimum wage, and the creation of family policy and family allowances. It also worked for taxes on income, profits, and products. Its social interventionism fitted admirably with the nation's tradition of state-led *dirigisme*. State intervention in economic matters, the protection of trade union rights, social laws for the protection of the family, and the promotion of the human person—all of these social and economic policies were and remain foundations of contemporary France, which explains why France is so reluctant to consider the notion that this policy of large-scale economic protection and intervention is perhaps the cause if its decline.

The MRP was also the party of Franco-German reconciliation and European integration *par excellence*. This orientation was largely the work of Robert Schuman, a German-speaking Alsatian, whose emphasis in this direction was not initially shared by the party rank and file, who were more anti-German and pro-Atlanticist in outlook, a line of thinking represented by Georges Bidault, for example. One only has to read the accounts of parliamentary debates on the ratification of the European Coal and Steel Community and European Defense Community treaties to realize how innovative Schuman's approach was and how widely misunderstood and opposed it was. The MRP was also the party that began to calm the long-standing debate over education by trying to secure the position of religious schools without calling into question the existing public education system. Its action helped to pave the way for the recognition of educational freedom in the Constitution of 1958, marking the beginning of the Fifth Republic, and the Debré law of 1959 on state funding for religious schools.

Since the end of the MRP in the 1960s, there has been no explicitly Christian party in French politics. The Catholic electorate was successfully wooed by the Gaullist Party, which succeeded in presenting itself as a party bridging the France of the past with the France of *laïcité*. The voting system used in presidential elections under the Fifth Republic has also favored more directly "political" positioning by candidates without reference to their religious convictions. In addition, the 1960s brought a rapid decline in religious observance and a generational break with the traditional idea of Catholicism as a system of binding beliefs and behavioral rules. The "Catholic vote" was now split across the whole party spectrum, with all parties of both the Left and Right now entirely secular.[32]

From this point onwards, Catholics were no longer a unified, static bloc. A growing minority among them began voting for the Left and to support corresponding opinions. From then on, European construction was no longer driven by a clear ideological motor in France, in contrast with the situation in other European countries, where Christian-Democratic parties continued to exist.

A Catholic "Imprint" on French Politics?

The Continuation of a Conservative Tendency

On the basis of data collected in 1966, Guy Michelat and Michel Simon were able to show that there was still, during that period of political polarization, a strong correlation between identifying oneself as a Catholic and voting for the Right.[33] Catholics voted more for the Right and less for the Left than non-religious people, and this was even more the case for practicing Catholics.[34] In similar studies conducted in 1990 and 1997,[35] Guy Michelat noted a lessening of this phenomenon, but not its disappearance. The erosion was due to a large extent to the work done in seeking political reconciliation during the 1960s and 1970s by political and labor activists close to the Confédération Française Démocratique du Travail (CFDT), a trade union federation formerly known as the Confédération Française des Travailleurs Chrétiens, and Michel Rocard's Parti Socialiste Unifié.[36]

In 1986, some 51 percent of those who believed in the existence of God voted for the Right, compared with 25 percent who voted for the Left; by contrast, 67 percent of atheists voted for the Left. The more the content of the Catholic faith is known and practiced, the higher is the probability of voting for the Right. Commenting on such findings, Yves Lambert suggests that electoral preferences still have a strong ideological dimension.[37] In the second round of the 1995 presidential elections, 59 percent of French Catholics as a whole voted for Jacques Chirac, compared with 41 percent for the candidate of the Left, Lionel Jospin.[38] According to Michelat, in the 1997 parliamentary elections, the Right (not including the extreme-Right National Front) took 57 percent of the vote among Catholics attending church every week, 46 percent among Catholics attending church once a month, 34 percent among occasionally practicing Catholics, 20 percent among non-practicing Catholics, and 8 percent among non-religious voters. Support for the Left was in inverse proportion to this: it took 44 percent of the vote among electors without any religion, 30 percent among non-practicing Catholics, 27 percent among occasionally practicing Catholics, 22 percent among Catholics attending church once a month, and 16 percent among those attending church every week. This negative correlation between a Catholic affiliation and support for the Left applied to all the main parties of the Left (Socialists, Communists, Greens, and Radicals), with the Communist Party particularly marked by this, as in the past. The abstention rate is particularly low among practicing Catholics (20 percent) and at its maximum among non-practicing Catholics and people with no religion (38 percent and 36 percent, respectively).[39]

Michelat infers from this that interest in politics is at its greatest among Catholics whom he characterizes as the most "undiluted" and is lower among those who in the past were more inclined to support the Left and who are today the most affected by a crisis in public interest in politics leading to doubt, party disaffiliation, and in some cases voting for the National Front. It is interesting that very few undiluted Catholics vote for the extreme Right. In the 1995 presidential elections, National Front leader Jean-Marie Le Pen took 16 percent of the vote among non-practicing Catholics and 15 percent among voters with no religion but only 8 percent of the vote among practicing Catholics.

The religious variable remains a heavy one in political sociology in explaining support for the Right. Weighing together the whole of the Catholic vote including regularly practicing Catholics and those who practice their religion monthly, occasionally, or not at all, estimates during the last thirty years show a certain stability. According to Michelat, the religious variable can be held to explain 68 percent of the vote for the Right in 1966, 70 percent in 1978, and 65 percent of this vote in 1997.[40]

A Cautious Attitude to a "Liberal" Europe

The most recent European vote reveals habits of mind deeply anchored among the French population that help to explain the rejection of the European Constitution in 2005. France had helped to build a vision of Europe shaped to a considerable extent by Catholics that included a commitment to substantive social policies through a consensus forged by Socialists and Christian Democrats in the 1950s around a principle which is now referred to as "solidarity," meaning policies designed to reduce social inequalities and eliminate social marginalization and exclusion, with a strong emphasis on equal opportunities and decent living conditions for all citizens in a Republic which is defined in article one of its constitution as "social" in nature. It would be a grave misreading of the fabric of French society to overlook the fact that a vision of an economically "liberal" Europe and a presentation of the European Constitution in essentially commercial terms was bound to offend both practicing and non-practicing Catholics, who together represent 64 percent of the electorate.

In the 1994 European elections, when the electorate in general tended towards hostility to Europe, showing a general lack of confidence and optimism, practicing Catholics showed themselves to be "Euro-optimists." That optimism had declined by the 1999 European elections, when the social policy dimension of the European Union appeared to be in decline in the most recent European treaties, which seemed to simply enshrine the idea of Europe as an ever larger and more efficient market with no real political project whether in terms of independence vis-à-vis the United States or on questions of social justice and peace. In an exit poll in 1999, 61 percent of French voters (and 62 percent of Catholics) said they wanted a Europe that was more independent from the United States and with stronger social policies, in a word a European welfare state. For Catholics as for the population as a whole, the top two priorities were the struggle against social inequalities and for greater personal security. If Europe were to pursue neither peace nor social justice, Europe would lose its purpose and its very soul.[41]

With hindsight we can see in the data from the 1999 European elections the onset of what was to become the great disavowal of 2005. The majority of Catholics, like the majority of the population as a whole, voted against the European Constitution in 2005 in the name of their own European ideal and they showed themselves more and more sympathetic to Euro-skeptics on both the Left and the Right, despite attempts by most party leaders to bring people back into line around a pro-European platform. In a pre-referendum opinion survey, while 53 percent of practicing Catholics said they intended to vote in favor of the European Constitution, only 40 percent of non-practicing Catholics said they intended to do the same,[42] despite the favorable position taken by the conference of French bishops and the Council of Christian Churches in France.[43] The rejection of the Constitution was also due to the defection of non–practicing Catholic voters, who until then had been loyal supporters of a Europe whose institutions they valued to the extent that they served the European population as a whole.

Conclusion: The Family—Last Political Bastion of French Catholics?

Today, very few French Catholics read papal or other ecclesiastical statements on questions of sexual morality, politics, or *laïcité*. They regard sex as a personal matter, are disillusioned about politics, and think *laïcité* is a very good system. With a historical consistency that goes back to Gallicanism, they firmly distance themselves from wholesale acceptance of the authority of Rome and ecclesiastical pronouncements. They maintain strong traditions of charity, expressed today under labels such as "solidarity" and "humanitarian aid." The Abbé Pierre, a Catholic priest who founded the Emmaüs charity for the homeless in 1949, was voted the most popular man in France in 2005. Millions of French Catholics are involved in voluntary associations and work on behalf of the disadvantaged both within France and abroad. Yet so too do other French citizens, making it difficult to see in this a specificity of Catholics socially or politically. This appears to leave one final bastion that, at an underlying level, seems still to distinguish Catholics from the values most commonly found among the rest of the population: the refusal to accept the same symbolic and legal status for homosexual as for heterosexual couples or the same status for same-sex parents as for opposite-sex parents.

This refusal has been forcefully articulated by Christine Boutin, a députée (member of Parliament) and former member of the centrist UDF Party who, for the last ten years, has argued for an implicitly Catholic view of the family in two main domains—the psychological and the legal—which she believes will resonate widely. She presents her discourse within the framework of *laïcité* as a contribution to social debate and as a normal use of the right of free expression available to members of civil society. Thus in its form and presentation, her Catholic cause uses a secular vocabulary containing few direct references to religious doctrine and thereby reaches a wider public than those whom Michelat calls "undiluted" Catholics.

In support of this cause, Catholic newspapers and magazines argue in common that human persons can best flourish when nourished by the authentic ties of a family led by opposite-sex parents who have not divorced or remarried. On this view of things, the true Catholic vision is that long-term commitments are the best way of enabling couples and children to develop to the full.[44] Similarly, the defense of the right of children to be educated in stable families is a recurrent theme among Catholic family associations, whose work in support of families has been recognized, a century after the 1905 law separating churches from the state, as a providing a public good.[45] While relatively muted compared with the pressures brought to bear in Spain in 2006 by bishops and lay associations against homosexual marriages during the visit of Pope Benedict XVI, there has been significant mobilization in France by Catholics opposed to the granting of marital and parenting rights to homosexuals. Christine Boutin was at the forefront of a coalition of religious forces opposed to the movement that eventually led, under the Socialist government of Lionel Jospin, to the law of 1999 establishing a form of civil union known as the PACS (Pacte Civil de Solidarité [Civil Pact of Solidarity]), granting legal recognition and financial protection to any couple regardless of gender or sexual orientation.[46] Against those who argued for this form of civil union as a means of safeguarding the future of individuals and of society at large, the opposing camp insisted that, in line with the thinking of sociologist Irène Théry, society would be mortally endangered if the symbolic status of marriage were to be undermined.[47] The strength of the mobilization against the draft law succeeded in watering it down considerably. This recent example shows that, when core family values are perceived to be threatened, French politics can still flush out into the open a Catholic electorate that is ordinarily more discreet, and has to take account of it.

Translated by Matthew A. Kemp and Alec G. Hargreaves

Notes

1. Marcel Gauchet, *Le désenchantement du monde, une histoire politique de la religion* (Paris: Gallimard, 1985).

2. Peter L. Berger, ed., *The Desecularization of the World: Resurgent Religion and*

World Politics (Grand Rapids, MI: Eerdmans. 1999). The French edition was published by Bayard Press in 2002.

3. Jean-Paul Willaime, *Europe et religions, les enjeux du XXIème siècle* (Paris: Fayard, 2004).

4. CSA survey for *Le Monde des religions*, http://www.csa-tmo.fr (accessed September 7, 2005).

5. Danielle Hervieu-Léger, *Catholicisme, la fin d'un monde* (Paris: Bayard, 2003).

6. CSA survey for *La Croix*, "Les Français et la Religion," http://www.csa-tmo.fr/dataset/data2004/0401664.pdf (accessed February 16, 2005).

7. Jean-Marie Donegani, *La Liberté de choisir. pluralisme religieux et pluralisme politique dans le catholicisme français contemporain* (Paris: Presses de la FNSP, 1993).

8. Guy Michelat, Julien Potel, Jacques Sutter, and Jacques Maître, *Les Français sont-ils encore catholiques?* (Paris: Cerf, 1991); see also Guy Michelat, Julien Potel, and Jacques Sutter, *L'héritage chrétien en disgrâce* (Paris: L'Harmattan, 2003).

9. These are categorized by Michelat as those who feel that the terms "Catholic," "believer," "Christian," and "religiously observant" define them very well.

10. Giancarlo Zizola, *Le Successeur* (Paris: Desclée de Brouwer, 1995), 18.

11. In this respect, Michelat distinguishes four categories of Catholics: those who go to church weekly, those who go once a month, those who worship only occasionally, and those who do not practice their religion at all. Guy Michelat, "Comportement électoral des catholiques," in *Dictionnaire du Vote*, ed. Pascal Perrineau and Dominique Reynié (Paris: PUF, 2001), 160-63.

12. Yves Lambert, "La religion en France des années soixante à nos jours," in *Données sociales—La société française* (Paris: INSEE, 2002), 565-79.

13. "Les Valeurs des Européens," *Futuribles* (July-August 2002); see also *Statistiques de l'Etat de la France* (Paris: La Découverte, 2002).

14. CSA poll for *La Vie-Le Monde*, "Les Français et leurs croyances," http://a1692.g.akamai.net/f/1692/2042/1h/medias.lemonde.fr/medias/pdf_obj/sondage030 416.pdf (accessed March 14, 2007).

15. CSA poll for *La Croix*, "Les Français et la Religion," http://www.csa-tmo.fr/dataset/data2004/0401664.pdf (accessed March 14, 2007).

16. "Le Christianisme en France. 'Vie privée-Vie publique-Laïcité,'" *La Croix*, June 19, 2003.

17. Guy Michelat, "L'Univers des croyances," in Michelat, Potel, and Sutter, *L'héritage chrétien en disgrâce*, 69-121.

18. This is the expression used by René Le Corre in "L'athéisme," in *L'Etat des religions dans le monde*, ed. Michel Clévenot (Paris: La Découverte and Le Cerf, 1987), 486.

19. Michelat, "L'univers des croyances," 69-121.

20. For the details of this survey see Martine Barthélémy, *Rapport final d'enquête, Les Français et la Laïcité*, December 2003 Survey, CEVIPOF, Institut d'Etudes Politiques de Paris, October 2004.

21. The data were first published in *L'Actualité religieuse dans le monde* on May 15, 1994, and can now be accessed online, "Ce que croient les Français," http://www.ipsos.fr/Canalipsos/poll/5319.asp (accessed March 14, 2007).

22. Jacques Sutter, "La culpabilité, un défi pour le devenir du fait religieux," in Michelat, Potel, and Sutter, *L'héritage chrétien en disgrâce*, 17-61, 83.

23. Jacques Sutter, "Dérive culturelle et catholicisme minoritaire," in Michelat, Potel, and Sutter, *Les Français sont-ils encore catholiques?* 288.

24. Martine Sévegrand, *Les enfants du bon Dieu. Les catholiques français et la pro-

création (Paris: Albin Michel, 1995).

25. Danielle Hervieu-Léger, *Catholicisme, la fin d'un monde* (Paris: Bayard, 2003), 168-212.

26. This expression is attributed to the German sociologist Ulrich Beck, author of *Risk Society: Towards a New Modernity* (1986; repr., London: Sage, 1992). The phrase is used by François de Singly, together with the distinction between the "horizontal" and the "vertical" family, in *Le soi, le couple et la famille* (Paris: Nathan, 1996).

27. As Françoise Subileau puts it, *laïcité* constitutes a code of political interpretation that is "less a body of constituted doctrine, than a system of political organization and perception—an interpretative and explanatory code for viewing the world." "Les militants socialistes et la laïcité" in *La laïcité, une valeur d'aujourd'hui: Contestations et renégociations du modèle français*, ed. Philippe Pontier (Paris: Presses Universitaires de Rennes, 2001), 175.

28. Martine Barthélémy, *Rapport final d'enquête, Les Français et la Laïcité*, December 2003 Survey, CEVIPOF, Institut d'Etudes Politiques de Paris, October 2004.

29. Jacques Maritain, *Christianisme et démocratie* (1943; repr., Paris: Desclée de Brower, 2005); Jacques Maritain, *L'Homme et l'Etat* (Paris: PUF, 1953), available in an English-language edition, *Man and the State* (Washington, DC: The Catholic University of America Press, 1996).

30. Catholics such as Edmond Michelet and André Colin were among the first to actively call for resistance. Some of the earliest resistance organizations were founded by Catholic activists such as Captain Henri Frenay, leading in 1941 to the creation of the Combat movement. Catholic priests and laypersons founded the Christian Democratic newspaper *Témoignage Chrétien* in Lyon in 1941. General de Gaulle's entourage in London included many Catholics such as Pierre de Chevigné, Maurice Schumann (official spokesperson for the Free French), Admiral Thierry d'Argenlieu, and Estienne d'Orves.

31. Pierre Letamendia, *Le Mouvement républicain populaire, histoire d'un grand parti français* (Paris: Beauchesne, 1995). These developments are also analysed by Jean-Luc Pouthier in "Emergence et ambiguïté de la culture politique démocrate-chrétienne," in *Les Cultures politiques en France*, ed. Serge Bernstein (Paris: Seuil, 2003), 303-34. See also Blandine Chélini-Pont, "Le christianisme, référence ou alibi dans la politique française depuis 1944," in *L'héritage chrétien dans le patrimoine culturel français, Actes du colloque de l'Institut de Droit et d'Histoire canonique*, ed. Jean Chelini (Aix-Marseille: Presses Universitaires d'Aix-Marseille, 1996), 155-85.

32. On left-voting Catholics, see Donegani, *La Liberté de choisir*, which presents a typology of Catholic identity models ranging from marginal through intermediary to unconditional. Pierre Bréchon, in *Attitudes religieuses et politiques des catholiques pratiquants. Enquête par questionnaire dans huit assemblées dominicales grenobloises* (Grenoble: BDPS-IEP, 1982), shows that practicing Catholics who translate their faith into social activism are more inclined to vote on the Left than those who are less socially active. This indicates that when Catholic belief is acted upon in terms of socially engaged altruism, it tends to equate with left-leaning political sympathies.

33. Guy Michelat and Michel Simon, *Classe, religion et comportement politique* (Paris: Presses de la FNSP, 1977), parts 2 and 5.

34. Michel Brulé shows that among regularly practicing Catholics (that is, 23 percent of the national population at this time), 72 percent voted for General de Gaulle or for Jean Lecanuet (of the moderate Right). Among irregularly practicing Catholics (36 percent of the national population), the proportion voting on the Right was 48 percent, compared with 23 percent for the Socialist candidate François Mitterrand. Among non-practicing Catholics (27 percent of the national population), the Left came out slightly

ahead: 34 percent voted for candidates of the Right and 37 percent supported François Mitterrand. "L'appartenance religieuse et le vote [présidentiel] du 5 septembre 1965," *Sondages* 28, no. 2 (1966): 17.

35. Guy Michelat, "Niveau d'intégration au catholicisme et vote," in *Données Sociales* (Paris: INSEE, 1990); Guy Michelat, "Intégration au catholicisme, attitudes éthico-politiques et comportement électoral," in Bernstein, *Les Cultures politiques des Français*, 209-35.

36. Michel Rocard, *Si la Gauche savait, Entretiens avec Georges-Marc Benamou* (Paris: Robert Laffont, 2005).

37. Yves Lambert, "La religion: un paysage en profonde évolution," in *Les Valeurs des Français*, ed. Hélène Riffault (Paris: PUF, 1994).

38. Survey conducted April 12, 2002, by TNS Sofres polling organization for *La Croix* which includes a statistical comparison between the 1995 and 2002 presidential elections. "Les catholiques et l'élection présidentielle," http://www.tns-sofres.com/etudes/pol/120402_catholiques_r.htm (accessed March 14, 2007).

39. Michelat, "Intégration au catholicisme," 209-35.

40. Guy Michelat, "Comportement électoral des catholiques," 163. More generally, in pre-enlargement Europe (that is, the fifteen-member European Union), non-religious people were more to the Left than non-practicing religious people, who were more to the Left than practicing believers, whatever their confession. See Bruno Cautrès, "L'influence de la religion sur les attitudes politiques: essai d'analyse spatio-temporelle dans l'Union européenne," in *Les enquêtes Eurobaromètres, analyse comparée des données socio-politiques*, ed. Pierre Bréchon and Bruno Cautrès (Paris: L'Harmattan, 1998).

41. CSA poll in *La Croix*, June 15, 1999. www.la-croix.com (accessed March 14, 2007).

42. CSA poll in *La Croix*, "Le oui des catholiques pratiquants," June 15, 2005. www.la-croix.com (accessed March 14, 2007); Ifop-*La Croix* Survey, "Le oui critique des catholiques à la Constitution européenne," May 26, 2005. http://www.ifop.com/europe/sondages/opinionf/debatdemocratique.asp (accessed March 14, 2007). One other poll gave the rate of 66 percent of regularly practising Catholics who voted for the European Constitution, CSA poll for *La Vie*, "Sondage: les catholiques ont voté 'non' à 52%," June 1, 2005, http://www.chretiente.info/spip.php?breve811 (accessed March 14, 2007).

43. Dossier, "La constitution Européenne. Repères: Les Chrétiens et l'Europe," *La Croix*, March 24, 2005, www.la-croix.com (accessed March 14, 2007).

44. According to research conducted by Sutter on the relationship between guilt and belief systems, 34 percent of the French regard marital infidelity as a personal matter while 56 percent regard it as either morally wrong (23 percent), a mistake (26 percent), or a sin (17 percent). See Jacques Sutter, "La culpabilité, un défi pour le devenir religieux," 55. After marital infidelity, the action most commonly regarded as a sin is abortion (13 percent classify it thus).

45. See Michel Chauvière, "L'enracinement confessionnel des associations familiales en France," in *Religions, Droit et Sociétés dans l'Europe communautaire*, ed. Blandine Chélini-Pont (Aix-en-Provence: Puam, 2000), 145-64.

46. Blandine Chélini-Pont, "Le mariage civil, thème de convergence inter-religieuse en France," in Chélini-Pont, *Religions, Droit et Sociétés dans l'Europe communautaire*, 229-44.

47. Irène Théry, *Couple, filiation et parenté aujourd'hui* (Paris: La Documentation française, 1998).

Part IV: Judaism

Chapter Seven

The American Jewish Experience

Michael Berenbaum

The Exceptionality of the Jewish Experience in America

Joseph Lieberman began his remarkable acceptance of the Democratic nomination for vice president with the words "Isn't this a great country" and he concluded it with the words "only in America," the paradigmatic statement of American exceptionalism. What is exceptional about the Jewish experience in the United States? The answers are many but can be stated concisely.

Government Neutrality and a Pluralist Society

First, despite the presence of anti-Semitism, only in America has the government itself been neutral with regard to religion; there was no established church and Jews were not a governmentally sanctioned separate entity, but rather chose of their own free will to constitute themselves as a community. This need not have been the case and perhaps only became so accidentally. When the first Jews arrived on the American shores in 1654, they posed a problem for Peter Stuyvesant, then governor-general of New Amsterdam. Stuyvesant had no love for the Jews, and was not inclined to accept them as refugees, for a very compelling reason—they were destitute and could not afford to move on. He appealed to his superiors in the Dutch West Indies Company, a company whose stockholders included several prominent Jews in Amsterdam—Jews who had found a haven in Amsterdam following the Spanish Inquisition—and these prevailed on their fellow board members to instruct Stuyvesant to accept their co-religionists.

Thus, early on, America became a community that made room for the Jews. The Jews had come to stay because they lacked any ability to leave. As Arthur Hertzberg points out, the best of European Jews did not come, nor did the most scholarly; it took more than a century and a half for any rabbinic leadership to arrive on this shore.[1] Therefore, the Jewish communities were led by lay people, which meant that whatever innovations occurred took place without the involvement, and particularly the resistance, of an entrenched religious leadership.

Anti-Semitism in American History

Second, anti-Semitism was not a large problem in America, especially when compared to its prevalence within Europe. In Europe, Jews were—to use the words of my Florida State University teacher Richard L. Rubenstein—cognitively dissonant, the one outsider community in Christian Europe; they could never quite shake their pariah status. In the United States, Jews were one of a series of outsiders, and were less despised and less problematic than others: Africans, Roman Catholics, Irish, and Italians. Further, the outsider status of the Jew was mitigated to some extent by the great respect given by the Puritans to the Hebrew Bible. This Puritan respect for the Jews is evident in the famous letter of George Washington to the Newport Hebrew Congregation on August 17, 1790:

> All possess alike liberty of conscience and immunities of citizenship. It is now no more that toleration is spoken of, as if it was by the indulgence of one class of people, that another enjoyed the exercise of their inherent natural right. For happily the government of the United States, which gives to bigotry no sanction. to persecution no assistance, requires only that they who live under its protection should demean themselves as good citizens in giving it on all occasions their effectual support. . . . May the children of the stock of Abraham who dwell in this land continue to merit and enjoy the good will of other inhabitants while everyone shall sit in safety under his own vine and fig-tree. and there shall be none to make him afraid.[2]

Washington's words were a prayer, a statement of principles and of aspirations that took many generations to be realized. Nevertheless, it is clear that these principles were present at the inception of the United States. Historians are fond of emphasizing that the sentiments expressed by Washington mirrored virtually word by word the statements made by the Congregational leadership in their letter of invitation, but whether initiated by Washington or merely echoed by him, they received his all-important imprimatur.

In 1820 the Jewish population was under four thousand, so the history of the Jews in this part of the New World was a history of individuals and small communities. Even in 1880 when the Jewish population had increased to

250,000, there simply were not enough Jews in the United States to fuel the growth of anti-Semitism. And in the 1880s, anti-Semitism took primarily a social form of exclusion from resorts, clubs, and places of residence rather than a more manifestly political form. Therefore, Jews came to this country for freedom, and the country they came to was primarily a land of opportunity. All immigration is a push/pull phenomenon. The push from Europe and later from other lands was primarily persecution: the Inquisition; the failed revolution of 1848 in Germany; Czarist pogroms and programs from 1881 onward; the so-called "one-third solution"—one-third shall leave, one-third shall die, and one-third shall assimilate; Nazism and the "final solution"; the rise of communism in the East; the failed Hungarian Revolution; the rise of Fidel Castro; and the fall of the shah and the rise of Ayatollah Khomeini. The stronger the push, the more open the shores of the United States, and consequently, the greater the immigration.

The pull was economic opportunity and the freedom to pursue it without being handicapped by one's faith. Jews had—and continue to have—a stake in the meritocracy of America. Economic opportunity came at a price, however. The rabbis of Eastern Europe called the United States a *goldene medinah* (a golden state), but a *treife* (unkosher) land. Again Hertzberg said it clearly. The best of the Jews did not come—certainly not the scholars and the rabbis—at least not for a very long time.[3]

The Effects of Freedom on the Contemporary American Jew

I had a conversation in Jerusalem the summer of Lieberman's nomination that was intriguing and disturbing. I walked into the office of a long-time—I am not quite ready to say old—friend, a fellow that I used to play basketball with at the local gym in Jerusalem on my first sabbatical in Jerusalem some twenty-eight years ago. He was the type of guy who came right at you, never backed off, and muscled his way in for the shot. He was aggressive and had little subtlety, but his concentration on the game was intense. We played together for six months before I learned that he was in my field of study, and indeed our interests coincided intellectually, as well as athletically. He said, "I don't understand how an Orthodox Jew can be a candidate for vice president. America has been a catastrophe for the Jews. More Jews have been lost as Jews in America than anywhere else except by death during Nazism. How can one pay homage to such a Jewish catastrophe?" His is an odd reading of American Jewish history and of the American Jewish experience. Still, the freedom that was unprecedented on these shores was not without its effects. Because Jews are free in the United States, there are no external coercions that force them to remain Jews or that limit their ability to be absorbed into the wider society. Two parallel phenomena characterize the contemporary American Jew.

Jewish Assimilation

On the one hand, the rate of assimilation has increased by almost any standard of measurement. To take just one example, intermarriage rates have increased. When I was an undergraduate student in the 1960s, Eric Rosenthal predicted that intermarriage rates might reach as high as 25 percent—they were then at some 3 percent. His statement, based on sound sociological methods, was so unacceptable that he became a pariah in the American Jewish community. The much challenged 1990 National Jewish Population Survey indicated that the intermarriage rate for young Jews was in excess of 50 percent. While its premises were questioned and its sample's validity dismissed, even the most severe critics spoke of an intermarriage rate in excess of 40 percent. One of the reasons that intermarriage rates have climbed in the past three decades has nothing to do with a decline in condemnation by the Jewish family, but rather with the greater acceptance by non-Jewish partners and their families of admitting a Jew into their family, welcoming a Jew as a potential spouse and partner.

Jewish Emancipation

About eight years ago a museum in Los Angeles hosted an exhibition on American Judaism in the 1950s entitled "Too Jewish," the content of which can best be described if we remember Philip Roth's marvelous short story "Eli the Fanatic" in which a suburban Jewish street is rocked by the fact that one of its members has become, to use a contemporary term, "a *baal teshuvah*," a returnee to traditional Judaism. With his beard and *caftan*, Roth's character reminds his newly Americanized, suburban neighbors of the Judaism they left behind, of the people who they did not want as neighbors.[4] We saw manifestations of "too Jewish" in Woody Allen's *Annie Hall* (1977), when the Jewish protagonist, Allen himself, seems to metamorphose into a Hasidic Jew at the dinner table of a Christian family.

The rule of emancipation was, "Be a Jew in your home and a man—universal person—in the street." When I was raised as an Orthodox Jew in New York City and attended school on the glitzy East Side, we were taught that the *yarmulke*, the skull cap, was an indoor garment. Like the gentlemen we were groomed to become, we were to wear hats (before John F. Kennedy overturned American fashion rules by going hatless) in the street. Subliminally, we were being taught even among the Orthodox not to be too Jewish, at least not in public, in the presence of non-Jews. In the 1950s, Irving Greenberg, who was an Orthodox rabbi and a Harvard Ph.D. student, would never walk with his head uncovered, but he did not feel free to wear a *yarmulke* at Harvard University. Several other Orthodox rabbis were in the same predicament.

In the aftermath of the Six-Day War, in the wake of Black Power and "Black is beautiful," and perhaps with the decline of Protestant domination, Jews now feel free to be Jews in public. At Harvard and at Yale University, the

Hillel House has moved to a prominent place near the center of campus. The fringes on garments, as required by scripture, once worn solely on the inside of a male's garments, have now been brought out of the shirt, and Jews can enjoy the freedom of a public Jewish life, which is thriving alongside assimilation. Lieberman himself is a manifestation of that freedom. The first Jewish vice-presidential nominee was not an assimilated Jew, but was rather very public about his religiosity and quite respected for it. Indeed, in heavily Roman Catholic Connecticut, instead of losing support because he is not a Christian, Lieberman is respected for his religiosity.

Therefore, as most students of American Jewish history acknowledge, a renaissance or a revival is taking place within American Judaism: religious life is intense and thriving from fundamentalism to liberal Reform Judaism. Jewish creativity is evident in films and documentaries, in poetry and literature, in music and art. Jewish scholarship is proliferating. In thirty-six years the members of the Association for Jewish Studies has increased by more than 1,000 percent and the quality and quantity of Jewish scholarship and learning in all of its forms have flourished.

American Influence on the American Jewish Experience

Make no mistake about it: the American Jewish community is an American community taking on the forms of American religion. I do not believe that I have to document this point with regard to the liberal religious community. Permit me only to address the paradox of the ultra-Orthodox or fervently Orthodox community—or the *haredi* community as they choose to be called in Hebrew—those who have been reticent to embrace or who have rejected modern values. It too is an American religion. Two examples will suffice.

ArtScroll is the English language publication firm that has taken much of the sacred literature of Jews and translated it into English. Although ArtScroll defines itself as a totally independent Torah publisher, without ties to any of the major institutions of Jewish public life, its editors and authors are intimately related to the *haredi yeshiva* world. ArtScroll's primary mission is to translate—in the sense of moving both from the sacred language to English, and from erudite to popular—Jewish canonical texts, supplanting what the press and its supporters regard as inadequate, distorted, or otherwise illegitimate representations of Jewish ritual practice, historical imagination, and theoretical knowledge, and replacing these with "corrected" editions. Unlike critical scholarship that deals with philological and archaeological evidence from diverse sources, the ArtScroll cadre seeks a return to what it defines as "Torah-true" interpretations of Jewish texts, the authenticity of which is secured by ArtScroll's close association with the luminaries of the *yeshiva* world. Essential to its success has been the combination of contemporary American design, initiated by its graphic de-

signer and owner Rabbi Meir Zlotowitz, with traditional content. It has succeeded economically and with regard to its mission in transforming the fervently
Orthodox world, and its Hebrew-language publications sell, not least because of
their contemporary design. It also bears witness, for better or for worse, to the
linguistic transition from Hebrew and Yiddish into English in the American
haredi world.

A similar Americanization has taken place within Habad Hasidism. Space
will not permit me to expand too greatly on the process of Americanization.
Permit me to confine myself to three points:

1. Habad has mastered the American tools of marketing, including a use of
television, even though one would not find this appliance in the homes of Habad
disciples.

2. It has followed the business practices of American corporations; the char-
ismatic leadership presented by the rebbe has been replaced by managerial institutional leaders. The picture of the rebbe remains only as the looming presence,
the guarantor of the authenticity, the name brand even in his absence from this
earth.

3. Habad operates as a franchise. Rabbinic leaders assume territorial responsibility and dominance. Local initiatives and decentralized management are the
keys to its success. Each territory must raise its own funding for its own opera-
tions.

I want to avoid the controversy of the rebbe as Messiah, except to point
out—as do some critics—that the possibility of maintaining the rebbe as a mes-
sianic figure after his death owes much to the subliminal absorption of American
Christian culture. In fact, one could argue that the entire fundamentalist Jewish
revival in the United States and elsewhere owes as much to the fundamentalist
religious revival in Christianity and within Islam as it does to purely Jewish factors. It is a response to the same forces within modernity—or postmodernity—
that drive fundamentalisms in other religious traditions.

Anti-Semitism and Empowerment

Seventeen years ago when I published my book *After Tragedy and Triumph:
Modern Jewish Thought and the American Experience,*[5] I wrote that American
Jews are living three questions, the answers to which we do not know. Two of
the questions were posed by European philosophers, the third by a first-century
rabbi. Jean Paul Sartre asked: Does it take anti-Semites to make the Jews? Fried-
erich Nietzsche asked: Is Judaism the religion of the powerless? And Yochanan
ben Zakkai asked: Are we one people or many?

Jews still do not know the answer to Sartre's question: Does it take anti-
Semites to make the Jews? We do know that anti-Semitism in the United States
is on a historic decline. Despite all the talk of its revival within the United
States, being Jewish is no obstacle to full participation in American life. Jews

find no barriers to participation in American political, economic, cultural, intellectual, and academic life. My parents knew obstacles; they understood what it was like to be excluded. My generation witnessed barriers falling. We took pride in "the first Jew to . . . ." Thankfully, my children's generation does not even remember that there were barriers to full participation. With the absence of external coercion and the cement of persecution to enforce Jewish unity, the question is whether Jews will remain a viable and distinct community *or* whether only those who feel exclusion and regard the external world as alien and threatening will remain Jews. The evidence is mixed; the answer is not yet in. There are those within the Jewish community—and not just within the Jewish defense organizations—who view the perceived increase in anti-Semitism as not altogether bad; it intensifies the need of Jews for one another and encourages parochial identification.

Concerning Nietzsche's question, American Jews are an empowered people. I know that talk of Jewish power makes people uncomfortable because of negative associations with the fantasies—nightmares—of anti-Semites. Yet by any scale of power, the American Jewish community is a powerful community, not quite as powerful as the anti-Semites proclaim, but far more powerful than we sense ourselves to be. And I would rather face the problems of empowerment than the vulnerabilities of powerlessness. Jews have wealth, power, and influence. They can be seen in the corridors of power in government and industry, in academia, and in the media. They face virtually no barriers to career advancement and they can advance without having to abandon or mute their commitment to Jewish faith and their proud membership in the Jewish people. We are not the Jews of the thirties and we are not hesitant to advance Jewish issues to the very center of the American national agenda. In fact, we are quite skilled at it, so skilled that American administration after administration has been responsive to Jewish issues, large and small, and supportive of Israel.

After the Yom Kippur War, Jews mistakenly thought that power in the last third of the twentieth century would be in the hands of those controlling natural resources, particularly the hands of Arabs controlling oil, the great addiction of the West. In fact, it turned out that over the past four decades, power was in the management of information, and Jews both in Israel and the United States were ideally positioned to benefit from the information revolution. Israel is an empowered country, having the third or fourth most powerful army in the world. Given the information revolution and its high-tech abilities, the Israeli standard of living ranks high; and in an era of globalization it seems likely to grow. Israel has withstood Intifada I and Intifada II, even a renewed war in Lebanon without missing an economic beat. Therefore, despite the heated rhetoric of some Jews who mistakenly compare contemporary anti-Semitism to the anti-Semitism of the 1930s, the most basic difference between the two is that anti-Semitism today is fueled by the anger of the disempowered. Anti-Semitism in the 1930s was the anti-Semitism of those in power.

Voting Patterns of Empowered American Jews

What then of values? Regarding Jewish voting patters—and much to the chagrin of the neoconservatives—Milton Himmelfarb has quipped that "Jews live like Episcopalians, but vote like Puerto Ricans." Jews are the only group whose voting patterns have not moved to the Republican Party with their own economic advancement. Two-thirds of the Jews in the 2004 election voted for John Kerry, only one-third for George W. Bush, despite the latter's manifest friendship with Israel and concerted efforts to change the Jewish vote. In the 2006 congressional elections exit polling found that Jews voted 88 percent for the Democratic candidate. Even the National Jewish Republican Coalition found that three out of four Jews voted for the Democrats. The only other constituency with such a disproportionate support for the Democratic candidate was that of African American voters. What was remarkable about the 2004 vote was that the dividing line in American Jewry was not economic but religious, with Orthodox Jews following the general voting patterns of evangelical Christians and the rest of the Religious Right. The more orthodox the Jew, the more likely he or she was to vote for the president.

There is a second significant element in Jewish voting patterns: age. In an off-the-record aside, an officer of the National Jewish Republican Coalition, the Jewish group that supports Republican candidates for office and the Republican Party in general, put it succinctly if not quite elegantly: "Those over seventy hate us and all that we stand for; we will have to wait for time to do its deed. Those under forty are 38 percent for us and 62 percent for the Democrats so at least we have a fighting chance." The generation that actually made the economic progression is firmly in the Democratic camp; their heirs less firmly so. Still, as a matter of values, Jews disprove the axiom that party affiliation is a function of economic success.

The Holocaust, Israel, the Death of God, and American Jewish Identity

I teach a course in American Jewish history and as part of that course I discuss Nathan Glazer's classic *American Judaism*, a book first written in 1956, reissued with a different introduction in 1972, and reissued again in 1989 with a very different conclusion.[6] In 1956, Glazer wrote of the American Jewish community. However, writing only a decade after the end of World War II, there is barely a word about the Holocaust. Instead, the postwar focus was on American Jewish soldiers returning home. Moreover, eight years after the establishment of the State of Israel, little was mentioned about Israel, which did not figure greatly into the content of American Judaism and the identity of American Jews. When the work was reissued in 1972, an epilogue was added because seemingly overnight in response to the Six-Day War, both the Holocaust and Israel became paramount to American Jewish identity as American Jews developed what Jonathan Woocher called the religion of "Sacred Survival,"[7] or what others called the narrative of "Holocaust and Redemption."[8]

Consistent with earlier forms of Jewish life in the United States, American Jews were building their identity not on what they were, but on what they were not. Most American Jews were neither Holocaust survivors nor children of survivors, and all American Jews had chosen not to be Israelis. Full participation in Israeli Jewish life was available for a one way ticket, and, while the most identified of American Jews visited Israel, all but a few bought a round trip ticket.

In earlier generations, American Jewish identity was also vicarious. The first post-immigrant generation of Eastern European Jews built their identity on the world they left behind. Real Judaism and real *Yiddishkeit* was in the world of Eastern Europe that they fled. Their descendants built their Jewish identity on what Irving Howe called "The World of Our Fathers" and what Ronald Sanders called "The Downtown Jews,"[9] worlds they too left behind as they moved across the bridge or uptown, out to Long Island and safely into the suburbs. They had no doubt that real Judaism and genuine Jewishness were found on the streets and in the stores, in the smells and restaurants, the synagogues and the *landsman-schaft* they had left behind. They hired paid professionals to be Jewish for them; and even today they may contribute to *Chabad*, for the latter represents Jewish authenticity, the world they left behind.

When I studied at Florida State University, the "death of God" was the mode of contemporary religious thought. My teacher was not alone in claiming the death of God as an existential fact of American culture when he wrote:

> I believe the most adequate theological description of our time is to be found in the assertion that we live in the time of the death of God. The vitality of death-of-God theology is rooted in the fact that it has faced more openly . . . the truth of the divine-human encounter in our times. The truth is that it is totally non-existent. Those theologies which attempt to find the reality of God's presence in the contemporary world manifest a deep insensitivity to the art, literature and technology of our time.[10]

Yet if any prediction proved wrong, it was the notion of the death of God. God is alive and well—perhaps too well in contemporary American culture and in contemporary world culture. If God was not spoken of in the synagogue of the 1970s and 1980s, because most Jews entered for other than religious reasons, God has returned to the center at least for many who enter the portals of the synagogue.

In 1989, Glazer characterized Judaism as a religion of survival: remember the Holocaust and save Israel. Religion, he cautioned, does not survive on instrumental values alone. What is different, he said, is that for the first time in the American experience of the Jews, Orthodox Judaism has not declined and is experiencing a modest revival; it has won the contest for Jewish authenticity. It is regarded as the genuine thing and its liberal counterparts are viewed as attempting to accommodate a clientele which may embrace the new package while disrespecting the lack of truth in advertising.

Ironically, and unbeknownst to Glazer at that time, a transformation had already begun. For some it can be dated to 1982, the war in Lebanon; for others it can be dated to the late 1980s and Intifada I; for some it can be dated to 1993 and the Oslo Accords, the overnight recognition by Israel of the Palestine Liberation Organzation (PLO), and the about-face change in attitudes toward that group, which had hitherto been recognized as a terrorist organization. For others, it was 2000 and onward with Intifada II; for some Orthodox, who are supporters of the now defeated "Greater Land of Israel" position, it was the 2005 disengagement from Gaza; and finally, for all, Israel has become less central and its support less certain, more divisive. Jewish organizational life in the United States, and certainly the political establishment, has yet to comprehend this monumental change.

Two recent works reflect that transition. Sociologist Steven Cohen and historian of religion Arnold Eisen wrote a work entitled *The Jew Within: Self, Family, and Community in America*,[11] based on a series of in-depth interviews with moderately committed Jews. Their conclusions were startling. Jewish identity in twenty-first-century America is deeply personal. Far from being vicarious, it is based on the deep experiences of the Jews. Its boundaries are permeable and do not require institutional justification and confirmation. The commitment of even those moderately committed to their Jewish identity is intense, inherent, and non-negotiable. Like J.J. Goldberg's findings in *Jewish Power*,[12] Cohen and Eisen found that there is no crisis in the American Jewish community, but a deep disconnection between Jews and the institutions of American Judaism. Part of the creativity of our time, part of what happens on the Internet is the creation of a new community and non-institutional modes of Jewish identification. Institutional Jewish life will catch up, perhaps even before it is too late.

Jonathan Sarna's *American Judaism*, which I now teach with Glazer's book of the same title in my course on American Jewish history, is a work of considerable importance that examines the same evidence as Glazer's work, but does so with a very different ending and comes to radically different conclusions.[13] Written by the dean of American Jewish historians—writing with deep awareness of Judaism and of American religion—it is fascinating for the questions it asks and not just for the significant information it provides. Unlike previous scholars who asked about the erosion of religious action and the loss of religious faith, Sarna had to account for its preservation both in its traditional and non-traditional forms. He had to grapple with the religiosity of Reform Judaism and the American versions of rejectionist Orthodoxy, and to see them both through the prism of Judaism and the American experience, to see them in fact through the lenses of interpretation that they might reject. The result is impressive; the effort is even more so.

The Jewish Experience in France

Because we are in dialogue with French and American scholars, let me stray from the topic and speak for a moment about French anti-Semitism. I think that we can swiftly come to several points of agreement:

1. There is a direct correlation between the situation in Israel and attacks on Jews in France; the more intense the violence in the Middle East, the more vehement the attacks on Jews.

2. The assaults against the Jews are related to the significant demographic changes in France; namely the emergence of a significant Islamic underclass that may be one-tenth of the French population. Further, France was doing little—precious little—to address the root of the problem, at least until the recent riots.

3. The Muslim population that attacked the Jews is *in* France, but not *of* France; thus the president of France could say, seemingly honestly, that "anti-Semitism is not France," even as it occurred throughout France.

4. The more assimilated the Islamic population is in France, the more accepting it is of French norms, which includes the full participation of Jews within French society.

5. As the government was slow to perceive the nature of the danger, no other segment of French society came forward to recognize the pattern of assault on the Jews; there was virtual silence from political leadership, the media, the church, the opinion makers, and even the Jewish community.

6. The most vulnerable Jews have been the least affluent, those who immigrated from Islamic societies and those who live alongside Muslims.

7. There are three elements of the Islamic community living in France: the assimilationists, the separatists, and those in-between. The separatists are the most numerous and the least exposed to French culture and French norms. They are nourished directly by extremist elements in Islamic culture.

8. The French government, French elite, and public opinion comfortably distinguish between Jews in France who they warmly welcome as fellow citizens and whose presence in French society and French culture is venerated, and the policies of the State of Israel, which are abhorred.

9. The vehemence of the attacks against Israel must raise the question that Richard Bernstein asked in the *New York Times*: "Does the ferocious moral condemnation of Israel mark a recrudescence of that most ugly of Western diseases, anti-Semitism? Or is it a legitimate, if crude, criticism of a nation's policies? Where does one draw the line? How does one judge?"[14]

10. The response of the government also underscores the importance of the American tradition of recognizing hate crimes.

Were similar assaults to have occurred within the United States, the response would have been quite predictable. A mayor or governor would have appeared at the site along with the police chief and the district attorney. They would have condemned the attacks in no uncertain terms and pledged to use all the resources of the law to apprehend and prosecute the criminals. The local clergy—Catholic, Protestant, and perhaps even Muslim—would have appeared together with the rabbi in a symbolic cleansing, and contributions would have flooded in to aid the institution that was desecrated and the victims of the crime. In America, hate crime is not petty crime but an assault on the community as a whole and hence identified as such and prosecuted as such. And thus, in the aftermath of hatred, there is a manifestation of community unity that defeats the hatred and reestablishes civil society. American Jews would have demonstrated in mass, with a number of non-Jewish politicians and civil and religious leaders joining them.

The Future of the Jewish Experience in America

What do we know of the future? In the mid-fifties, Will Herberg wrote his famous work *Protestant, Catholic, Jew: An Essay in American Religious Sociology*,[15] observing that while Jews constituted some 3 percent of the population, they were one-third of the American religious experience, something that will manifestly not be the case in the twenty-first century when the practitioners of Islam and Asian religions—Chinese, Japanese, and Korean—will far exceed the number of Jews. Evidence of the shift can already be found in the fact that the National Conference of Christians and Jews is still the NCCJ, but is now termed the National Conference of Community and Justice. Jews will diminish in number—both absolutely and as a percentage of the population. Those Jews who remain will be more intensely Jewish—more religious, better educated, and more observant than ever before. Only such people will remain Jewish. We are going through a religious revival worldwide. It has taken one form in America, but the truth is that the religious revival is the result of the failure of secularism to answer the problems of modernization.

The final question of the three I posed in *After Tragedy and Triumph: Modern Jewish Thought and American Experience* is whether the Jews will remain one people or bifurcate in many unexpected ways: Israelis and Jews, liberals and fundamentalists, Orthodox and non-Orthodox. Two trends are quite apparent: First, for the non-Orthodox Jews, the boundaries of Judaism are permeable and the formal, quasi-official boundaries of membership in the community are no longer applicable. Second, the unity of the Jewish people depends on the form that fundamentalism takes over the next generation. Will it be a fundamentalism that includes or excludes, that regards the outsider—even when Jewish—as alien or welcomes and includes him or her into the community? That direction will not only be charted by fundamentalist Jews alone, but also by the character of fundamentalism in the twenty-first-century world.

Notes

1. Arthur Hertzberg, *The Jews in America: Four Centuries of an Uneasy Encounter* (New York: Simon and Schuster, 1989).

2. Morris U. Schappes, ed., *A Documentary History of the Jews in the United States*. 3rd ed. (New York: Schocken Books, 1971), 80-81.

3. Hertzberg, *Jews in America*, 101-18.

4. Philip Roth, *Goodbye Columbus and Five Short Stories* (Boston: Houghton Mifflin, 1959).

5. Michael Berenbaum, *After Tragedy and Triumph: Modern Jewish Thought and the American Experience* (Cambridge: Cambridge University Press, 1990).

6. Nathan Glazer, *American Judaism*, 2nd ed., rev. (Chicago: University of Chicago Press, 1989).

7. Jonathan Woocher, *Sacred Survival: The Civil Religion of American Jews* (Bloomington, IN: Indiana University Press, 1986).

8. Jacob Nesuner, *Stranger at Home: "The Holocaust," Zionism and American Judaism* (Chicago and London: University of Chicago Press, 1981).

9. Irving Howe, *World of Our Fathers* (New York: Simon and Schuster, 1976); Ronald Sanders, *The Downtown Jews: Portrait of an Immigrant Generation* (New York: New American Library, 1969).

10. Richard L. Rubenstein, *After Auschwitz: Radical Theology and Contemporary Judaism* (Indianapolis: The Bobbs-Merrill Company, 1966), 245-46.

11. Steven M. Cohen and Arnold M. Eisen, *The Jew Within: Self, Family, and Community in America* (Bloomington, IN: Indiana University Press, 2000).

12. J. J. Goldberg, *Jewish Power: Inside the American Jewish Establishment* (Reading, MA: Addison-Wesley, 1996).

13. Jonathan D. Sarna, *American Judaism: A History* (New Haven, CT: Yale University Press, 2004).

14. Richard Bernstein, "The Word: Ugly Rumor or an Ugly Truth," in *The New York Times*, August 4, 2002.

15. Will Herberg, *Protestant, Catholic, Jew: An Essay in American Religious Sociology*, rev. ed. (Chicago: University of Chicago Press, 1960).

Chapter Eight
From Assimilation to Post-Republicanism: Jews in France

Michel Wieviorka

Throughout the world, Jews like to ponder and ask the question: what does it mean to be Jewish, and what is Jewish identity? If the question arises so frequently—if not insistently—it is because there is no easy response, or at least, no response that is acceptable to everyone, in all places, and at all moments in history.

What does it consist of today, as seen from the French perspective? Before examining this question, let us underscore a point that is unique to the French language. If the word is used with a religious referent and solely with such a referent, the word *juif* in French is written with a lower case "j"—*un juif, les juifs*—whereas when it is written with a capital "J"—*un Juif, les Juifs*—it refers to the idea of a people or a nation in a much larger sense. By the same token, whether we are talking about *juifs* or about *Juifs*, it is impossible to reduce the debate or the analysis to purely religious dimensions.

An "Uncertain Assimilation"

To understand the present question, a step back is first necessary: this will enable us to see the nature of the paradigm within which, starting from the nineteenth century, French Jews settled in France through to the 1960s. This will then allow us to better understand the issues at stake in the changes that have taken place since then.

Contrary to many accepted notions, in the France of the Ancien Régime the Jewish question was a minor one, and the status of Jews varied from one locality to another, making it impossible to speak of a unified Judaism before the Napoleonic Empire. They lived in a fragmented world racked by tensions, and as Patrick Gérard indicates in a convincing work, their communities "were theocratic societies, autocratically governed by a hated and detested financial oligarchy. Far from being micro-societies where one could live well in the warmth of a comforting fraternity, these communities were additionally undermined by the reduction of Judaism to a sterile formula of orthodox practice and by the diffusion of heterodox opinions peculiar to the Jewish world, or by the diffusion of new ideas acquired through contact with the non-Jewish world."[1] Enlightenment philosophers played a role both in their intellectual emancipation, notably through the Concours de Metz in 1788 and the Malesherbes Commission, and also in their practical emancipation when a number of local authorities, even before the Revolution, put an end to socio-juridical discrimination against them.

Was the French Revolution a powerful accelerator of this logic, or perhaps even truly the moment when a rapid process of emancipation was initiated? This seems doubtful. In drawing up a balance sheet of revolutionary activity, Patrick Gérard is particularly severe on this point, at least when it comes to the emancipation of the Jews. It was only on September 27, 1791, on the eve of the separation of the Constituent Assembly, that the Revolution resolved to extend the emancipation of Jews to include those in the eastern part of France; for the rest, the "granting of civic rights to other Jews of the kingdom was not in the strict sense its [the Revolution's] work."[2] The Revolution demonstrated towards the Jews "an overall attitude that was not particularly honorable," reflected in "the combined manifestation of indifference, hostility and lukewarm procrastination."[3]

In view of this, should we therefore attribute to Napoléon Bonaparte a decisive role in the implementation of a model that put an end to the diverse formulae which had characterized the Ancien Régime? The convocation in 1806 of an assembly of Jewish notables followed, in 1807, by the installation of the "Grand Sanhedrin" of Paris, and then by measures that were, in fact, brutal and hostile to Jews, starting with the "infamous decree" of March 17, 1808, (in fact, two decrees) which abolished certain rights for Jews and submitted them to special restrictions, causes us to doubt this, particularly when one examines the concrete policies of the emperor. "Two years earlier," notes the great historian Simon Doubnov, "he had declared to the Council of State that it was necessary to apply not the civil code, but the 'political' code to the Jews; now he applied his martial code to them, using war and expropriation as his principal levers."[4]

In fact, if ideas for emancipating the Jews were in circulation before the Revolution, and if their message became blurred and was sometimes even refuted during the Revolution and Napoleonic Empire, this period was one of intense debates and of a process of politicization that, above all, prepared for what followed with the crystallization, under the Third Republic, of the republican model for the treatment of the Jewish question. In any event, starting from the end of the eighteenth century, a number of important changes led French Jews to enter into a new model that was never perfectly defined or stabilized, a model that the historian Annie Kriegel has described as an "uncertain assimilation."[5]

Throughout the nineteenth century, Jews participated in French political and institutional life in an increasingly active fashion, sometimes acceding to ministerial responsibilities. Many of them not only integrated themselves into the nation, but also displayed patriotism, in particular during the Franco-Prussian War of 1870 and at the moment of defeat, as many Jewish families chose to leave Alsace so as not to be subjected to German domination. The Crémieux decree of October 20, 1870, granted the same political and civic rights of French citizenship to Algerian Jews, which distinguished them from Muslims but also obliged their communities to submit to the directives of the Central Consistory of Paris, thus abandoning their autonomy. The tendencies towards Jewish assimilation were therefore very powerful, and the dominant model for them became associated with the term "Israelite": they were Jews in a discreet and sometimes entirely private sense, and their Jewishness was therefore anything other than communitarian in spirit. Their affirmation of Jewishness was limited to the religious domain. It is true that the moment of acceleration for these tendencies was also marked by a rapid passage from a classic anti-Judaism—which did not quite disappear—to a modern anti-Semitism that was highly politicized, largely anti-republican, often nationalist and chauvinistic, and that denounced the emancipated Jews for having allegedly turned France into an atheist country, pushing it into the disastrous war against Prussia, ruining it to the profit of their own interests, and finally betraying it—as was claimed during the Dreyfus affair.

But overall, despite the existence of an anti-Semitism that up to the Second World War took the form of an opinion rather than of a program of action, the Jews of France for the most part aligned themselves with the categories of the republican idea. They were hardly visible as such in the public space, where they were individuals like everyone else, conforming to the celebrated formula of the Count of Clermont-Tonnerre, who declared during an important session of the National Assembly in December 1789 in response to Father Maury that "the word 'Jew' serves to designate not a sect but a nation." He went on: "To Jews, as a nation, we must refuse everything; but to Jews as men, we must grant everything." The Jews of France liked to think of themselves as citizens of Israelite belief, as free individuals with equal rights, and some among them, in the words of Pierre Birnbaum, were "Republican fanatics," "State Jews" who put themselves passionately at the service of the state, displaying a great love for the *patrie* (fatherland).[6]

New arrivals from Central Europe, that is, those who emigrated and regrouped in France in substantial waves most notably after the First World War, also showed a strong adherence to this model. Of course, other tendencies also existed, with some Jews distinguishing themselves from this model for religious reasons (most notably Orthodox Jews), or because they adhered to Zionism. But even the Second World War, and the actions of the Vichy State, did not really break this overall logic. It was only in the 1960s that everything changed.

The Great Change

The elements that together constituted a profound change had the particularity of converging at the same moment, reflecting a global phenomenon, a linking together of global dimensions and factors unique to French society.

At the world level, the most decisive changes occurred in Israel, but also in North America. In Israel, two key moments sent out shock waves that would extend far beyond the frontiers of the Hebrew state. In 1961, the head of the Israeli government, David Ben-Gurion, announced the arrest and future trial in Jerusalem of Adolph Eichmann. The Nazi criminal had been arrested and brought secretly from Argentina by the Israeli secret services, and he would be judged by the Israeli justice system in front of envoys from across the world, including Hannah Arendt who wrote an account for the *New Yorker*. This trial would be the occasion, for the first time on this scale, to speak within Israel itself of the destruction of the Jews of Europe and would usher in what Annette Wieviorka has called the "era of testimony."[7] From this point on, the Jews appeared to the world as a state capable of assuring their own justice, and it also enabled them to put behind them a kind of shame, combining now the identity of a victim with a constructive identity, that is, that of a nation or a people capable of taking action itself. In May 1967, the war known as the Six-Day War reinforced this image of a people capable of acting—including militarily—when Israel was confronted with a coalition of Arab states that attempted to attack it, only to be defeated by a lightning war.

The fears felt by Jews around the world rapidly gave way to pride, and in this context, the Second World War was again discussed, including the camps and the genocide—themes that, contrary to what one might think, did not yet have the importance that they would then acquire in Israel.

In the United States, the impact of the Eichmann trial was considerable, and lively polemics followed the publication of Hannah Arendt's account of the trial. In 1964, the Broadway presentation of *The Deputy*, the Rolf Hochhuth play that targeted Pope Pius XII for his behavior in the face of Nazism, led to a scandal. As Peter Novick wrote, all of this "put a definitive end to 15 years of silence over the Holocaust in American public discourse."[8] This was the period when the Shoah—which would long be referred to as the "Holocaust"—entered into Western consciousness, and became increasingly a cause with which Jews of the diaspora identified themselves.

What occurred in Israel and, less directly, in the United States, exerted an influence over French Jews, who were in any case undergoing similar experiences: Jews in France were starting to become visible as Jews in the public sphere—one could say that they were tending to Americanize or ethnicize themselves. Various factors specific to French society worked in this direction. Some were demographic and geopolitical: at the end of the 1950s and the beginning of the 1960s, decolonization resulted in the arrival in France of large numbers of Jews from North Africa. They brought with them tremendous communitarian vitality, a greater devotion to religious practices, and also other political and cultural sensibilities. In particular, they were less attached to the cult of the Republic. They were far from being able to recognize themselves in the figure of the Israelite: a Jew in private, invisible in the public sphere.

In addition, France at the end of the 1960s was entering into a general phase calling into question universalist conceptions of progress and reason, including the republican idea, and Jews were not immune from this process, which led to the highlighting of various forms of particularism in the public sphere—in the regional domain, for example.

These changes in France were also linked to foreign policy changes that General Charles de Gaulle chose to introduce once the Algerian War ended (the Evian Accords, which ended the war, were signed in 1962). This seemed to him to be the moment to mark a real distance vis-à-vis the State of Israel in order to return to the grand project of a policy addressing the Arab world. During a press conference in 1967, de Gaulle spoke of the Jews as "an elitist people, who are sure of themselves and dominating." Here, he targeted the State of Israel, but his words were like a cold shower for Jews, some of whom saw his remarks as a sign of anti-Semitism, a sort of throwback to a repressed Maurrassian tendency. Raymond Aron spoke in his memoirs of the shock he experienced. Many Jews inferred from this that the republican model, which had already been shown to offer far from absolute protection in the late 1930s, did not offer them any real guarantees and they began to ask themselves if they should not now assert themselves more visibly in the public space.

Thus began to take shape a partial retreat from the republican model. The Jews of France identified themselves far more than before with the State of Israel, and at the same time they began to assert the cause of what was not yet called the Shoah—that is, the destruction of the Jews of Europe by Hitler. Following this, another dimension of this change started to take shape: the examination of the role of Vichy in the destruction of the Jews. Out of this came the success of Marcel Ophuls's film *Le Chagrin et la pitié* (1971), and the considerable impact of the book by American historian Robert Paxton on *La France de Vichy* (1973).

At the same time, Jews in France tried hard to revive more or less moribund cultural traditions such as the use of Yiddish or Ladino. In universities, Jewish studies programs really took off, as did specialized publishers on Jewish themes and private Jewish schools. In addition, the forms of Jewish religious life underwent a very observable process of renewal and diversification.

The 1980s and 1990s were thus a period in which the Jews of France took some distance from the canonical republican model. They stopped being "Israelites" and defined themselves, in a complex fashion, in terms of a diverse network of more or less visible relationships with the State of Israel, with religion, and with certain forms of cultural affirmation. At the same time they renewed the fight against anti-Semitism, which caused them renewed concern periodically, by declaring themselves to be Jews, sometimes in the streets, when the situation seemed particularly menacing, for example at the time of the Rue Copernic bombing of 1980, which targeted a synagogue. By the end of the 1990s, the Jews of France had become the rather successful figureheads of a mild form of multiculturalism *à la française*. They seemed to happily combine an attachment to the universal values of law and reason, to the Republic, and to the nation, with the assertion, in the public sphere as elsewhere, of a particularism that was not only religious, but also cultural, historical, and inseparable from more or less clear sympathies with the State of Israel, the existence of which became for them an absolute, incontestable, and non-negotiable reality.

The Decomposition

But this new model was fragile and soon showed itself to be transitory. On the one hand, it contained within itself a centrifugal logic, leading French Jews to transform this multiculturalism into *communautarisme* (ethnic community formation often seen in France as a form of factionalism). Statistics from a study by Erik Cohen clearly show these tendencies, for example, the fact that 28,391 children were attending Jewish schools in 2002 compared with 15,907 at the end of the 1980s; or the fact that only 18 percent of Jewish heads of household today say they have no involvement in the Jewish community, compared with 35 percent in 1988.[9]

The transitory model of multiculturalism has also been unraveling if one considers the attachment of Jews to the State of Israel. That model has either been transforming itself into the form of an actual departure—the *alya*—or, for a significant number of French Jews and a fortiori their community leaders, has begun to take on the appearance of unconditional support for the policies of this state.

There is more at work than simply *communautarisme* and unconditional support for the Hebrew state. For the Jews of France, the beginning of the new millennium has also been a time of renewed fears in the face of anti-Semitism, which has found a new lease of life without it initially being recognized as such by the media or by political leaders who do not seem to have perceived its damaging effects. If the Jews of France are sending their children to private schools more and more frequently, it is, for certain people at least, not for religious reasons, but more often because they believe that state schools can no longer ensure their safety. In addition, state schools seem incapable of dealing properly with the Shoah, the evocation of which sometimes leads to shocking reactions among certain youths. The feeling is spreading that republican institutions no longer fulfill their mission, or at least not sufficiently well, and a recent work, which has had quite a large degree of success among the Jewish population, makes this point: Emmanuel Brenner's book, *Les territoires perdus de la République* (The lost territories of the Republic [Paris: Mille et une Nuits, 2002]). Under these conditions, whether one speaks of a "new Judeophobia" essentially to denounce a form of anti-Semitism linked to Islamism or to leftist excesses linked with radical support for the Palestinian cause, a new tendency among French Jews is observable: a return to the classic republican model, but without necessarily abandoning the gains made in the past, and thus without ceasing to declare support for the State of Israel, while also trusting Jewish community institutions to ensure their symbolic protection.

All of this leads to a situation which is impossible to manage dispassionately. The return to the model inherited from Enlightenment intellectuals and the Republic effectively implies the end of visibility in the public space, and therefore the opposite of *communaitarisme*, and an end to displays of unqualified support for the State of Israel. Yet visibility has now become a resource for Jews in France, if only in confronting anti-Semitism. So how can they turn towards the Republic and demand to be treated as individuals and not as a "nation," when such demands are actually being put forward by organizations that are *communautaire* in nature, and accompanied by behavior that reinforces *communautarisme*? How, in other words, can the republican model be reestablished on a basis that is pulling in a different direction? And moreover, how can Jews adopt the discreet posture that the republican model calls for if, at the same time, they are campaigning for the idea of a strong link between French Jews and Israel?

The republican model was invented before the creation of the Jewish state and, more broadly, it can only truly function if the population as a whole is able or potentially willing to adapt itself to that mold. Today, global trends such as transnationalism and diasporic phenomena in general are endangering that model, and from this point of view, the Jews of France are not alone. It is even more difficult for them to remain silent in public for they are constantly called upon to speak about Israel while other actors are actively mobilizing with reference to the Israeli-Palestinian conflict.

The Jewish question today relates not just to a resurgence of anti-Semitism. It is also, and above all, that of a population that identified itself in the past with a now exhausted republican model of uncertain assimilation, that witnessed a sort of multiculturalist golden age in the 1980s and 1990s, and that now poses the question: Is it possible to reestablish a republican model that would construct its own *aggiornamento* in such a way as to authorize a certain visibility in the public sphere? Have the Jews of France not entered into a delicate period, without a clear future direction, in which they lack the capacity to elaborate or grasp a real proposal capable of mobilizing them in their entirety, around satisfactory institutional and political projects?

A Post-Republican Phase

These questions have become all the more pressing in recent years, partly with reference to events in the Middle East, then in response to the kidnapping, torture, and death of a young Jew, Ilan Halimi, early in 2006, and more generally in relation to upsurges of group memories leading to a kind of "competitive victimhood" calling into question the symbolic and historical status of the Shoah.[10]

Until the beginning of the new century, anti-Semitism in France seemed to be an essentially domestic matter. But a new upsurge of anti-Semitism since then, notably among minorities of North African immigrant origin, often claiming to speak for the cause of Palestinians and/or of radical forms of Islam and sometimes for both, coincided so closely with the beginning of the second Intifada that it appears more "global" in nature, combining supranational dimensions from outside the country with elements specific to France. Jews now became the targets of escalating forms of anti-Semitism, sometimes verbal, sometimes in the form of attacks or attempted acts of arson against buildings such as synagogues or Jewish schools, in which Jews were identified with the State of Israel and with Israeli policies and more generally with the West, seen as bent on pursuing a "clash of civilizations" agenda hostile to Islam. Against this backdrop, *l'alya* (the departure of Jews to Israel) almost doubled from a thousand to two thousand a year, with the Israeli government exhorting French Jews to leave a country depicted as profoundly anti-Semitic.

In 2005, the situation appeared somewhat calmer and outside Jewish circles anti-Israeli sentiments were seen as less pronounced, or at any rate less militant, perhaps because of the policy turn taken by Ariel Sharon. Sharon had notably decided unilaterally to withdraw from the Gaza strip and to leave Likud in order to suddenly form a new party striking a stance that was centrist instead of right-wing. For a time, Israeli policy thus appeared less shocking in the eyes of some of those in France who found it unacceptable, and anti-Semitism fueled by or grounded in opposition to Israeli policy lost some of its appeal. At the time of this writing, it is too soon to assess the impact of the fighting during the summer of 2006 between Israel and Hezbollah but it is noteworthy that Jewish organizations in France generally sought to avoid appearing to give unconditional support to Israeli policy. In the discourse of its representative organizations, the Jewish Diaspora in France thus appears somewhat less rigidly bound than in the past to the unequivocal defense of Israeli policy.

The Fofana affair of 2005, named after the leader of a gang of kidnappers who abducted, tortured, and left for dead Ilan Halimi, had an unquestionable anti-Semitic dimension. It was because he was a Jew, and therefore was supposed to be rich, that Halimi was targeted for kidnapping so that a ransom could be demanded in exchange for his release. The affair also manifested the post-republican turn taken by Jews in France. In this respect, two events in particular should be noted. The first of these was the participation of the nation's highest representatives in a ceremony held in a synagogue in memory of Halimi. The second was the organization of a mass demonstration in which the main Jewish organizations in France invited every one in the country committed to democratic and republican values to join with them in their protests. In both cases, Jews were seen as very visible actors in the public space, with high levels of media exposure, confirming their break with the more classical republican model; at the same time, they underscored their attachment to republican values and the expectations associated with these, most obviously their protection from anti-Semitism. This new configuration, in which republican values go hand in hand with the relinquishing of traditional forms of behavior, may be fairly described as a post-republican phase.

A third element is also at work. In its new forms, anti-Semitism in France today draws on an additional theme: the idea that, through the Shoah, Jews have been attempting to monopolize the historical space of collective suffering. All sorts of groups are now demanding recognition as victims of the past. It is true that in some cases, Jews in France seem to claim the right to speak with some sort of exclusive status: as they see it, is not the Shoah not only exceptional and unique but also the only genocide that can truly be described as such? Still more importantly, extremism and hatred are clearly driving certain discourses of victimhood articulated by individuals and groups who accuse the Jews of being responsible for the historical ills suffered by those other groups and for the failure of the state and society at large to give due recognition to their suffering. A particular example of this is the humorist Dieudonné, who has built an image for himself in France as a defender of the cause of blacks by making anti-Semitic comments, notably in accusing Jews of having played an important role in the slave trade (which is historically untrue) and of having done everything in their power to prevent discussion of the slave trade so as to retain their monopoly of suffering and victimhood (which is also untrue). Many groups have been asking France to acknowledge its historical guilt in matters such as slavery, the slave trade and colonization, as well as the guilt of other states, such as Turkey in the matter of the Armenian genocide of 1915, and in most cases these claims have been advanced without any anti-Semitism. But this upsurge of historically based claims has fueled identity-based debates that were launched by Jews in France during the 1970s, and that are out-of-keeping with the classical republican model since they bring into the public space very visible and active collective identities. The post-republican phase was, so to speak, adumbrated by Jews and it is now very plain to see, with many other groups involved in it. Jews in France now feel rivaled or even threatened, not as a minority rejected by the nation and suspected of undermining social unity, as was the case from the late nineteenth century onwards and during the classical republican period, but as a minority that has successfully integrated and that is now blamed by other groups for their own exclusion. Many among those groups resent the fact that Jews have a significant presence in the core institutions of the Republic, are protected by their own institutions, and have the respect of the nation in official histories (school programs, for example) where the Shoah now has a significant place.

Jews today are thus in the paradoxical situation of finding themselves no longer a minority suffering rejection, exclusion, discrimination, and scorn, but a successfully integrated minority, protected by a range of institutions, and resented by others precisely because they are thought to no longer suffer from discrimination.

Translated by Matthew A. Kemp and Alec G. Hargreaves

Notes

1. Patrick Gérard. *La révolution française et les juifs* (Paris: Robert Laffont, 1989), 14.

2. Gérard, *La révolution*, 10.

3. Gérard, *La révolution*, 15.

4. Simon Doubnov, *Histoire moderne du peuple juif* (1933; repr., Paris: Les Amis de Simon Doubnov/Cerf. 1994).

5. Annie Kriegel. *Les Juifs et le monde moderne, Essai sur les logiques d'émancipation* (Paris: Seuil, 1977).

6. Pierre Birnbaum, *Les fous de la République. Histoire politique des Juifs d'Etat de Gambetta à Vichy* (Paris: Fayard. 1992).

7. Annette Wieviorka, *L'Ere du témoin* (Paris: Plon, 1998).

8. Peter Novick, *L'Holocauste dans la vie publique américaine* (Paris: Gallimard, 2001); first published in English as *The Holocaust in American Life* (Boston: Houghton Mifflin, 1999).

9. Erik H. Cohen. *Les Juifs de France, valeurs et identité* (Paris: Fonds social juif unifié, 2002).

10. Jean-Michel Chaumont. *La concurrence des victimes* (Paris: La Découverte, 1997).

Part V: Islam

Chapter Nine
To Vote or Not to Vote:
The Politicization of American Islam

Liyakat Takim

The twentieth century witnessed a dramatic increase in the migration of Muslims to the American shores. As Muslims migrated here in waves, Islam became an integral part of the American religious landscape and gradually, Muslims became a visible part of the fabric of American society.

Between 1900 and 1914, several hundred settlers comprising diverse religious backgrounds migrated from the Middle East. Many of these migrants came from Lebanon and settled in Detroit to work for the Ford Motor Company.[2] Thereafter, migration by members of the Lebanese community increased further between 1918 and 1922.[3]

The second wave of immigrants arrived after the end of World War II, when the United States encouraged students from the newly independent Arab states to study at American universities with the expectation that once they returned to their home countries, they would constitute an important asset to United States interests.[4] Later on, migrants came from other parts of the Muslim world. Given the more favorable economic and political circumstances, many of them decided to settle in the United States.

Immigrant Islam and the "Back-Home" Phenomenon

Whereas the early Muslims came primarily from the Arab world, postwar immigrants represented a wide array of linguistic, cultural, and national origins. Increased immigration from various parts of the world has resulted in the American Muslim community becoming more fragmented as bonds of common faith are replaced by efficacious ties to common origins, ethnicity, and culture. The process of ethnicization involves the formation of associations that are bound by distinctive cultural and ethnic characteristics. These include shared language, cultural norms, and the affirmation of a common history of a people. It is these homeland settings that construct social identities among Muslims in America.

As newer immigrants held nostalgic views regarding their homeland, the "back-home" phenomenon became intertwined with the "myth of return." As a matter of fact, many Muslim immigrants refused to accept America as their permanent home and hoped to return to their native lands after significant economic gains. While in America, they continued to speak their native languages, refused to integrate in the mainstream American society, and often restricted their interaction to members of their own ethnic or faith groups, establishing, in the process, ethnic islands within America. Many immigrants also imposed a conservative and extraneous expression of Islam and exhibited a general disdain of American culture and norms.

Apart from cherishing the dream of returning to their homeland countries, the back-home phenomenon also meant that immigrant Muslims fashioned Islam in America along the same lines as it was practiced back home. America was seen as a temporary residence, one in which the traditional expression of Islam was to be imposed and perpetuated. In addition, to protect the younger generation from the perceived corrupt, secular American society, it was deemed important to practice Islam the way it was done back home. Hence, it is correct to state that the major characteristic of immigrant Islam is that it universalizes the back-home Islam and imposes its understanding of Islam as the only possible construction of the Islamic ethos. Any other expression of Islam is construed as invalid and even heretical. In the view of the immigrants, immigrant Islam is not subject to interpretation or reformulation. It can only be transferred from one location to another in an unadulterated form.[5]

Immigrant Muslims tend to experience Islam through a cultural prism that is highly resistant to change. In their centers, Islam is mediated in a culturally conditioned form. They decide on how the mosques are to be run, and on what is acceptable in terms of dress, language, and political behavior. In addition, they have imposed their authority on indigenous Muslims especially as many African Americans had no authoritative spokesman to speak about Islam. Thus, the increase in immigrant Muslims meant that all that was alien to immigrants was seen as alien to Islam itself.[6] Before the 1970s, Islam in America was defined and understood through the prism of indigenous Muslims, primarily the Nation of Islam. Increased migration of Muslims meant that the African American community largely lost its interpretive voice.

Even after their arrival in America, immigrant Muslims were more concerned with addressing foreign rather than domestic issues. The back-home mentality meant that American issues like those of affirmative action, racism, joblessness, education, housing, and urban violence were replaced by foreign issues like Palestine, Kashmir, and lately Iraq. This emphasis was compounded by the importation of political ideas through foreign movements whose vision did not enhance Muslim participation in the American political culture. Their vision was focused on topics like the establishment of an Islamic state, implementation of the *shari'a*, removal of *jahiliyya*, abstinence from an infidel culture, and so forth. Muslim aversion to involvement in American social and political discourse was accentuated by the fact that many Muslims saw America as *dar al-kufr*, the abode of infidels. Hence, any participation in the American domestic agenda was construed as being involved in an infidel government, one that contravened Islamic jurisprudence. Ironically, Islam became the cause rather than solution to the lack of Muslim political activism.[7] Such a position undermined Muslims' ability to assert any influence in the American political culture. Voting, lobbying, and holding political office were all frowned upon, if not proscribed.

The Indigenization of American Islam

In 1964, President Lyndon Johnson ratified an immigration act increasing quotas from non-European countries. The new immigration laws allowed immigrants to migrate from all areas of the Arab and Muslim world. New immigrants were more representative of the ethnic, national, and religious diversity of the Muslim world. In addition, there was a gradual change in the Muslim constituency. Conversion rates to Islam increased as did the number of Muslims born or raised in America.

As the immigrants settled here and the Muslim population increased, Muslims came to identify America as their permanent home. They realized that they could not remain socially invisible or politically neutral. In addition, the Islam that was transposed from abroad was challenged not only by converts but also by Muslim youth who appropriated a distinctly American culture. In many Islamic centers, services were conducted by immigrants along the same lines that were held in their own countries, with little or no concern for the needs of the members in this milieu. The imposition of an alien culture in the centers estranged the youth in the Muslim community. As one youth states: "We are less likely to identify with the home-sick mosque culture and more likely to assert a very active political role for the Islamic center, and to do it as an American Muslim community—not as Egyptian, Pakistani, or Malaysian expatriates, but as Americans."[8]

There was another factor that made Muslims accentuate their American as opposed to their homeland identity. This was the threat posed by the characterization in the media of Islam as a militant and violent religion, a depiction that has become increasingly apparent in the past fifteen years. Attacks against Israel and other American interests abroad revived American prejudices of Islam as a religion that promotes violence and of Muslims as an inherently militant and irrational people.

In recent times, the American global "war on terror" and the invasion of Iraq have further revived the stereotypes and suspicions against Muslims, especially those of Middle Eastern origins. Furthermore, the vitriolic attacks on Islam and the Qur'an by some Christian fundamentalists have clearly exacerbated the current conflict in America. They have projected Islam as inherently violent and incompatible with Western values and norms. Such attacks tend to engender hatred and destroy rather than build bridges.

Due to the activities of terrorists, American Muslims have come to the realization that both their Islamic identity and American citizenship are at stake. The Muslim community has acknowledged that the silent majority syndrome has to end simply because Muslim acquiescence has encouraged an extremist expression of Islam. Thus, many Muslims have felt the need to integrate themselves into mainstream American society so as to make their voices heard. This indigenization of American Islam represents a silent revolution that many Muslims have been engaged in.[9]

Indigenization of American Islam is the process of identifying, understanding, and relating to the culture, heritage, and the history of America. Indigenization also means carving out a space for oneself in American society, being more appreciative of American values while remaining authentic to Islam. An essential element of the indigenization of American Islam is Muslims' identification with American culture and values, and their distancing themselves from a back-home mentality. Indigenization also means viewing American secular culture as a challenge to be comprehended and tolerated rather than a threat to be confronted, for the latter approach can breed a culture of negative isolation and fear of the "other."

Indigenization of American Islam does not mean the Arabization or Indianization of Islam; rather, it means interpreting its message so that it is suitable to the American Muslim without sacrificing its doctrinal integrity. Thus, it is correct to state that indigenization is an internal process, one that cannot be imposed from abroad.[10] It has to be formulated, articulated, and expressed by those Muslims who are familiar with the American milieu and culture.

Indigenization has also meant that American Muslims have increasingly expressed themselves through a properly articulated intellectual discourse, so that they can be both physically and intellectually visible. Thus, American Muslims have sought to go beyond the history of hostility, caricature, and power struggles that have characterized relations between Christians and Muslims in the past. It is correct to state that the Muslims' struggle in America has been not only to coexist with the "other," but also to make themselves comprehensible in the American milieu, to "de-mythify" and decode Islam and to challenge the negative characterization of Islam.

The process of the indigenization of American Islam is intertwined with the construction of a distinctly American Islamic civic identity. This process has expressed itself in a myriad of forms. Muslims have joined forces with various peace and anti-racist movements. In addition, since September 11, 2001, various Islamic centers have facilitated "open-mosque" hours and have tried to become more "people friendly" by encouraging their non-Muslim neighbors to visit mosques.

Instead of denouncing American society and values, Friday sermons delivered in many mosques have focused on devotional, ethical, and historical topics. The community has also embarked on coalition building with human rights, religious rights, and civil rights groups. Muslim groups have been involved in various social programs like food drives and have sought to help homeless Americans.

Indigenization has also meant that rather than focusing on American foreign policy, Muslims now tend to concentrate more on reconstituting their identity as American Muslims. In all probability, this is because as the second generation of Muslims in America identify with and assimilate in American culture, they develop a sense of patriotism leading to a greater politicization of the community and a sense of American national consciousness. Furthermore, Muslims have realized that unless they become more vocal and American, they could become foreigners in their adopted homeland.

Muslim Institutions in America

Since the early immigrants did not intend to stay in America, they did not invest in any religious or socio-political leadership that could offer an intellectual or political vision to the community. Thus, the early Muslim institutions did not engage in political activity. Rather, most of the early Muslim organizations were social, ethnic, or religious in nature. Societies like the Syrian and Lebanese American Federation of the Eastern States, the National Association of Syrian and Lebanese-American Organizations (formed in 1932), and the National Association of Federations were quite indifferent to U.S. foreign or domestic policies. In 1952, under the leadership of Abdullah Ingram, immigrants from the Middle East formed the Federation of Islamic Associations in the United States (FIA). This was meant to be an umbrella body that would unite twenty immigrant associations and provide for the social, cultural, and religious needs of the community. However, it did not raise Arab political consciousness.[11] Until the 1960s, there is little evidence to indicate that the majority of Muslims in the U.S. had any awareness of events overseas or the geography of the Middle East.[12]

However, the Israeli-Palestinian conflict forced American Muslims to reconsider their apolitical stance. American hostility towards Arabs during the Six-Day War and the ignorance of the American public regarding the Middle East conflict led to the formation of the Association of Arab-American University Graduates (AAUG) in 1967. The AAUG was established by graduate students, professionals, university professors, lawyers, doctors, and veterans of the Organization of Arab Students (OAS).[13] Most of the organizations were formed by American Arabs who sought to establish a platform where the Arab-Muslim voice could be expressed. They also tried to have an input into the shaping of American foreign policy.[14]

In the 1970s, other organizations were founded with the intention of informing and educating the American public about the Arab world. In 1971, Lebanese Americans organized the National Association of Arab Americans (NAAA). The leadership sought to educate Arab Americans about the political process as well as arrange for them to meet with members of Congress to discuss issues that concerned the community. The American-Arab Anti Discrimination Committee (ADC) was founded by former Senator James Aburezk and James Zogby, both of Christian-Lebanese origin. The Arab American Institute (AAI) was established in 1984 when Zogby split from the ADC. It encourages Arab Americans to participate in the American political system, working to get Arab Americans to vote and to run for office.[15]

The 1980s and 1990s witnessed increased animosity towards Arabs and Muslims in the United States. In all probability, domestic groups like the conservative wing of the Republican Party, Christian fundamentalist groups, and the pro-Israel lobby were responsible for encouraging the anti-Islamic rhetoric. American hostility toward Islam and Muslims was also precipitated by various events oversees. These included: the Six-Day War in 1967, the Yom Kippur War and oil embargo of 1973, the Islamic Revolution in Iran in 1979, the hostage crisis in Iran and Lebanon, PLO attacks against Israeli targets, the Rushdie affair of 1989, and the Gulf Wars. Such events precipitated measures that led to the targeting and racial profiling of Arabs and Muslims, along with a growing atmosphere of hostility towards Islam. As a matter of fact, a scheme known as Operation Boulder placed Arab Americans under FBI surveillance in the early 1970s.[16]

Increased government surveillance and discriminatory policies forced Muslims to abandon their traditional ambivalent stance toward political intervention. They quickly realized that it was only by participation in the American constitutional order that Muslims could enjoy protection against government agencies that disregard the Constitution and violate civil liberties. Political activism could also persuade policymakers to counteract American resentment against Muslims. In addition, the Muslim community perceived the need to bring its members closer, especially as many of them had settled in remote parts of America. These factors led to the establishment of various Islamic institutions.

In 1963, the Muslim Student Association (MSA) was formed by students at the University of Illinois-Urbana. By the 1970s, the MSA had helped to establish branches on college campuses throughout the United States. In 1981, the MSA established the Islamic Society of North America (ISNA). Unlike earlier institutions that catered primarily to the Arab American community, organizations such as ISNA assisted individuals from different ethnic groups to meet in its conferences and encouraged its members to associate with other ethnically defined Muslims. Soon, other immigrant organizations, such as the Islamic Circle of North America (ICNA) and the Islamic Association of North America

(IANA) were established. They held annual conventions, published magazines, built mosques and Islamic centers, reaching out, in the process, to hundreds of thousands of American Muslims.

As Muslims continued to experience intimidation, discrimination, misunderstanding, and even hatred, they saw the need to educate Americans about Islam, correct some of the anti-Islamic stereotypical images portrayed in the media, and protect the interests of the Muslim community. Hence, more Muslims organizations were established in the 1980s and 1990s. Their aim was not confined to educate Americans about the Arab-Israeli conflict. Rather, these institutions encouraged Muslims to address political and civil right issues that impacted the rights of the growing community.

In 1988 the Muslim Public Affairs Council (MPAC) was established by the multi-ethnic Islamic center of Southern California in Los Angeles. This political lobby has made important contributions in the last few years. It has established close ties with Hillary Clinton and with officials at the Department of State. Through its efforts, the First Lady hosted two events to celebrate the end of the month of fasting of Ramadan (*eid al-fitr*) events.

In 1989, the American Muslim Alliance (AMA) was established in northern California by a political scientist of Pakistani origin. The goal of the AMA was to empower Muslims to become politically active by voting and running for office. On the East Coast, the American Muslim Council (AMC) was established in 1990 in Washington, D.C. The AMC has established relations with various branches of the government. It has also sought to have Muslim religious leaders invited to offer an opening prayer before congressional deliberations.

At the national level, the Council for American Islamic Relations (CAIR), which was established in June 1994, has challenged the misrepresentation and defamation of Islam and Muslims in the workplace. Since 1996, CAIR has issued an annual report documenting incidents of anti-Muslim discrimination and violence. CAIR's 1999 report noted that despite the persistence of discrimination, an increasing number of employees have eased their objection to Muslim women's *hijab*.[17]

Since the events of 9/11, Muslims have had to endure the USA PATRIOT (Providing Appropriate Tools Required to Intercept and Obstruct Terrorism) Act of 2001. The act sanctions the monitoring of individuals, organizations, and institutions without notification. Its provisions have been protested by the American Civil Liberties Union. Several Arab and Muslim organizations have recently sued the American government insisting that the act is unconstitutional. Recent disclosure of secret wiretapping of suspected terrorists and the federal government's admission that, in search of a terrorist nuclear bomb, it has run a far-reaching, top secret program to monitor radiation levels at over a hundred Muslim homes, businesses, and mosques in the capital region and in other areas, have all augmented Muslim concern regarding their civil rights. In numerous cases, the monitoring required investigators to go on to the property under surveillance, although no search warrants or court orders were ever obtained. In December 2005, under the Freedom of Information Act (FOIA), CAIR filed a request to access all government records relating to this program. Due to its efforts to safeguard the interests of the Muslim community, CAIR has emerged, in the eyes of many Muslims, as the Muslim equivalent of the Jewish Defense League.

These Muslim public affairs groups have been able to make the stereotyping of Muslims a matter of public debate and have documented many incidents of harassment, discrimination, and defamation against Muslims. They have also monitored and publicized discriminatory measures by government agencies and civic groups and have highlighted the distortion of Islam in the media.

By convening seminars, publishing articles in magazines and Islamic newsletters, delivering lectures at various conventions and workshops, organizations such as ICNA, ISNA, AMC, CAIR, MSA, and MYNA (Muslim Youth of North America) have altered the way Muslims think about the United States and about themselves. As the back-home mentality gradually faded in the mid-1980s and early 1990s, these organizations shifted Muslim political and civil discourse in America to how Muslims could interact with Americans and yet maintain their own distinctive identity. Muslims also grappled with issues like the scope and nature of Muslim participation in the American public square. The vision was now on repositioning Islam as an element of American national interest and not as a threat to it.

The four leading American Muslim political organizations (AMA, AMC, MPAC, and CAIR) engage in political lobbying and encourage Muslims to run for electoral office. In 1999, these four institutions agreed to coordinate their activities under the umbrella of the American Muslim Political Coordinating Council (AMPCC).[18] Through their various activities, these groups have provided a vision for Muslim engagement with America's political institutions. In the process, they have had to confront not only a hostile American media and an unsympathetic U.S. government, but also traditional Muslim scholars who decried any involvement in the American public sphere.

Resistance to Muslim Political Discourse in America

Attempts at making American Muslims a viable and active political force have met with firm resistance from within the Muslim community. As mentioned earlier, certain segments within the community have resisted integration or political discourse with American society, claiming that America is an infidel state that is based on secular values and laws. Those advocating such a perspective include foreign-based movements like the Tablighi Jamat, a group of propagators that started in India and is now a transnational movement. Tablighis try to permeate mainstream Muslim life, using mosques as bases for their activities. Their primary objective is to preach to Muslims, urging them to return to the *sunna* (practices) of the Prophet and early companions.[19] In their view, only God has the prerogative of framing the law. Hence, obedience to or participation in the policies of a secular state is deemed to be *haram* (religiously proscribed).[20]

The Salafis have also tried to sway Muslims to their way of thinking. They emerged from Saudi Arabia and other parts of the Middle East. They see the Western world as a morally corrupt society that must be shunned. Their emphasis is on maintaining proper belief and a return to the Islam of the pious ancestors (*salaf*), that is, the early Muslim community. The Hizb al-Tahrir, a foreign group that attempts to resurrect the caliphate, claims that registering to vote is tantamount to registering to commit a religiously forbidden act. This is because participating in the American political process is tantamount to implementing man-made laws, which, in their understanding, is prohibited in the Qur'an. During the 2000 elections, their motto was, register to vote, register to commit *haram*.[21] Thus, many Muslims have eschewed any participation in the American political system as they believe America to be a secular state. Any involvement in it would violate the traditional Islamic model regarding the proper relationship between church and state.

Similarly, Shi'i aversion to American politics can be discerned from the following anecdote. In 1996, there was a major discussion on the Shi'i based internet discussion group called the "ahl al-bayt discussion group" (ABDG) as to whether Shi'is should support candidates running for federal elections. The majority felt that since they were living in a non-Muslim country, Shi'is should eschew all political involvement. Others even argued that, given American penchant toward Israel, voting for a candidate would be tantamount to supporting the Israeli cause. Therefore, they decreed that it was *haram* to support or vote for a candidate. A small minority disagreed, arguing that voting for a candidate of their choice might help the Shi'i cause in America and perhaps influence American foreign policy.

The distinctive views of the various groups have been propagated in the Muslim media, Friday sermons, workshops, and over the Internet. In the process, the question of political participation in America has become a battle of rhetorical devices, with Muslims employing Qur'anic hermeneutics and traditions from the Prophet to vindicate their respective points. America has become a battleground for Muslim minds and voices as traditional differences between those who call for political engagement and isolation have resurfaced, engendering further fragmentation of the Muslim community.

Immigrant Muslim aversion to political involvement is further evidenced when we examine the cases of two former Muslim congressional candidates, Riaz Hussain of New York and Bill Quraishi of California. Both candidates sought Muslim votes, but conservative Islamic groups disliked the candidates' perceived accommodation to Western culture. They were blamed for not keeping a beard and for adopting a Western name.[22]

Muslim Engagement in American Politics

Up to the late 1970s, most of the immigrant Muslims did not organize or mobilize themselves as a political force within the American universe of political
lobbies. However, this attitude changed significantly in the second generation of
Muslims because of their greater assimilation into American culture and their
adoption of an American identity. In addition, the denigration of Islam and hostility toward Muslims in America demanded a more positive Muslim response.

The process of indigenization that I described above meant that there was a
definitive shift in Muslim political discourse. With the establishment of Muslim
civic and political institutions, Muslims became increasingly aware of the U.S.
government's domestic as opposed to foreign policies, especially those that impacted their daily lives. Muslims also concluded that political power can be only
be enhanced by the politics of engagement between American Muslims and the
political system. It was to the advantage of Muslims to seek ways of influencing
governance, especially with regard to policy formation. They realized the need
to monitor and influence American foreign and domestic policies, and that self-
denial of voting power would make Muslims more vulnerable.[23]

Muslims also realized that the politics of numbers can benefit the community in a positive manner and that the source of power in America lies in the
mobilization and institutionalization of statistical advantage, that is, by the
channeling of votes, political lobbying, and influencing the views of senators
and congressmen. As a matter of fact, Muslims have made significant progress
in attaining symbolic recognition, perhaps more so than any other group, in the
past few years. Since the middle 1980s, several political action committees
(PACs) have been established. The first was the Houston-based All American
Muslim Political Action Committee (AAMPAC) in 1985. Other PACs were
later formed in California and Michigan.[24] Even ISNA established an umbrella
PAC body called ISNA-PAC.[25]

Similarly, Warith al-Deen Mohammed and his associates have founded the
Coalition for Good Government to provide political vision for American Muslims. Warith al-Deen's view of engagement with, rather than denunciation of,
the American political culture has led to greater Muslim presence in local and
national political life.[26] By the mid-1980s, ISNA felt the need to coordinate local
political activities and make Muslims a political force. In 1986, a report issued
by its planning committee stated: "In order to exert influence on the political
decision-making [sic] and legislation in North America, ISNA should launch a
campaign to educate Muslim citizens about their voting rights and mobilize
them to vote on issues affecting Islam and Muslims. On a longer term basis,
ISNA should develop communication with and among politically active Muslims and establish a separate organization in due course."[27]

As the Muslim community became more visible and vocal in the 1990s,
senators, congressmen, and even the White House paid increasing attention to
the American Muslim community. Muslims were being recognized as an inte-

gral part of American society. In the fall of 1995, Vice President Albert Gore became the highest-ranking U.S. official to visit a mosque.[28] President Bill Clinton's speech on religious freedom on July 12, 1995, acknowledged Muslims several times. African American Muslim leaders Siraj Wahhaj and Warith al-Deen Muhammad delivered invocations in the House and Senate, respectively. Friday prayers are now held regularly in the U.S. Capitol building for Muslim staffers, federal employees, and other Muslims in the area. Since 1998, a crescent and star is displayed on the White House lawn alongside a menorah and Christmas tree.[29]

President George H. W. Bush began a tradition of wishing Muslims a happy holiday on *Eid*, which President Clinton expanded upon by holding an *Eid* celebration in the White House, usually attended by the First Lady. Despite negative coverage in the media, the Clintons opened the White House to Muslims.[30]

In the run up to the election in 2000, the struggle between Muslims who advocated for engagement with and those who wanted to isolate from American politics intensified. The isolationists were largely marginalized as Islamic organizations succeeded in mobilizing Muslims to vote in large numbers, making a difference in the crucial state of Florida.[31] Increasingly, American Muslims have realized that political isolation is detrimental to their interests in America.

Muslims have become more assertive and made positive contributions in the political arena. In the 2000 presidential elections, they sent delegates to Democratic and Republican election conventions; they ran in various local, state, and congressional district elections; they made financial contributions to various campaigns; and they also voted in large numbers. In its national gathering, the American Muslim Alliance featured the theme "How to Get 2000 Muslim Americans Elected to Public Offices in 2000." Its focus was to empower Muslims so that they could serve on school boards, in municipal posts, and as mayors and state legislators.[32] These facts indicate a clear paradigm shift in Muslim political consciousness from complaining about the inequities of American policies to seeking measures to redress them.

During the 2000 presidential election, at both the Republican and Democratic national conventions, Islamic prayers were offered for the first time, broadening the symbolic boundaries of American religious culture to include Islam. Various Muslim groups endorsed George W. Bush for president. For example, the Political Action Committee of the American Muslim Political Coordination Council (AMPCC-PAC) endorsed Bush due to his outreach to the Muslim community and his stand on the issue of secret evidence. Furthermore, during the presidential debates, Bush questioned the fairness of profiling Arabs and Muslims. Muslims even sent delegates to the party conventions before the 2000 elections, seven to the Republican convention, twenty-six to the Democratic convention.[33]

Increased political activity can be seen from the fact that Muslims have participated in the electoral process as candidates. The website of the American Muslim Alliance (AMA), whose main purpose is to promote Muslims seeking public office, listed eleven Muslim candidates running in various local, state, and congressional districts in the 2000 elections. Eric Vickers, a St. Louis Muslim lawyer and member of the board of directors of AMA, received 6 percent of the vote in his congressional district in the Democratic Party primary on August 8, 2000.[34]

Other Muslim candidates won some electoral seats at the state and local levels. In 1996, Larry Shaw became a state senator in North Carolina—the first Muslim ever to occupy such a position in any state. Several other Muslims have won city council seats, including Yusuf Abdus-Salaam in Selma, Alabama; Yusuf Abdul-Hakeem in Chattanooga, Tennessee; and Nasif Majid in Charlotte, North Carolina. According to the American Muslim Alliance, two dozen Muslims were elected to party conventions at precinct, county, state, and national levels in 1996.[35]

Muslims attained prominent positions in other spheres too. In 1991, Charles Bilal, an African American Muslim, was elected mayor of Kountze, Texas, becoming the first Muslim mayor of an American city. Another Muslim, Adam Shakoor, served as deputy mayor of Detroit, which has a large Muslim community, in the early 1990s.[36]

Muslims have also made financial contributions to various political campaigns. Many supported the political campaigns of candidates directly; others channeled their contributions through political actions committees (PACs). The Democrats received $357,506 and the Republicans $249,672 in the 1998 and 2000 elections (combined totals).[37]

Muslims are also voting in increasing numbers. Exit polls conducted by *Minaret Magazine* and MPAC of four hundred randomly selected Muslims indicated that 65 percent registered to vote; another survey by *Minaret* in 1996 shows 76 percent of the Muslims surveyed voted in the elections.[38]

The project Muslims in the American Public Square (MAPS) that was initiated under the auspices of Georgetown University also conducted a survey in 2000. It indicated that 79 percent of the Muslims registered to vote; 40 percent voted for Democrats, 23 percent for Republicans, and 28 percent for independents. According to Karen Leonard, African Americans are more likely to vote for Democrats, Pakistanis are more inclined towards the Republicans, and Arabs are evenly divided.[39]

In January 2006, CAIR launched an *Eid*-voter-registration drive, in which it urged American Muslims to register at *Eid al-Adha* events. The *Eid*-voter-registration drive was part of a major non-partisan Muslim political mobilization effort to be conducted during the 2006 election cycle. The effort was to include in-person and online voter registration drives, candidate forums, production of voter guides, get-out-the-vote campaigns, conducting research on and surveys of American Muslim voters, and other grassroots activities. CAIR also stated that it would be calling on Muslim students to volunteer in political campaigns.[40]

Even allowing for some exaggerations, the figures quoted above indicate enhanced Muslim political awareness and participation. They also reflect how Muslim institutions like CAIR, AMC, and MPAC have mobilized the community to exert political pressure on lawmakers and legislators in America. The various figures quoted above also testify to the growing Muslim awareness that, to be a political force, they must reposition their focus from mosque construction and community projects to political mobilization and interest articulation.

Shi'i Political Discourse

Unlike the Sunni community, the American Shi'i community has not been politically active. Lack of Shi'i involvement in the American political process can be attributed to the relatively young age of the Shi'i Islamic centers. Most Shi'i centers in America have been established since 1985. Thus, Shi'is have used their limited financial resources to build and consolidate their centers rather than to engage in political activity or make financial contributions to campaigns.[41] Shi'i political inactivity is also explained by the fact that the Shi'is have yet to form nationwide institutions like CAIR, AMC, or AMA. Hence, there is no institution that can unite the Shi'i community or address issues that are of political concern. It is only in the past three years that the United Muslim Association of America (UMAA) has been established. However, this nascent organization has yet to formulate any definitive direction for the Shi'i community, nor has it been able to bridge the chasm that has divided different ethnic entities within the community.

Shi'i political aspirations in America have yet to crystallize into a concrete body with a properly formulated political agenda. In the absence of such political institutions, political activism manifests itself in public discourse on moral and social issues that impact the community.

In a few isolated cases, some Shi'is have nominated themselves to run for Congress by seeking votes from local Shi'i and Sunni communities. However, most of these candidates run independently and are not directly supported by any Shi'i institution. In some areas of America, Shi'i political activity has taken the form of establishing eclectic bodies that transcend sectarian boundaries, cooperating with Sunnis to create a unified and effective challenge for local posts. Shi'i institutions like al-Khu'i Foundation in New York have persuaded their members that their votes and involvement in the political process can make a difference in their lives in America. Thus, some Shi'is cooperate with Sunnis to provide Muslim candidates for school boards, municipal posts; they also work together for the election of Muslim mayors and state legislators. The intent is to get Shi'is to vote for fellow Muslim candidates, planning for an eventual Muslim presence in Congress or the Senate.[42]

Lack of Shi'i political involvement is further discerned from the fact that during the elections in 2000, there was little discussion within the Shi'i centers on any involvement in the Muslim election campaign. Another striking point is that the Shi'is are not represented even within the Muslim organizations that participate in American civic society. Thus, there are no Shi'i representatives in the American Muslim Council, the Council of American Islamic Relations, or in the Islamic Society of North America. For Muslims to collectively make a significant impact in the American political process, they will have to set aside their ethnic, sectarian and nationalistic differences.

Conclusion

Relaxation of immigration laws in 1964 meant that new waves of Muslims from overseas were dominated by students and professionals who established new institutions in America. Changes in the Muslim population occurred due to the immigration of a large number of highly educated Muslims from various parts of the Muslim world, specifically from the Middle East and Southeast Asia. These migrants built new institutions that have effectively shaped Muslim political consciousness. Thus, it is correct to state that in recent decades, Muslims have sought to indigenize Islam, and to foster a distinctly American Muslim identity.

The struggle among American Muslims for the definition of the self, to give meaning to their new identity as American Muslims, and to the new sociopolitical context of their existence is manifesting itself in tensions between the liberal and conservative, indigenous and immigrant, young and old, and between Sunni and Shi'i Muslims. Conflicts have arisen due to an immigrant community having to come to terms with an alien culture. The American Muslim community is split between those who are willing to engage the larger American society and those unwilling to do so. In the last three decades, through the efforts of Muslim activists and various organizations, Muslim focus has shifted from battling the West to building bridges with it. In the battle for American Islam, Muslims have gradually marginalized their coreligionists who advocated for resistance to and disengagement from the American public sphere. Paradoxically, the very institutions that are supposed to unite Muslims (such as mosques) have become a catalyst for the perpetuation of a distinctive ethnic ethos.

Notes

1. On the waves of Muslim migration see Yvonne Haddad and Adair Lummis, *Islamic Values in the United States: A Comparative Study* (New York: Oxford University Press, 1987), 13-14.

2. Linda Walbridge, *Without Forgetting the Imam: Lebanese Shi'ism in an American Community* (Detroit: Wayne State University Press, 1997), 16-17.

3. Walbridge, *Without Forgetting*, 17-18.

4. Yvonne Haddad, *Not Quite American? The Shaping of Arab and Muslim Identity in the United States* (Waco, TX: Baylor University Press, 2004), 5.

5. For an excellent discussion on the tension between immigrant and indigenous Islam see Sherman Jackson, *Islam and the Blackamerican: Looking Toward the Third Resurrection* (New York: Oxford University Press, 2005), chapter 2.

6. Jackson, *Islam and the Blackamerican*, 70.

7. Jackson. *Islam and the Blackamerican*, 73.

8. Steven Barboza. *American Jihad: Islam after Malcolm X* (New York: Doubleday. 1994), 58.

9. See Liyakat Takim, "From Conversion to Conversation: Interfaith Dialogue in Post-911 America," *The Muslim World* 94, no. 3 (2004): 343-55.

10. On the difference between indigenization and assimilation. see Jackson. *Islam and the Blackamerican*, 169.

11. Yvonne Yazbeck Haddad. "American Foreign Policy in the Middle East and Its Impact on the Identity of Arab Muslims in the United States." in *The Muslims of America*, ed. Yvonne Yazbeck Haddad (New York: Oxford University Press, 1991). 225-26.

12. Haddad. *Not Quite American?* 17.

13. Haddad. *Not Quite American?* 20.

14. Haddad. *Not Quite American?* 49-50.

15. Haddad. *Not Quite American?* 22.

16. Haddad, "American Foreign Policy." 220.

17. Mohammed Nimer, "Muslims in the American Body Politic," in *Muslims' Place in the American Public Square: Hope, Fears, and Aspirations*. ed. Zahid H. Bukhari, Sulayman S. Nyang, Mumtaz Ahmad, and John L. Esposito (Walnut Creek, CA: AltaMira Press, 2004), 149.

18. Karen Leonard, *Muslims in the United States: The State of Research* (New York: Russell Sage Foundation, 2003). 18.

19. On the mass movements in Sunni mosques in America see Barbara Metcalf, "New Medinas: The Tablighi Jama'at in America and Europe." in *Making Muslim Space in North America and Europe*, ed. Barbara Metcalfe (Berkeley and Los Angeles: University of California Press, 1996), 113.

20. See Omar Khalidi, "Living as a Muslim in a Pluralistic Society and State: Theory and Experience," in Bukhari et al.. *Muslims' Place in the American Public Square*. 67-68.

21. Ihsan Bagby, "The Mosque and the American Public Square." in Bukhari et al., *Muslims' Place in the American Public Square*, 329.

22. Asma Gull Hasan. *American Muslims: The New Generation* (New York: Continuum. 2001). 152.

23. Ali Mazrui, "Muslims Between the Jewish Example and the Black Experience: American Policy Implications," in Bukhari et al.. *Muslims' Place in the American Public Square*, 127.

24. Steve A. Johnson, "Political Activity of Muslims in America," in Haddad. *The Muslims of America*, 116.

25. Jane Smith, *Islam in America* (New York: Columbia University Press. 1999). 186.

26. Smith. *Islam in America*, 186.

27. Quoted in Steve A. Johnson, "Political Activity of Muslims in America," in Haddad, *The Muslims of America*, 111.

28. Hasan, *American Muslims*, 153.

29. Hasan, *American Muslims*. 153.

30. Mazrui, "Muslims Between the Jewish Example." 128.

31. Muqtedar Khan, "Living on Borderlines: Islam Beyond the Clash and Dialogue of Civilizations," in Bukhari et al., *Muslims' Place in the American Public Square*, 106.

32. Smith, *Islam in America*, 185.

33. Hasan, *American Muslims*, 157.

34. Nimer, "Muslims in the American Body Politic," 161.

35. Nimer, "Muslims in the American Body Politic," 161.

36. Hasan, *American Muslims,* 159.

37. For details of other Muslim financial contributions see Nimer, "Muslims in the American Body Politic," 160-61.

38. Hasan, *American Muslims,* 157.

39. Leonard, *Muslims in the United States,* 101.

40. See the press release issued by CAIR over the Internet, "CAIR Launches Eid Voter Registeration Drive," January 5, 2006, http://www.cair.com/default.asp?Page=artic leView&id=1938&theType=NR (accessed February 26, 2007).

41. See Liyakat Takim, "Multiple Identities in a Pluralistic World: Shi'ism in America," in *Muslims in the West: From Sojourners to Citizens,* ed. Yvonne Yazbeck Haddad (New York: Oxford University Press, 2002), 218-32.

42. Takim, "Multiple Identities in a Pluralistic World," 218-32.

Chapter Ten
From Migrants to Citizens: Muslims in France

Catherine Wihtol de Wenden

The widespread disturbances that erupted in disadvantaged areas of French cities in November 2005 refocused attention on the ethnicization of poverty and violence in France. They also called into question the so-called French model of "integration" and renewed the debate about the role of Islam as a factor of provocation or pacification, overshadowing the December 5 commemoration of the 1905 law separating churches and state. During the last three decades, these and related issues have becomes leitmotifs in debates about French politics and society. These debates have been all the more heated in so far as the terms and categories of analysis have been imprecise, lending themselves to marked politicization. The term "Muslim" is complex: does it refer to the faith and religious practice of Islam, to Muslim culture, which is itself multi-facetted, and/or to sociological Islam, that is, to the everyday behavior of populations of Muslim culture including the descendants of immigrants who are presumed to belong to this religion? More fundamentally, why is it that these questions have arisen?

Following the example of some of her European neighbors, France suspended economic migration from non-European Community countries in 1974. This decision was to have the effect of accelerating family reunification, most notably among Maghrebis (North Africans), and placed the question of "integration" at the center of the French debate over immigration.[1] More than thirty years later, the question is just as pertinent, but is now set against a context marked by new security questions, actions designed to curb Islamic radicalism, the challenges arising from social inequalities, and the growing importance of the European Union as a policy actor. At the same time, at an everyday level we can see the often overlooked integration of the majority of immigrants, together with spectacular social successes, relatively exceptional in nature, alongside serious problems of social exclusion. In this context, new actors, new issues and new institutions have emerged in France. These include young people of immigrant origin also known as the "second generation";[2] civic *Beurs* involved in associative actions;[3] cultural mediators in socially disadvantaged urban areas;[4] Muslim women who live out their religion in many different ways; Muslims who are identified as such by the nature of their heritage, their religious practices or political activism, including some practicing militant Muslim identities; and middle class and more elite actors of immigrant origin. Among the issues they raise are questions of citizenship, the struggle against social exclusion, the business of "living together," urban policies, the institutionalization of Islam, and the struggle against discrimination at the level of attitudes and institutions.

Out of an estimated population of approximately 12 million people of immigrant Muslim culture in Europe, France accounts for more than 4 million. France has indeed the largest Muslim population of any West European country, although their numbers cannot be counted precisely since French censuses do not currently include any questions relating to religious affiliation. Estimates are based, for example, on the number of foreigners from countries of Muslim culture (the countries of the Maghreb, Turkey, sub-Saharan West Africa, Pakistan, and the Near and Middle East), the estimated numbers of young people of immigrant background, the number of *harkis* (former auxiliaries of the French army repatriated from colonial Algeria) and their children, to whom must be added people of French origin who have converted to Islam. This population is very diverse. The majority of it is made up of Maghrebis and their children, with some of them (notably Algerians) having often been present in France for several generations, whereas others, such as Turks, sub-Saharan Africans, Pakistanis, and other people from the Middle East, are more recent immigrants. As Sunnis of the Malekite branch, the Maghrebis have set the tone in France in matters of integration and Islam and in negotiating their ways of being Muslim with institutions that seek a dialogue with them. An increasing number of them possess French citizenship by virtue of having been born in France and due to peculiar legal provisions applying to the children of Algerian immigrants, and most also have dual nationality due to the application of *jus sanguinis* (citizenship through filiation) in all Muslim countries. Whether they practice the religion or not, they are all considered to be of Muslim culture because in their countries of origin Islam is the religion of the overwhelming majority, although one does also find there some firm adherents of secularism, such as in Turkey, and indeed some atheists among the intelligentsia even though Islam forbids renunciation of the religion (that is, apostasy).

If we look at the interaction between actors of Muslim culture, integration policies, and the various ways in which Muslims have lived their religion in French society, we can distinguish three periods in the integration of "Muslims" in dialogue with the society around them.

1974-84: From Immigrant Workers
to the March of the Beurs

Immigrant workers

Following the first oil shock of 1973, in July 1974 the French government decided to suspend the immigration of salaried workers from non-European Community countries. This decision would have an important impact on immigration from the Maghreb, which had already begun to result in the settlement of family groups in France, though many migrants still made frequent journeys to and from the country of origin (a phenomenon known as *noria*). Now family reunification in France accelerated, paradoxically spurred in part by the fact that Algeria had, in 1973, unilaterally decided to stop further emigration following a wave of racist attacks in the city of Marseilles. The minister for immigration, André Postel-Vinay, who had been appointed by President Valéry Giscard d'Estaing, took the decision to suspend all further economic immigration in 1974, but resigned after only a month on the grounds that he lacked the necessary means to implement an appropriate housing policy for migrants already in France. His successor, Paul Dijoud, then pursued a policy of what he called integration with reference to immigrants, among whom Muslims were regarded as a secondary presence since groups such as Italians, Portuguese, Spanish, Polish, and Yugoslavians were more numerous. It was still customary at this time to talk essentially of "immigrant workers," without any reference to the Muslim culture of many migrants. As viewed by the majority population, immigrants from Muslim countries were simply unskilled foreign workers living without families in social spaces that were confined to the factory, hostels, and other cheap forms of housing, and cafés frequented by co-ethnics in neighborhoods such as la Goutte d'Or and Barbès in Paris or la Porte d'Aix in Marseilles. Most kept a low profile and participated little in the life of the receiving country, as they were constrained by their work schedule (relentless patterns of shift work), by reluctance to meddle in politics, and by illiteracy, which some sought to remedy through taking literacy classes. The main public policy concerns related to the reception of families and the provision of housing (the elimination of shantytowns, decided by Jacques Chaban-Delmas in 1969, had not yet been completed). Foreigners campaigned for new rights in the workplace (equal trade union and social protection rights with those of French nationals were acquired in 1975), and associations such as the FASTI (a federation of associations working in support of immigrant workers) called for the recognition of political rights and the freedom of association. A long conflict (1976-80) between residents and managers in hostels for immigrant workers was fought over a number of issues including demands for places of Islamic worship to be established within such hostels. But political and social issues were still dealt with mainly with reference to the world of work, often with the involvement of associations sponsored by immigrants' home states, such as the highly influential Amicale des Algériens en

Europe (Organization of Algerians in Europe), with a status similar to that of a *wilaya* (prefecture), independent associations often in conflict with home states (such as the Association des travailleurs marocains en France [the Association of Moroccan Workers in France]), and trade unions. Cultural and religious expression was rare, if not entirely absent.[5] With their families still in the country of origin, young workers of Muslim culture were often more influenced by trade unions than by other organizations and they tended to put off until later concerns about arrangements for practicing Islam, limiting themselves to abstaining from the consumption of pork and to a lesser extent from alcohol.

A recurrent debate dividing opinion in relation to those described as "non-Europeans" took the form of cost-benefit analyses of immigration, focusing on the idea that immigrants cost more than they brought in. Many people subscribing to this viewpoint were persuaded that it was time to put an end to immigration and hoped to see Maghrebis, Turks, and Africans return to their countries of origin. Although a study directed by Anicet Le Pors, with detailed figures supporting the findings, demonstrated that these economic arguments were unfounded,[6] the integration debate focuses repeatedly on questions such as hospital fees, the housing of immigrants with and without families, and social benefits. During the 1930s, the idea of immigrants as a "burden" and as carriers of disease (tuberculosis was widespread at that time) was already very common with regard to Maghrebis.[7] Financial aid designed to encourage immigrants to return to their countries of origin, launched by the new minister for immigration, Lionel Stoleru in 1977, was a failure: Maghrebis, who the aid package had been designed to encourage to leave, showed little interest in the scheme while Spanish and Portuguese immigrants, who policy makers would have preferred to see remaining in France, took up the repatriation packages more readily. Another initiative aimed at helping immigrants to return to their countries of origin, accompanied by measures to assist reinsertion there, was launched in 1983, again with minimal results with regard to Maghrebis.

Young People of Immigrant Origin

At the end of the 1970s, the "second generation" of Maghrebi immigrant background, who were either born in the country of origin and had arrived in France at a very young age, or were born in France and had lived in shantytowns and high-rise apartment buildings in poor working-class neighborhoods, started to protest their living conditions through new associations such as the JALB (Jeunes Arabes de Lyon et Banlieues) in Lyon, which denounced police violence (a significant number of children and teenagers had been killed in incidents with the police) and deportation orders, demanding in their place equal rights, respect, and freedom of association. Freedom of association for non-nationals was granted in 1981, and although the right to vote in local and other elections was refused to foreigners, these new rights would profoundly modify the relationship between populations of Muslim culture and French society, even if the visibility of newly created associations often exceeded the intensity of grassroots activism. It was particularly with the nationwide March of the *Beurs*—which after setting off from Marseilles arrived in Paris on December 1, 1983, where its representatives were received by President François Mitterrand at the Elysée Palace—that these young people, of Maghrebi origin for the most part, began to create social movements and new forms of expression that were very different from those of their parents. Young women participated and often took up positions of leadership. These included Djidda Tazdaït, spokesperson for the JALB who had worked with Christian Delorme, a Catholic priest in Lyon, and Halima Thierry-Boumidienne, president of the EMAF (Expressions maghrébines au féminin) in Aubervilliers. Media attention was attracted by these new forms of activism, which were often festive in nature (theatre, rock, rap, raï, and so forth). New demands were also put forward, ranging from antiracism, citizenship based on residence rather than nationality, a ten-year *carte de séjour* (residence permit), the right to plural identities, and cultural hybridity. Long-standing and still-unsatisfied demands were also maintained such as the right for foreigners to vote in local elections (that is, a citizenship "for immigrant parents"). The main issue at stake was to negotiate a form of collective belonging in French society, as Arabs and Muslims, just as the extreme right-wing National Front was making its electoral breakthrough in the municipal elections during the spring of 1983, campaigning on the issues of French identity and immigration.

During these years, Maghrebi, Turkish, and African immigrants settled in poor working-class areas (*banlieues*) that had been abandoned by French nationals, and in dilapidated neighborhoods of large towns that were awaiting redevelopment, such as in La porte d'Aix in Marseilles or in Très Cloîtres in Grenoble. Gradually, the classic image of the Algerian immigrant—as a former member of the FLN pro-independence movement, a member of the Communist-led CGT trade union federation and a member of the state-sponsored Amicale des Algériens, a man caught between two stools as described by Abdelmalek Sayad[8]— gave way to the meritocratic model of the *Beur* (*Arabe* in back-slang), that is, a second-generation Maghrebi born of an illiterate father and brought up in a shantytown or a poor working-class neighborhood, now infused with republican values and associative civic activism. In reality, very few of the associative civic leaders fit this mold, for many were in fact "inheritors"—that is, the products of mixed marriages or of a small immigrant middle class. But many did owe their access to the "beurgeoisie," that is, a middle-class stratum of *Beurs*, to forms of social mobility and professionalism to which the associative movement gave them access,[9] playing a kind of catch-up role, compensating in many cases for inadequate schooling, although their school baggage was far from negligible.

1984-94: Citizenship, Security, and Radicalization of Islam

The Rise and Fall of the Beur Movement

The *Beur* movement reached its peak during the late 1980s and then declined, giving way to a more difficult period marked by forms of Islamic violence and the rise of security concerns vis-à-vis those who, more and more, became designated as Muslims. Yet the mid-1980s had been promising: 1984 saw the granting of the ten-year *carte de séjour* (residence permit), which was no longer conditioned by employment status but by length of residence, and that as such was seen as a major victory for the associative movement. There were also major conflicts with the automobile manufacturers Renault, Citroën, Talbot, and Peugeot, in which demands relating to Islam featured alongside the labor contract demands of unskilled workers.[10] This period also saw the birth of two major civic associations of young people of immigrant background: SOS Racisme and France Plus, which sought to promote antiracism and civic rights. And there was also a new approach to integration, now seen by Minister for Social Affairs Georgina Dufoix as a process of "living together," combining concessions made to collective identities with republican ideals.

These ten years were also marked by a legislative frenzy concerning the entry, settlement, and integration of immigrants. Institutional advances and setbacks included the 1984 law granting the ten-year residence permit to long-term residents; the Pasqua law of 1986 on the entry and settlement of foreigners, known notably for its mass expulsions of illegal immigrants; the Joxe law of 1989, which granted judges a more important role in such matters; the social development of disadvantaged neighborhoods and the beginning of new urban policies in 1990; and debates over the reform of the nationality code. After an initial project abandoned in 1988, nationality laws were reformed so as to restrict access to citizenship based on residence (the Pasqua-Méhaignerie law of 1993) and through marriage (the second 1993 Pasqua law on entry and settlement).

The period was, above all, rich in forms of activism which demonstrated the many different postures adopted by populations of Muslim culture in French society. Between 1983 and 1986, amid the conflicts with automobile manufacturers, demands for prayer rooms in workshops and breaks during Ramadan appeared, with Muslim union leaders using Islam to strengthen other demands, supported in this by the most secular of trade union organizations, such as the CGT, which saw in this a means of gaining ground during these conflicts, gaining the loyalty of imams and claiming responsibility for the opening of prayer rooms in automobile factories.[11] This also enabled unions to widen their field of intervention and membership recruitment during a period of economic downturn and declining union activism. One of the Muslim trade union leaders, Aka Ghazi, became a Moroccan member of Parliament. But there was in general no crossover from these labor conflicts into politics. By contrast, associative civic movements did aim to move into politics through slogans such as "new," "active," "participative," or "concrete" citizenship. Inspired by the principles of 1789 and ideas such as the "right to be different" (SOS Racisme) or to be "undifferentiated" (France Plus), they promoted the registration of young people on electoral lists, and the promotion of *Beur* candidates in the municipal elections of 1989. By the end of the 1980s, the *Beur* movement had reached its zenith, spreading a positive image of young people of Muslim culture who were engaging with republican institutions and secularism to establish a place for themselves in French society. The multi-ethnic "Festival of Friends" organized by SOS Racisme in the Place la Concorde in June 1985, the participation of young Maghrebis in the bicentennial celebrations of the French Revolution four years later, the proliferation of civic, national, and local associations, the election of *Beur* city councilors in the municipal elections of 1989 were a measure of the successful integration of the most militant, who were actively courted by the political parties of the Left and the Right.

Islam and Integration

Islam continued to progress in everyday life,[12] while the media served up disturbing images for public opinion, such as prayer rooms in the basements of high-rise apartment buildings located in poor neighborhoods (the *banlieues*); Muslims prostrating themselves in the streets during prayers; religious trade unionists involved in labor conflicts; the appearance of a visible market for Islam with *hallal* butchers, Muslim bookstores, and Muslim clothing; the building of mosques with minarets in urban locations such as Evry; children of mixed marriages sequestered by their fathers in their country of origin; religious clan wars in Turkish and Kurdish neighborhoods; polygamy and excision among sub-Saharans; and many other representations feeding fears of Islamic subversion. In 1989 the Rushdie affair gave rise in France to protests by Pakistanis, and later that year the headscarf affair, revolving around the wearing of headscarves by three young girls in a French public school, reinforced a widespread feeling that people of Muslim culture were not integrating in France because of Islam. Expressions of a collective identity built around Islam, sometimes as a point of refuge for the least integrated, but more often as a negotiated identity within the acceptable limits of citizenship, met with a hostile reception in public opinion that frequently confused Islam, Islamism, and fundamentalism, and mixed together into the same category negative stereotypes of Muslims, illegal immigrants, and delinquents.[13]

Yet social and political debates such as those surrounding the reform of the French nationality code (1987-93) showed that people of Muslim culture had a strong desire to be part of the French society into which they had been socialized through years of living alongside the majority ethnic French in schools, through their housing, and so on.[14] Refusing to be French citizens merely on paper or even in spite of themselves, as the extreme-right National Front and the Club de l'Horloge portrayed them, these "different" French citizens negotiated collectively their presence and their communal belonging. Out of these contradictions, new figures emerged in French society: cultural intermediaries and those known as "older brothers" in the *banlieues*; mediators between the grassroots and the state, between "here" and "there," and between the Republic and Islam; female intermediaries in poor neighborhoods combining modernity with rural traditions; and ethnic entrepreneurs. At the dawn of the 1990s, as the *Beur* movement began to decline, some chose to focus on working with local politicians within the framework of urban policy, which delegated a certain amount of authority in the domain of integration to "get things done" in a way that was reminiscent of the colonial period. In this way the institutions of the Republic in effect created the *communautarisme* (ethnic community formation and/or factionalism) that was castigated in their discourse: instead of implementing local policies designed to provide a place for cultural pluralism, the state delegated to these intermediaries the management of relations between these supposed communities.

This ambiguous mixture of republicanism and *communautarisme* is illustrated clearly by the example of *harkis* in both the discourse of their spokespersons and that of the public authorities. Through new types of jobs invented by city halls, young people of immigrant origin were able to move forward in the labor market, though at the risk of losing their activist credentials and being labeled as "token Arabs" and "traitors" by their peers. The most opportunistic or the most talented placed their know-how at the service of political parties on virtually all parts of the political spectrum, promising to serve as gateways to the mobilization of hypothetical Arab or Muslim electorates. This was a time in which people fell back on local, everyday concerns: in the struggle against "urban violence," many municipalities used local associations and "older brothers" to restore social order, negotiating in some cases with Islamic fundamentalists to buy social peace and combat illegal drugs in disadvantaged neighborhoods.

During this time, integration continued to progress. A study undertaken in 1992 by Michèle Tribalat involving twelve thousand people showed that among the five groups questioned, Algerians were the best-integrated with regard to the criteria adopted: the number of mixed marriages, a low observance of Islamic religious practices, and use of the French language in private life.[15] The Turks, by contrast, were the least well-integrated due to linguistic obstacles, a tendency to remain within their own community (notably among women), arranged marriages, and high dropout rates at school. If deindustrialization caused many foreign workers of the first generation to become unemployed in the sectors in which Maghrebis were the most numerous (such as the automobile and steel industries), this also affected their children, who lacked the network of small businesses through which the Portuguese and Turks found social incorporation. Younger generations of Maghrebi immigrant origin have suffered high unemployment levels, which have been exacerbated by discrimination and their reluctance, having been educated in France, to do the same low-status types of work as their parents. Unemployment has led to the phenomenon of *hittistes* (that is, young men who spend their days leaning on walls in the streets of their neighborhood), to urban violence that is often linked to territorial clan conflicts or to illicit trafficking known as *trabendo*, and to confrontations with the police when subjected to identity checks and searches. Radical Islam, seen in the 1995 bomb attacks on the RER (express subway) stations of St. Michel and Place de l'Etoile in Paris, recharged the debate over the integration of those referred to as Muslims, even though such attacks were the work of only a very small number of people among a Muslim population whose members mainly practiced moderate forms of Islam.[16]

Another population of Muslim culture that is often forgotten is that of the *harkis* and their descendants. This population began to make itself heard at the end of the 1980s and the start of the 1990s. After fighting on the side of the French against the nationalist insurgents in Algeria, the *harkis* had entered France at the end of the Algerian War in 1962 with the support of some of their military leaders, despite the opposition of President Charles de Gaulle and his interior minister Louis Joxe. On arrival, they went through a sorting process and those judged to be unsuitable for industrial work were placed in camps.[17] Some of these settlements, which have since been renamed, still exist today in the south of France, often in forested areas. Many *harkis*, who have not recovered from the trauma and transplantation arising from the Algerian War, have continued to live in a state of dependence on French public welfare.[18] With the exception of small elites emerging from this group,[19] the children of *harkis* have struggled to integrate themselves, despite their French nationality, which they proudly carried and used during this period to demand (sometimes through hunger strikes and through other forms of collective action) recognition of their rights and the honoring of their memory. Long officially described as French Muslims (a paradoxical practice in a secular Republic), they adhered for the most part to a "quiet" form of Islam, like many first generation immigrant workers. Unlike the latter, who did not initially expect to settle in France permanently, the *harkis* knew that they would not return to Algeria so soon and sought to establish prayer rooms and other types of religious infrastructure such as Muslim burial areas in cemeteries and animal slaughter facilities meeting their needs. It remains to be seen how long they will continue to be considered as fundamentally separate from the mainstream French population.

The end of this second period was marked by the hardening of French public policy: the second Pasqua law of 1993 restricting entry and settlement and the 1993 Méhaignerie law that restricted access to French nationality, reversing a century-old trend of enlarging the right to citizenship based on residence (the laws of 1889, 1927, 1945, and 1973). The European Community reinforced this repressive climate through the implementation of the Schengen Accords (adopted in 1985), and the Dublin Accords of 1990, which criminalized illegal movements between frontiers, and strengthened external border controls. This context was not conducive to the integration of populations of Muslim culture, who as non-Europeans were the most affected, in terms both of entry visas and settlement conditions.

During these ten years, research on Muslims developed considerably in France and in Europe as a whole, which had become an important place of settlement for Islam.[20] The Islam of working-class, especially Maghrebi, immigrants, now found itself living as a minority religion in a secular state dominated by Christian culture. Turkish Islam, which had a relatively secular flavor and was organized into brotherhoods, as was also the case for sub-Saharan Africans, attracted less attention in emerging debates on the institutionalization of a republican and secularized French Islam (a Gallican Islam, as some called it) that was already represented by the great Mosque of Paris, constructed in the 1920s as a way of thanking Muslim soldiers for their sacrifices in the war of 1914-18. Adapting a question formulated long ago by Montesquieu, it became increasingly common to ask: "How can one be Muslim in France?" The question was especially asked of young French people of Muslim culture, notably during debates over the reform of the nationality code, and then in a more provocative fashion during the first Gulf War of 1991, when small numbers of young people in the *banlieues* found in Saddam Hussein a provocative rallying call ("Long live Saddam!").[21] In an attempt to respond to the questions posed by Islam to French society, Interior Minister Pierre Joxe set up the Comité de réflexion sur l'Islam en France (Council for Deliberation on Islam in France) in 1990, a fragile institution contested by those who saw themselves as poorly represented within it.

1994-2005: From the Security Syndrome to the Emergence of New Citizens

Radicalization and Citizenship[22]

This third phase opened in 1995 with a wave of bomb attacks in Paris and Lyon, committed by young people representing a radical form of Islamism, the most publicized of whom was Khaled Kelkal, a second-generation Algerian raised in the *banlieues* of Lyon. The public authorities, now less interested in supporting minority ethnic civic associations aimed at mobilizing young people and calming the *banlieues*, became more cautious in their funding. Financial support for associations from the publicly funded Fonds d'Action Sociale (Social Action Fund) decreased and many associations refocused their activities on local initiatives, on the struggle against social exclusion, and on educational and preventive measures against delinquency, working in association with city councils supported by nationally funded urban policies. A number of Muslim associations created through the 1981 law (there were around 1,500 of these) also became involved in social work. The people running Muslim associations of this kind often resembled those who had held leadership positions in *Beur* civic associations ten years earlier but with a weaker legitimacy in the republican space: they often held university degrees, were around age thirty, were upwardly mobile, and were seeking to make a place for themselves in French society as both citizens and as Muslims.

Among young people of immigrant background, while social exclusion persisted, most notably in the form of ethnic and spatial segregation in the *banlieues*, the process of social inclusion was also progressing. Most were French citizens, making them potential voters; as such they were increasingly courted by all of the main political parties including the National Front. Concerned to give a multicultural look to their lists of candidates in the hope of capturing a hypothetical "Arab" or "Muslim" vote—but still not ready to offer "token Arabs" winnable positions—political parties offered few positions of national responsibility to minority ethnic members (the rise within the Socialist Party of Malek Boutih, a former president of SOS Racisme, was a rare exception to this rule) and not a single *député* of Maghrebi origin was elected to the National Assembly. Three or four members of Maghrebi origin gained seats in elections to the European Parliament. Most belonged to the Socialist Party or the Greens, reflecting the leftist orientation of Maghrebi voters. Some, weary of the hypocrisy with which they felt they had been treated, turned to alternative forms of politics, mobilizing around issues such as the struggle against discrimination, equal rights for women, the recognition of collective identities in the republican space, and the abolition of deportation orders against foreigners convicted of criminal offenses. Examples included the *Motivé(e)s* list of candidates put forward in municipal elections in Toulouse, social movements such as the MIB (Mouvement Immigration Banlieues), or, in a different civic register, the association Ni putes ni soumises campaigning on behalf of young Muslim women threatened on the one hand by the hell of gang rape in the *banlieues* and on the other by forced marriages to cousins in their countries of origin.

Overall, the picture was complex and variegated. Most Muslims were becoming integrated, simultaneously feeling part of "here" and "somewhere else," both republican and Muslim. Rates of religious observance were quite low but many Muslims still liked to situate themselves around a common identity validated by emblematic personalities such as Zinedine Zidane, star of France's victory in the 1998 soccer World Cup, or the junior minister for sustainable development from 2002-4, Tokia Saïfi. Conscious of the limited visibility of this part of the French population, state officials began to force the pace by publicly proclaiming in 2003 the appointment of a Muslim superintendent of schools and a Muslim prefect, who were in fact civil servants of Algerian origin who had arrived in France at an adult age. Officials also talked about the need for the army and the police force to reflect the diversity of the national population,[23] including persons of Muslim culture, but movement in this direction was cautious. While the public authorities gradually supported the emergence of a republican Islam respecting the code of *laïcité*, notably through the creation in 2002 of the Conseil français du Culte musulman (French Council of the Muslim Religion), marking the institutionalization and "citizenization" of Islam, this was also a time of worsening financial fortunes for minority ethnic civic associations that were finding it difficult to recruit young activists to replace those stepping down from office. Newer generations of minority ethnic youths had no direct experience of the earlier successes scored by such associations and the personal benefits to which these gave access and they felt disillusioned over the perceived careerism of older activists, by whom they felt the broad mass of their peers had been abandoned.

Exclusion and Inclusion

Ongoing unemployment, lack of educational opportunities (few minority ethnic youths gain admission to France's elite *grandes écoles* nor to the preparatory classes which lead to them), poor housing, difficult relations with the police,[24] and above all discrimination in access to work—all of these factors served to keep part of the population in a state of social exclusion, leaving it prey to the temptations of the parallel economy and to the Islamic fundamentalism of certain associations (sometimes Wahhabite in inspiration, which is strongly present in Saudi Arabia, and sometimes Salafist, insisting on strict traditional observance). Yet such forms of Islam are in fact more an invention of new ways of being Muslim than the perpetuation of ancestral practices. It is a process of "making oneself a Muslim." For example, young women who decide to wear the headscarf do not do so in the same way, nor do they wear headscarves for the same reasons as their mothers. In some cases they are motivated by a desire for emancipation in a form that is acceptable to their family (enabling them to go outside the family home freely, while simultaneously reassuring their parents). In other cases, it signifies a new way of living their religion that is significantly different from the rural tradition of their parents.[25] Similarly, the practice of polygamy among Malians is less an indicator of conservatism than a compromise linked to migration whereby the polygamous husband shows the family back home that he has not broken with Muslim customs and has succeeded in France to the point where he can afford more than one wife. The reading of the Qur'an, which has been gaining ground since the mid-1980s in France and elsewhere in Europe, can also be interpreted as a new approach to Islam rather than a simple return to it. Because of their illiteracy, many heads of immigrant families have no direct textual knowledge of the sacred texts. When their children learn classical Arabic and read the Qur'an they are able to free themselves from traditional village practices by following the letter of Muslim prescriptions. Of the five pillars of Islam (the profession of faith, prayer, Ramadan, the ritual giving of alms, and the pilgrimage to Mecca), some are more practiced than others, notably Ramadan due to its festive dimension and its way of marking a collective identity in Western society, as well as the demand for the respect of dietary proscriptions, for specially designated areas in cemeteries, and for the presence of imams in places where there are Catholic chaplains such as the army, prisons, and hospitals. Only about 5 to 10 percent of Muslims in France practice their religion regularly, a proportion similar to that found among Catholics. The security worries that surround Islam today serve to isolate these citizens if their religion is considered to lack legitimacy in the public space (through the construction of large-scale mosques, such as in Lyon, and the general acceptance of the practicing of Islam). The attacks of September 11, 2001, did nothing to help the image of Islam, the second largest religion in France: a number of potential terrorists were interned at the Guantanamo Bay prison, having been arrested in Afghanistan where they had gone to train. Another—the presumed would-be twentieth hijacker, Zacarias Moussaoui, who became separated from the other hijackers—is a French citizen of Moroccan origin, raised "in the French way" in a Toulouse *banlieue*, and then in England. If social exclusion can lead to a person seeking refuge in Islam, it nevertheless appears that the main terrorist actors are people who have taken upwardly mobile professional paths inside the receiving countries.

Other phenomena are a reflection of a constant but conflictual interaction with mainstream French identity: the "incivilities" and urban violence of those who are described as "wild youths" (*sauvageons*) by the former minister of the interior, Jean-Pierre Chevènement; the hostile whistling of "La Marseillaise" during a friendly football (soccer) match between France and Algeria in 2001; and acts of petty delinquency in disadvantaged neighborhoods. Yet such acts are more an indication of persistent social inequalities than a failure of integration. When, during the presidential elections of 2002, the National Front managed to reach the second round in place of the Socialist Party, many young people of Maghrebi immigrant background, who had been strongly abstentionist, protested in the Place de la République in Paris, asserting the importance of citizenship while in some cases displaying the Palestinian flag. The Arab-Israeli conflict, American intervention in Afghanistan, and the invasion of Iraq in 2003 have all had an impact on people of Muslim culture, all the more so now that they are able to watch the Arabic-language television channel Al Jazeera, and programs from their own countries of origin. The anti-Semitism found among a number of young people of Muslim culture is fed by satellite-media images that tend to support existing regimes in the Arabo-Islamic world, and nurture feelings of identification with them.

In response to the disaffection and uncertain loyalties associated with the multiple identities of French Muslims, the state has been attempting to reestablish the rule of republican principles in fields where some fear these are under threat (for example, through the law of 2004 banning the Islamic headscarf from state schools) while at the same time hesitating to implement positive discrimination measures regarded as incompatible with the spirit of republican equality. By pursuing a spatial approach to integration policy (as in the Borloo "anti-ghetto" law of 2003), the state appears wedded to a policy approach conceived in terms of certain categories of urban areas rather than targeting assistance at socially defined groups.

Conclusion

The blind side of French public policy has been counterbalanced by the recent recognition of the memory of immigration as a constituent aspect of French identity. Gradually, the weight of immigration of Muslim culture is also being taken account in the formulation of foreign policy,[26] as in the Euro-Mediterranean and Middle East dialogue. In the winter of 2005-6 these debates reached a crescendo that forced the government to rescind a law passed in February 2005 requiring history teachers to teach the "positive" role of French colonialism, notably in North Africa.[27] Between France and its populations of Muslim origin and Muslim culture, a new relationship has thus been emerging in which measures taken by the state in the name of republican values have had sometimes the paradoxical effect of encouraging *communautarisme*,[28] which some Muslims have in turn sought to strengthen while outwardly playing on republican values. As Rémy Leveau has written, the Maghrebis who have settled in France are no longer exactly immigrants and are not yet full citizens, but members of a minority community seeking recognition by mainstream society.[29]

Translated by Matthew A. Kemp and Alec G. Hargreaves

Notes

1. Catherine Wihtol de Wenden, *Les immigrés et la politique. Cent-cinquante ans d'évolution* (Paris: Presses de la FNSP, 1988).
2. Catherine Wihtol de Wenden, "La seconde génération," *Projet*, no. 171-72 (1983): 100-11.
3. Dossier, "Immigration, citoyenneté, nationalité," *Les Cahiers de l'Orient*, no. 11 (1988); Dossier, "Citoyennetés sans frontiers," *Hommes et Migrations*, no. 1206 (1997).
4. Dossier, "Immigration: à la recherche des intermédiaires culturels," *Migrations Société* 4, no. 22-23 (July-October 1992).
5. Daniel Linhart cites the case of an Algerian hiding behind boxes to pray in the workshop where he was employed in *L'établi* (Paris: Le Seuil, 1977).
6. Anicet Le Pors, *Immigration et développement économique et social* (Paris: La Documentation française, 1976).
7. Catherine Wihtol de Wenden, "L'immigration maghrébine dans l'imaginaire politique français," in *L'Islam en France*, ed. Bruno Etienne (Paris: Editions du CNRS, 1990), 127-38
8. Abdelmalek Sayad, "Etat, nation et immigration: l'ordre national à l'épreuve de l'immigration," *Peuples méditerranéens*, no. 27-28 (April-September 1984): 187-205.
9. Catherine Wihtol de Wenden and Rémy Leveau, *La beurgeoisie. Les trois âges de la vie associative issue de l'immigration* (Paris: CNRS Editions, 2001).
10. Jacques Barou, "Pratiques religieuses en entreprise," in *Ouvriers spécialisés à Billancourt*, ed. Renaud Sainsaulieu and Ahsène Zehraoui (Paris: l'Harmattan, 1995); and Jacques Barou, "L'islam, facteur de régulation sociale?" *Esprit* 6 (1985): 207-15. See also René Mouriaux and Catherine Wihtol de Wenden, "Syndicalisme français et Islam,"

Revue Francaise de Science Politique 6 (October 1987): 782-93; Jacqueline Costa-Lascoux and Emile Temime, *Les hommes de Renault-Billancourt 1930-1992* (Paris: Autrement, 2004).

11. Catherine Wihtol de Wenden, "Syndicalisme français et islam," in *Les musulmans dans la société française*, ed. Rémy Leveau and Gilles Kepel (Paris: Presses de la FNSP, 1988), 39-64.

12. Gilles Kepel, *Les banlieues de l'Islam* (Paris: Seuil, 1987).

13. Catherine Wihtol de Wenden, "Le rapport imaginaire aux flux migratoires en France et en Allemagne," in *Politiques méditerranéennes entre logiques étatiques et espace civil*, ed. Jean-Robert Henry and Gérard Groc (Paris: Karthala, 2000), 303-16.

14. Marceau Long, *Etre Français aujourd'hui et demain* (Paris: La Documentation française, 1991). See also Patrick Weil, *Qu'est-ce qu'un Français?* (Paris: Grasset, 2002).

15. Michèle Tribalat, *Faire France* (Paris: La Découverte, 1995).

16. Bruno Etienne, *L'Islamisme radical* (Paris: Hachette, 1987). See also, Bruno Etienne, *La France et l'Islam* (Paris: Hachette, 1989); and Bruno Etienne, ed., *L'Islam en France* (Paris: Editions du CNRS, 1990).

17. Dossier, "Les harkis et leurs enfants," *Hommes et Migrations*, no. 1135 (1990).

18. Thierry Samper, "Le cas des harkis," *Panoramiques* 49 (October 2000): 175-78.

19. Djamel Oubechou, the son of a *harki*, earned a degree from the elite Ecole Normale Supérieure and was advisor to Michel Vedrine, minister of foreign affairs.

20. See notably Jocelyne Cesari, *Etre musulman en France: associations, militants et mosquées* (Paris: Karthala, 1994); Jocelyne Cesari, *Etre musulman en France aujourd'hui* (Paris: Hachette, 1997); Jocelyne Cesari, *Faut-il avoir peur de l'Islam?* (Paris: Presses de Sciences-Po, 1997); Jocelyne Cesari, *L'Islam à l'épreuve de l'Occident* (Paris: la Découverte, 2004); see also Dossier, "Musulmans en terre d'Europe," *Projet*, no. 231 (1992).

21. Catherine Wihtol de Wenden, "Les beurs et la guerre," *Esprit*, no. 172 / *Les Cahiers de l'Orient*, no. 6 (1991): 102-7.

22. This term was developed in a dossier by *CEMOTI*, "Musulmans d'Europe," *CEMOTI*, no. 33 (November 2002).

23. Rémy Leveau, Catherine Wihtol de Wenden, and Christophe Bertossi, *Les militaires issus de l'immigration* (Paris: Centre d'Etudes en Sciences Sociales de la Défense, 2005).

24. Sophie Body-Gendrot and Catherine Wihtol de Wenden, *Police et discriminations. Le tabou français* (Paris: L'Atelier, 2003).

25. Valérie Amiraux, *Acteurs de l'islam entre Allemagne et Turquie* (Paris: L'Harmattan, 2001).

26. Similar developments are reflected in the creation in January 2005 of a National Center for Immigration History under the direction of former French culture minister Jacques Toubon.

27. Béatrice Gurrey, "Mémoire coloniale: Jacques Chirac temporise," *Le Monde*, December 11-12, 2005.

28. Catherine Wihtol de Wenden, "Ambiguités de l'intégration à la française des populations d'origine maghrébine," *Némésis* 5 (2004): 141-49.

29. De Wenden and Leveau, *La Beurgeoisie*.

Part VI: Conclusions

Chapter Eleven
Current Issues in France

Jean Baubérot

Continuity and change closely intersect in the relationship between religion and politics in modern France. France, like the United States, is today still marked by the memory of its origins and founding myths. At the same time, structural differences between the two Republics are reflected in differences between their founding myths. The founding of the United States may be seen as an extension of the founding of English America, and Thanksgiving Day may be seen as similar to the national holiday of the Fourth of July. France's two founding references do not go at all in the same direction. The first reference concerns the baptism of the Frankish leader Clovis, which is believed to have taken place in 496 CE, and that is regarded as marking the unification of what was to become France with the rejection of the Aryan "heresy" in favor of the "Apostolic Roman Catholic" Christian faith. The second reference concerns the foundation of modern, republican France through the French Revolution. Considered as an indivisible entity (as Clemenceau would later say), this second foundation, that of French political modernity, was built amid a frontal and violent conflict with Roman Catholicism.

From the beginning of the nineteenth century through to the beginning of the twenty-first century, these two elements have formed the symbolic infrastructure of relations between politics and religion in France. But these relations have taken on different forms depending on the dominant problems of the time. Three main periods may be distinguished. The first period, stretching from the Revolution itself (which very quickly acquired the status of a founding narrative) to the separation of the churches and the state, was that of a conflict between two Frances: the France of Clovis and the France of 1789 confronted each other, and tried in vain to reconcile themselves in a war between two competing civil religions. The second period is that of the *pacte laïque* (the secular pact)"[1]—that is to say, a gradual process of reconciliation, with its ups and downs, with the principal remaining areas of conflict concerning the status of schools. Tensions provoked by an initial Catholic refusal to apply the law of separation began to abate from 1908 onwards. The principal milestones of this process were the *Union Sacrée* (the sacred union) of 1914, in which church and state put aside their differences during World War I, the enshrinement of *laïcité* in the Constitution of 1946 (despite the fact that the prime minister of the day was a member of the Christian Democratic Party), and finally, the failure of the Left's attempt to end public financing of confessionally based schools in 1984. But new conflicts began to emerge from 1989 onwards with the first "Islamic headscarf" affair. In 2005, the centenary of the 1905 law separating churches and the state was characterized at one and the same time by a general reconciliation of the two Frances, as defined earlier, and by the emergence of new problems of this kind. Today, we see sometimes latent and sometimes open tensions between France and religious minorities such as Muslims and Protestants. France has so far been unable to construct a *nouveau pacte laïque* (a new secular pact) in response to the developments marking this third phase.[2]

In this chapter I will discuss this most recent period and examine essentially contemporary problems. But we can understand neither this period, nor the problems that it has thrown up without taking into account their historical and symbolic underpinnings. As a recent study shows very clearly, the real and mythical history of the United States causes atheism to be viewed virtually always with suspicion, whereas the real and mythical history of France causes religion to be viewed almost always with suspicion, or at any rate as being deeply ambivalent.[3] The United States and France have in common the fact that they both declared freedom of belief during the last quarter of the eighteenth century. Yet it seems that they do not understand the concept of "freedom" in exactly the same way. The conflict between the two Frances was above all a conflict over national identity. During most of the nineteenth century, this conflict fueled the instability of political regimes (of which there were around ten different ones between 1789 and 1875), seen most obviously in the conflict between monarchical and republican forms of governance. When Pope Leo XIII asked French Catholics to rally to the Republic in 1892, this did nothing to end the head-to-head conflict in the sense that the Republic to which Catholics were being invited to rally was seen as destined to have a Catholic identity. Significantly, the crisis that accelerated the process of separation between the churches and the state was provoked by the visit of the president of the French Republic, Emile Loubet, to the king of Italy. In the eyes of Pope Pius X, this visit by the head of state of a Catholic nation was inappropriate. He did not take the same stance towards the emperor of Germany.

The most painful aspect of separation for practicing Catholics was not the *laïcité* of the state (that is, the separation church and state), which to a large extent had already been acquired, but the religious neutrality of the nation.[4] The greatest conflicts arose over schools, which is hardly surprising given that schools teach not only a way of thinking, but also a certain vision of the nation. The nation's young were seen as being divided into two camps learning two different visions of France at state schools observing the code of *laïcité* on the one hand and at confessional Catholic schools on the other.[5] After many new twists and turns (and here is not the place to trace all of the details), the years of 1982-84 saw the failure of an attempt at unifying all school institutions, both private and public (with a degree of flexibility) under a shared umbrella of *laïcité*. Private schools, Catholic for the most part, which had received substantial financial subsidies from the state since 1959, continued to receive funding.[6] By now, after the Second Vatican Council, the majority of the public did not feel that the vision of France taught by a "Catholic school" was different from that taught by a "republican school." Many parents in fact wanted to derive other benefits from the competitive relationship between the two different types of school.[7]

Has the conflict between the two Frances irreversibly ended? For some, this conflict has shifted from being one related to political and educational issues to one of values. The media highlighted the comments of Pope John Paul II, who condemned the supposed laxity of modern societies in this regard. We know that it is in this domain that a refocusing began after the Second Vatican Council: in 1968, Pope Paul VI's *Humanae Vitae* maintained the condemnation of modern forms of contraception. A survey taken at the time of Pope John Paul II's death in 2005 provides extremely interesting data on the opinion of French people, and notably Catholics, on the official position of the Catholic Church with regard to values.[8]

In this, as in other surveys, around two-thirds of the French population declared themselves to be Catholic, and around a quarter stated that they had no religion. The rest were members of other religions, or refused this type of classification altogether.[9] But if 66 percent of French people refer to themselves as Catholic, only 8-9 percent are regularly practicing Catholics, the remainder being divided equally between non-regularly practicing Catholics and non-practicing Catholics.[10] Among the questions posed in the 2005 survey, several concerned values, and it is interesting to look at the responses of regularly and non-regularly practicing Catholics, who together account for a little more than one-third of the French population, and who constitute the most important body of Catholic public opinion (with regularly practicing Catholics forming the "hard core").

Eighty percent of regularly practicing Catholics and 91 percent of non-regularly practicing Catholics want the pope to authorize contraception; 73 percent of the first group and 90 percent of the second group want the pope to "tolerate abortion under certain conditions"; and 76 percent and 95 percent, respectively, want the pope to "authorize the use of condoms to combat AIDS." Only 24 percent of regularly and non-regularly practicing Catholics want the pope to "condemn homosexual couples" (72 percent and 69 percent being of the opposite opinion). To put it another way, three-quarters of regularly practicing, and nine-tenths of non-regularly practicing Catholics wanted to see a change in the positions of the Catholic Church in the matter of values and were in agreement with the dominant French opinion on these subjects.[11]

The official attitude of the Catholic Church could lead one to believe that the conflict between the two Frances is not over, but rather, has simply been displaced. In fact, this would be a misleading impression. There is no longer a "conflict between two Frances," but there does exist a latent, internal conflict within the Catholic Church between, on the one hand, the magisterium of Rome and those who accept it, and on the other hand, the broad mass of Catholics. This hypothesis is confirmed by two other indices: On the one hand qualitative work—for instance, priests whom we have interviewed say that the majority of their parishioners live outside "canonic norms."[12] On the other hand, survey questions focusing more specifically on the Catholic Church point in the same direction, albeit less acutely. Thus 61 percent of regularly practicing Catholics and 81 percent of irregularly practicing Catholics wanted the pope to "authorize marriage for priests" (compared with 36 percent and 16 percent respectively who were opposed to this), and 51 percent of regularly practicing Catholics and 67 percent of irregularly practicing Catholics wanted the pope to accept "the ordaining of female priests" (compared with 44 percent and 31 percent respectively who were opposed to this). Unfortunately the survey did not include any questions on bio-ethical issues (such as cloning for medical purposes). But, such as they are, the results indicate a clear general tendency. In embracing the dominant values of modernity a majority of Catholics desire a fresh *aggiornamento* (renewal) on the part of their church.[13]

On May 29, 2005, a referendum on the treaty proposing a European constitution was held in France. The treaty was rejected by 54.68 percent of voters, with 45.32 percent voting in favor. A survey of 5,216 registered voters, carried out by the CSA polling organization on the day of the referendum, showed that religion remained a significant factor in respondents' attitudes.[14] Among those who voted, around two-thirds of regularly practicing Catholics voted in favor of the Constitution (67 percent in favor, 33 percent against) while two-thirds of people with no religion voted against it (65 percent against, 35 percent in favor). Occasionally practicing Catholics were more or less evenly divided (49 percent voting yes, 51 percent voting no), while non-practicing Catholics, as is often the case, exactly mirrored French opinion as a whole (45 percent in favor, 55 percent against). Protestants voted 43 percent in favor, 57 percent against, and Muslims voted 46 percent in favor, 54 percent against, again very close to the overall distribution of public opinion.

It should be noted that the division between regularly practicing Catholics and people without any religion is not the only one to be strongly accentuated. There are also less notable, but relatively significant differences according to age (41 percent of eighteen- to twenty-four-year-olds and 38 percent of twenty-five- to twenty-nine-year-olds voted in favor of the Constitution, compared with 57 percent of those aged sixty-five to seventy-four, and 59 percent of those over seventy-five). Above all there are equally important differences depending on level of education (39 percent of people without a school diploma or with only a primary school diploma voted in favor, compared with 69 percent of those with a university diploma), and even more clearly depending on monthly household income (35 percent of people with incomes under 1,500 euros per month voted in favor, compared with 74 percent of those with incomes of over 4,500 euros per month) and political affiliation (16 percent of those who had voted for the extreme Left in the 2004 European elections voted yes in the 2005 referendum; among those who had voted for the Left in 2004, 42 percent supported the European Constitution, compared with 76 percent who had voted for the Right, and 17 percent of those who had voted for the extreme Right).[15] As is shown in numerous surveys, regularly practicing Catholics are less young, more likely to have a degree, have better incomes, and vote more for the Right (but less for the extreme Right) than the general French population. There is therefore a convergence here, although it is not possible to determine precisely the importance of the religious factor. However, an indicator that suggests that the religious factor has not been negligible is connected with newspaper readership: the readers of the daily paper *La Croix*, who are devout Catholics, voted 74 percent in favor of the treaty (readers of *Le Figaro* voted 68 percent in favor, and readers of *Le Monde* voted 52 percent in favor).[16]

Two religious minorities, who are too small to be properly taken into account in most surveys, were large enough in this survey to constitute two sub-samples.[17] Protestants, who have long been considered to be more to the Left than the French average,[18] were hardly distinguishable in their "no" to the over-all vote, and Muslims voted, for the most part, in line with the overall population. This last result is even more interesting in that Muslims are far closer to the Left than the national average.[19] They therefore voted for the treaty in larger numbers than was the case among the political tendency that they usually support and the social class to which most of them belong. We can see here a legitimist reflex[20]—a desire for integration. And the fact that regularly practicing Catholics showed themselves to be more favorable to the European Constitution than the French population as a whole also reflects their general belonging to what may be called "the establishment." Undoubtedly, other surveys show that their belonging to the Catholic religion can be a significant factor in voting for the Right, but this refers to what, significantly, is known in France as "the republican Right" as distinct from the extreme Right. Thus, ideologically and politically, the old conflict between the two Frances is clearly over.

Further support for this interpretation can be found in a third survey relating to *laïcité*,[21] which, let us recall, was the key dividing factor in the conflict between the two Frances. Five responses were offered to the question, "For you, what does the principle of *laïcité* mean above all?" Only one response could be chosen. For each response, we give below (1) the percentage opting for it among the sample as a whole; (2) the percentage among Catholics; and (3) the percentage among people with no religion:

"placing all religions on the same level of equality" (32, 26, and 30 percent)
"separating religions from politics" (28, 29, and 24 percent)
"ensuring freedom of conscience" (28, 28, and 34 percent)
"reducing the influence of religion in society" (9, 13, and 8 percent)
"none of the above" (1, 3, and 4 percent)
non-respondents (2, 1, and 0 percent)[22]

The results are highly informative. Respondents were fairly evenly divided between the first three options, with a relative majority giving primary emphasis to equality between religions, which seems to be a major preoccupation among members of minority religions. Equality between religions was ranked third among Catholics, six percentage points lower than the average for the sample as a whole, and was ranked second by people with no religion, two percentage points below the average. The second option, the separation of religions and politics, was chosen by only 24 percent of non-religious respondents (four points less than the average, and five points less than for Catholics). While this could be interpreted in a number of ways, for this group the principle of *laïcité* does seem to mean above all respect for freedom of conscience (including more specifically the right not to believe) whereas Catholics appear here to be in line with the general population. We should also note the low scores gained by what we might call combative *laïcité* (9 percent), even if Catholics opt for this a little more than others (13 percent), while people with no religion gave it a low rating (8 percent). Let us also note that the French readily situated themselves within the range of proposed responses, as may be seen by the low numbers responding "none of the above" or giving no response at all.

Finally, to round off this part of my analysis, let us examine responses to the question: "Is *laïcité*, according to you, an essential, very important, or not at all important element of France's identity?" Seventy-five percent of French people responded "essential" (23 percent) or "very important" (52 percent). The percentage was 80 percent among Catholics, with a very different distribution: 12 percent stating "essential"; 68 percent stating "very important." People with no religion mirrored the average French response: (78 percent, made up, respectively, of 24 percent saying "essential" and 54 percent "very important"). One can therefore say that if Catholics are a little less commonly outright zealots of *laïcité* than other respondents (which will surprise nobody), they have—in the vast majority of cases[23]—interiorized the fact that *laïcité* is part of French identity.

That said, as already noted, the dominant vision of religion in France is ambivalent, for if 78 percent of French people judge the religious factor to be an essential need in their existence, 59 percent are afraid of an excessively large influence of religion in the world (and 47 percent in France).[24] The conflict between the two Frances has been a politico-religious conflict, and religion has shown itself, from a very early stage, to have a political signification in France. This is why, shortly before the law of 1905, hopes were expressed that the separation of churches and state would favor the birth of a "republican Catholicism,"[25] just as today many politicians speak of the need for a "moderate Islam," and indeed of a "republican Islam." It is also in this context that the republican state must guarantee freedom of thought against unduly invasive religious phenomena.[26]

Political authorities began to worry about religious groups, or more exactly about the boundary between religious and non-religious groups (the latter being qualified as "cults") starting in the mid-1980s and, following various affairs, this preoccupation became important in the 1990s.[27] At a juridical level, this led to the law of June 12, 2001, against "cults undermining human rights" (the initial draft of the law had targeted "associations or groups of a cult-like character").[28] Although specifically titled a law against "cults," it has been controversial in its application: for the *rapporteur* who steered it through the French Senate (the upper house of the French Parliament), the law applies to any group whose activities have as their "goal or effect the creation, maintenance, or exploitation of the psychological or physical subjectivity of persons participating in these activities" (article 20), which gives it a general character. By contrast, the *rapporteur* in the National Assembly (the lower chamber in the French Parliament) stated: "Under no circumstances can trade unions, professional groups or political movements be targeted," which would give the law a discriminatory character.[29]

Beyond this ambiguity in the legislative process,[30] the wider context has been characterized by an unmistakable attitude of distrust on the part of civil servants (whose importance in political governance is enormous) towards what may appear not to be "religiously correct." In 2003, a document produced by the Protestant Federation of France (FPF) denounced "the increase over the last 15 years of a climate of suspicion with regard to religion and notably, in the view of the Protestant Federation, with regard to evangelical associations which, when working to take care of young people for example, suddenly see taken away from them aid which they had previously been granted."[31] The president of this federation, Jean Arnold de Clermont, reiterated this sentiment on September 4, 2004, during the annual Assembly of Protestants at the Musée du Désert (commemorating the resistance of the Camisards against the banning of Protestantism effected in 1685 by Louis XIV). Meanwhile, in February 2005, the mayor of Montreuil, a suburb of Paris, had—under the pretext of carrying out building inspections—interrupted the celebration of religious services by Haitian, West Indian, and African Protestant communities.

The Protestant Federation is also calling for the law of 1905 to be modified in two respects in particular: by changing the fact that, at present, any modification to the 1901 general law on associations automatically applies to the 1905 law too; and by changing article 19 of the law, which defines associations of religious worship. As currently worded, article 19 says that "these associations must exclusively have as their objective the exercise of a religion"; the FPF wants the word "exclusively" to be replaced by "principally." This second demand, arising from practical problems encountered by local churches engaged in social work, touches on a sensitive symbolic point, for the law intended to estab-

lish a clear distinction between the religious and the political. This brings us
back to the question of "cults," for one of the main problems, at the level of social representations of them, lies in the displacement and verbal camouflaging of
the frontier between the religious and the non-religious. Because of this, the
FPF's concerns have been given little attention, and this has had a paradoxical
consequence: that of casting the Catholic Church as a defender of the 1905 law,
when in reality the Catholic Church has benefited from special provisions introduced by the laws of 1907 and 1908, and by the agreement reached with the
Holy See in 1923-24 after Pope Pius X's order to French Catholics not to apply
the law of 1905.

The frontier between the religious and the non-religious is also a major issue in debates concerning Islam. Toward the end of 2003, the weekly magazine
Elle published a manifesto signed by actors and intellectuals in favor of a law
banning "the Islamic veil in schools and in public administration" and, more
broadly, "all visible religious signs." The article presenting this manifesto stated:
"the veil is not a religious symbol (there is no consensus over the interpretation
of Islam on this question) but the branding of one sex by another, a tool of oppression inherited from a long patriarchal tradition aiming to designate women
as eternally impure beings in the eyes of men, and eternally minor in their social
status. And this dialectic of obscurantism and fundamentalism is revolting."[32] On
the other hand, opponents of the law point out that this kind of discourse denies
the possibility for a woman to freely wear the Islamic veil, a position very much
in line with a brand of antifeminism adhered to by certain proponents of *laïcité*
who for many years argued that women should be denied the right to vote on the
grounds that they were held under the sway of clericalism, and therefore had to
be educated and emancipated by republican *laïcité* (and this would be a long and
endless process).[33] It is clear that the dominant positions of feminists on this
question on each side of the Atlantic are diametrically opposed, and there has
been no real dialogue between them.

Since 1989, the question of the "headscarf" or the "Islamic veil" has occupied an important place in French political life.[34] The first "affair" (in the fall of
1989) occurred shortly after the fatwa issued by Ayatollah Khomeini against the
writer Salman Rushdie in February of 1989. This strongly contributed to a view
held, rightly or wrongly, among members of the intelligentsia according to
which the "veil" was held to threaten freedom of thought. In addition, this affair
occurred just after the adoption of the Jospin law of July 1989, giving increased
rights to pupils, and the affair was considered by some to be the first consequence of this law. Similarly, today, some individuals are indignant that certain
Muslim women refuse to undress in front of male doctors and blame this behavior on the influence of their husbands.[35] Similar issues have arisen in the context
of the Kouchner law of 2002, giving rights to the sick.[36] Within the framework
of the conflict between the two Frances, educational and medical institutions
played a role of legitimation for republican regimes grounding themselves on
the legacy of 1789. As they were unable to legitimize themselves through religion, these regimes opposed alleged religious passivity by championing the

"march of progress" and the concordance of technical and scientific progress with social and moral progress. School and medicine were consequently invested with a level of veneration that was stronger than in other democratic countries; today, the loss of veneration for secular institutions and changes in the balance of power between institutions and individuals have greater political significance in France than elsewhere.[37] Through its specific cultural and religious characteristics, and through the position its members hold in French society, Islam exemplifies these politico-symbolic changes. And in the absence of a deeper analysis, many people see this exemplarity as the cause of the changes.

A reversal of the dominant political perceptions of religions has taken place if we compare those prevalent at the end of the nineteenth and the beginning of the twentieth century with those dominant at the end of the twentieth and the beginning of the twenty-first century.[38] A century ago, the dominant secular and republican ideology judged, rightly or wrongly, that congregations—and indeed "clericalism" as a whole—were a political threat that had to be resisted.[39] This ideology regarded Islam more favorably than Catholicism.[40] We can group together the arguments that were put forward under three main headings.

The first relates to the representation of the theological structure of the two religions. Catholic dogma,[41] such as the Trinity, transubstantiation, the virgin birth of Jesus, the resurrection, and so forth, were considered to be offensive to reason and to science. New dogmas such as the immaculate conception of Mary and papal infallibility exacerbated this apparent "obscurantism." By contrast, the Islamic insistence on the unity of God and the simplicity of the Muslim religion in matters of dogma accorded relatively well with the imagination of the spiritualist tendency among freethinkers.

The second reason relates to the institutional structure of the two religions. Islam seemed to be a less "clerical" religion than Catholicism: it had no pope, no bishops, no hierarchy—not even a clergy, or at least, no celibate priests making vows distinguishing them from laypersons. Here, again, Islam appeared to favor an individual form of piety that was closer to republican spirituality than Catholicism.

The third and final reason invoked was that in contrast with Catholicism and its notorious Inquisition, Islam was considered to be historically a relatively tolerant religion that had allowed the presence of Christian and Jewish minorities on its soil.

Who in France today could expect to be regarded as credible if they propounded the idea of Islam as a more enlightened, less clerical, and more tolerant religion than Catholicism? On the contrary, at the start of the twenty-first century, it is commonplace to draw contrasts between, on the one hand, a Christianity that knows how to "render unto Ceasar that which is Ceasar's" and "to God, that which is God's," and that supposedly lies at the "origin" of *laicité* and, on the other hand, an Islam which now and for ever more is prone to mix religion with politics. During the Stasi Commission hearings, a former minister at the center of the political spectrum insisted that from the point of view of the Republic, "all religions are not of the same worth," from which it followed that Christianity and Islam cannot be placed on the same level.[42]

The discourse of the "threatened Republic" has thus shown itself to be recurrent in France, but the enemy has changed. While it undoubtedly corresponds to certain realities, it also possesses an ideological function. The "threat" that may have existed in the past was ideologically overestimated at the time and is ideologically underestimated (or implicitly denied) today, when it is commonplace to criticize the type of republican discourse that was dominant in France at the beginning of the twentieth century.[43] How will the dominant republican discourse in France today be judged in a century—or, perhaps, in less than a century?

Translated by Matthew A. Kemp and Alec G. Hargreaves

Notes

1. On the *pacte laïque* (the secular pact), see Jean Baubérot. *Histoire de la laïcité en France.* 3rd ed. (Paris: PUF, 2005).

2. See Jean Baubérot, *Vers un nouveau pacte laïque* (Paris: Seuil. 1990).

3. Blandine Chélini-Pont and Jeremy Gunn, *Dieu en France et aux Etats-Unis, quand les mythes font la loi* (Paris: Berg International. 2005).

4. Seventeen eighty-nine had proclaimed this principle, Napoléon had politically imposed it, for the most part, and the Third Republic reestablished what by then had been whittled away, and introduced various additional measures.

5. This was not untrue, but there were variations between schools, and one must remember that the nation's young were also divided and schooled in different ways within the public education system according to their social class. See Jean Baubérot. *Laïcité 1905-2005 entre passion et raison* (Paris: Seuil, 2004), 34ff.

6. A contract with the state required them. notably, to respect the official curriculum laid down by the Education Ministry, even if specific activities (linked to the unique character of these establishments) could be added.

7. The two types of schools are charged with different obligations. as the Constitutional Council recalled in 1994. when it ruled against a new increase in possible subsidies.

8. CSA survey for *La Vie*. "Les attentes des Français à l'égard du prochain pape," April 15, 2005. www.csa-fr.com (accessed March 14, 2007).

9. Sociologists of contemporary religion emphasize the individualization of religion, including *bricoloage* (mixing and matching) between diverse religious traditions. It seems to us that if a question taking this new situation into account were proposed in opinion surveys, it could resonate not only among those classified as the "rest" but also in other categories of responses.

10. These data come from a survey, discussed in further detail below. carried out among a representative national sample of a little over 5.200 French people during the referendum over the European Constitution: 8.5 percent of respondents referred to themselves as regularly practicing Catholics; 27.5 percent as occasionally practicing Catholics, and 31 percent as non-practicing Catholics; 2 percent declared themselves to be Protes-

tant: 2 percent indicated they were Muslim: and 23 percent indicated they were without religion. This corresponds overall to what one finds in other survey investigations. CSA opinion survey conducted for *France 3, Radio France, Le Parisien,* and *Aujourd'hui en France,* "Le vote au referendum sur le traité constitutionnel," May 29, 2005, www.csa-fr.com (accessed March 14, 2007).

11. Except for the question of homosexuality, for which a section of non-practicing Catholic opinion shared the reservations of the official Catholic Church position. CSA survey for *La Vie,* "Les attentes des Français à l'égard du prochain pape," April 15, 2005, www.csa-fr.com (accessed March 14, 2007).

12. Young people having extra-marital sex, couples practicing contraception, divorces, and so forth.

13. CSA survey for *La Vie,* "Les attentes des Français à l'égard du prochain pape," April 15, 2005, www.csa-fr.com (accessed March 14, 2007).

14. CSA opinion survey conducted for *France 3, Radio France, Le Parisien,* and *Aujourd'hui en France,* "Le vote au referendum sur le traité constitutionnel," May 29, 2005, www.csa-fr.com (accessed March 14, 2007).

15. Criteria based on votes in the European elections of 2004. CSA opinion survey conducted for *France 3, Radio France, Le Parisien,* and *Aujourd'hui en France,* "Le vote au referendum sur le traité constitutionnel," May 29, 2005, www.csa-fr.com (accessed March 14, 2007).

16. CSA opinion survey conducted for *France 3, Radio France, Le Parisien,* and *Aujourd'hui en France,* "Le vote au referendum sur le traité constitutionnel," May 29, 2005, www.csa-fr.com (accessed March 14, 2007).

17. The sample of each minority (a little more than one hundred persons) may appear small; it must, however, be recognized that surveys typically take a sample of between eight hundred and one thousand people and, therefore, this represents the equivalent of a sub-sample of more than 10 percent of these surveys.

18. As confirmed by surveys undertaken on this group.

19. See Syvlain Brouard and Vincent Tiberj, *Rapport au politique des Français issus de l'immigration* (Paris: CEVIPOF, 2005).

20. Political leaders on both the Right and the Left (with the exception of Laurent Fabius) had called for a vote in favor of the treaty.

21. CSA survey conducted for CNAL (Centre National d'action laïque), "Les français et la loi de 1905," February 2-3, 2005, www.csa-fr.com (accessed March 14, 2007).

22. At this level, we may distinguish within the sample as a whole three subcategories: Catholics, those without religion, and (by default) others. The CSA Institute did not respond to our request to provide the respective size of these three sub-categories. It is highly probable that regularly and non-regularly practicing Catholics identified themselves almost unanimously as "Catholics." It is, on the other hand, plausible that non-practicing Catholics, because they were not able to identify themselves as such in the survey, may have been divided between "Catholics" and "others." In this survey, therefore, Catholic opinion has a relatively wide span.

23. Only 8 percent of Catholics think that *laïcité* is "not at all important in French identity" (compared with 9 percent of those without religion, and 7 percent of the sample as a whole; it is probable that members of other religions are far less likely to choose this response). CSA survey conducted for CNAL (Centre National d'action laïque), "Les français et la loi de 1905," February 2-3, 2005, www.csa-fr.com (accessed March 14, 2007).

24. CSA survey conducted for *Le Monde des religions* in June 2005, www.csa-fr.com (accessed March 14, 2007).

25. But the law of 1905 turned its back on such a possibility, notably through article 4, see Maurice Larkin, *Church and State after the Dreyfus Affair: The Separation Issue in France* (London: Macmillan, 1974).

26. See Jean Baubérot, "Laïcité, sectes, société," in *Sectes et Démocratie*, ed. Françoise Champion and Martine Cohen (Paris: Seuil, 1999). 314-30.

27. See especially Assemblée nationale, *Les sectes en France. Rapport fait au nom de la Commission d'enquête sur les sectes* (Paris: Assemblée Nationale. 1996).

28. For what followed, see Patrice Rolland, "La loi du 12 juin 2001 contre les mouvements sectaires portant atteinte aux Droits de l'Homme. Anatomie d'un débat legislatif," *Archives de sciences sociales des religions* 121 (January-March 2003): 149-65.

29. Rolland, "La loi du 12 juin 2001," 149-65.

30. Rolland. "La loi du 12 juin 2001." 157.

31. Protestant Federation of France. *La Laïcité*, September 19. 2003 (unpublished document submitted to the Stasi Commission; see note 35).

32. "Elle s'engage." *Elle*, December 8. 2003.

33. Among democratic countries, France is the one with the greatest time difference between the granting of the right to vote to men (1848) and to women (1944). The conception of republican universalism is largely the cause of this (see Pierre Rosanvallon. *Le Sacre du citoyen* (Paris: Gallimard, 1992), 396, 411ff.

34. The choice of term often reflects the position of the social actor using it. It should be noted that those inclined to tolerate this garment in the name of freedom of conscience speak of the "headscarf," whereas those who want to ban it call for a law forbidding "religious signs" and speak of the "Islamic veil."

35. This form of behavior, which nobody has attempted to quantify, was regarded as particularly significant by certain members of the Stasi Commission, which was given the task by President Jacques Chirac of studying the problems posed by the application of the "principle of *laïcité*."

36. In an interesting paradox. French doctors of the nineteenth century refused access to medical studies to women, on the grounds that the exercising of this profession would offend their sense of modesty. The first woman authorized to register for such studies was allowed to do so at the Faculty of Algiers precisely so that she could treat female Muslims in colonial Algeria.

37. Baubérot, *Laïcité 1905-2005.*

38. On the first dominant representation see notably the *Grand Dictionnaire Universel* (published between 1866 and 1876, and still largely used at the start of the twentieth century by republican cadres). On the second representation see notably Olivier Roy, *La laïcité face à l'islam* (Paris: Stock, 2005).

39. I give a fictionalized representation, but one that is based on archival work, of the climate and the events of 1902-5 in my historical novel: Jean Baubérot, *Emile Combe et la princesse carmélite. Improbable amour* (Paris: L'Aube, 2005).

40. See the report of Emile Combes on Islam in Baubérot, *Emile Combe*, 73-74. This did not prevent, however, the desire to control Islam in Algeria.

41. In fact, apart from transubstantiation (considered to be particularly absurd and obscurantist) and the new dogmas of the nineteenth century, these dogmas were common to Christianity. But in Protestantism, they were either contested or the object of spiritualist interpretations.

42. These comments were made by the centrist political leader François Bayrou on October 7. 2003, during a hearing before the Stasi Commission, of which I was a member.

43. Today it is said that "the Republic [was] against congregations" (the title of a

work by historian Christian Sorrel. *La République contre les congrégations* [Paris: Le Cerf. 2003]). whereas at the time. moderate republicans considered that it was the congregations that were against the Republic.

Chapter Twelve
Politicized Religion in France and the United States: Different Histories, Common Ideals, Similar Dilemmas

Amanda Porterfield

This concluding essay offers a summary overview and comment on *Politics and Religion in France and the United States*. Calling attention to common ideals and similar dilemmas faced by the two countries as they struggle with the effects and implications of highly politicized forms of religious activism, the essay argues that France and the U.S. have different strengths and shortcomings when it comes to handling these matters, and that comparative analysis contributes to greater clarity about these strengths and shortcomings. Cognizant of the seriousness of these issues, I hope my perspective as a historian of religion sheds some light on the interplay of religion and politics in the two countries.

Both countries are committed to principles of liberty and equality. These principles are ingrained in the laws of both nations and many citizens in both places revere these principles as ideals the whole world might live and profit by. Our Statue of Liberty is a gift from France and symbolizes important ties of historical and philosophical kinship. As Sébastien Fath pointed out during discussion at the conference where the essays in this volume were first presented, it is no coincidence that John Calvin, whose ideas on conscience David Little's essay shows to be so important in the early development of religion and politics in America, was a Frenchman. As part of the shared commitments to equality and freedom of conscience, both nations have long traditions of resistance to perceived misuse of religious authority.

171

These traditions of resistance have included resentment and hatred. Prior to the twentieth century at least, many celebrants of freedom of conscience in both America and France viewed the Catholic Church and its supporters with animosity. In earlier eras of American history, Protestant conceptions of American nationhood have often turned on a distinction between the integrity of American Protestant government and the degeneracy of European states infected by Romish superstition, absolutism, and corruption. In French history, as will be discussed further below, the Catholic Church as been the target of considerable resentment.

Along with resistance to the perceived misuse of religious authority and shared idealism with respect to liberty and equality, there are numerous differences in the ways the people and governments of the two nations have understood the relationship between religion and reason and conceptualized the proper role of religion in politics and public life. While the French have more often looked to reason as a means to social order and reform, Americans have more often looked to religion to solve social difficulties. Rather than being as consistent as the French in casting reason as the chief defender of liberty and individual rights, Americans have tended to conceptualize both the individual and liberty in more thoroughly religious terms. Americans have often wanted to clear the way for individual conscience and initiative because of religious perceptions of the individual as the principle conduit of grace and the basic and essential entity through which the liberty of God is revealed. In this schema, both church and state are purposively weakened.

The rational consistency with which liberty and equality are defined and institutionalized in France as rights guaranteed to individual citizens stand out in some contrast to the U.S., as does the great respect for rational analysis that permeates French culture. In the U.S., anti-intellectual tendencies are more firmly ingrained in national culture. Americans have often been partial and inconsistent in their enthusiasms for liberty and equality and blatantly religious in selecting who should be equal to whom and whose liberties should be protected first and foremost.

At the same time, religious pluralism and multiculturalism have flourished more openly and exuberantly in the U.S. than in France and contribute significantly to the dynamism of many aspects of American life, from politics and the economy to religion and the arts. With little systematic governance or rational oversight, American multiculturalism is a source of enormous creativity and vitality but also prey to the forces of a market economy and consumer driven culture, and to periodic violence and a good deal of religious hatred and repression. As France struggles to make more public space for the kind of multiculturalism and religious activism that is so prevalent in the U.S., the rational management of society becomes more difficult and religious violence escalates. In France as in the U.S., competing religious groups often show little interest in making sure other groups are treated with the same degree of respect and equality they demand for themselves. The liberal principles of liberty and equality are not entirely compatible with multicultural religious activism, in which competing groups jostle for space and ascendancy. On the other hand, discouragement of religious activism creates more problems than it solves and runs up against the principle of religious freedom to which France is committed.

In elaborating on these points, I want to call attention to the comparative setup of this volume and to the kind of insight that is yielded by methods of comparative analysis. Comparing the interplay of religion and politics in two different nations can reveal distinctive aspects of that interplay within each nation that analysis of one nation alone might not discover. To briefly illustrate this methodological point, let us take Rémy Schwartz's discussion of the strong exercise of government neutrality with respect to the headscarf issue in France. His discussion provides a nice foil against which the relative weakness of American concepts of government neutrality can be perceived and better understood. *C'est l'interdit qui libère* is not something one can easily imagine coming out of the mouth of U.S. government officials. The idea that any imposition of government rule could be liberating runs against the grain of American culture, to the extent there is such a thing as American culture, as does the presumption, so reasonable in the French context, that government can speak for conscience or impart a constructive rule of freedom. Schwartz's discussion of the French government's strong exercise of religious neutrality enables us to think more deeply about the greater aura of religious sanctity protecting religious expression in America, and about the tendency of Americans, unlike the French, to interpret the principle of religious freedom in terms of *resistance* to government intervention.

Jeremy Gunn offers telling examples of how strange and contradictory American culture seems to outsiders, with a separation of church and state like that of France but with a public square full of religion, with presidential oaths on Bibles, "In God We Trust" on money, and the pledge of allegiance to "one nation under God" in public schools. This apparent contradiction makes sense to many Americans because of their belief that religion flows into public life primarily through individuals, not through the state or even the churches, although those institutions are important conduits for the religious energy that individuals receive.

Many Americans operate on the theory that the ideal form of government is self-government, nurtured by religion, education and family life, with the state providing common security and public education. Americans disagree over questions about how religion, education, and family life should be defined. Should intelligent design be taught in public schools? Should same-sex marriages be legalized? Does common security include universal health care? These serious disagreements about the definition of terms often presuppose an underlying notion that self-government is where all government should start and end. This commitment to individual responsibility is not the same thing as moral relativism. Avid proponents of individual responsibility in the U.S. have helped to build an enormous prison system that incarcerates a significant percentage of the young black male population and that, in many states, includes capital punishment, despite strong moral opposition to that form of punishment in many other countries and among American liberals as well.

Jean Baubérot's discussion of the founding myths of the two countries points to some of the differences between France and the U.S. with respect to attitudes toward government authority. Desire for freedom from the heavy hand of government is paramount in the two American founding mythos of Thanksgiving and the Fourth of July story. The seventeenth-century Pilgrims commemorated in the annual holiday of Thanksgiving sought sanctuary in America to practice their faith; the eighteenth-century revolutionaries commemorated on Independence Day resisted what they perceived to be the tyrannical authority of the British crown. As Baubérot observes, both stories point in the same general direction in contrast to the French stories about the baptism of Clovis in the late fifth century and Bastille Day at the end of the eighteenth century, which point in opposite directions with respect to freedom and government authority. While religious freedom and reasons for its defense come to the fore in the American stories, tension between religion and reason characterizes the emergence of French nationalism. The tension is represented in the juxtaposition of the two founding myths—the baptism of Clovis symbolizes pride in the rule of a Catholic monarchy while Bastille Day symbolizes pride in its overthrow. French respect for reason as a combatant and regulator of religion stands in contrast to American assumptions about their ultimate harmony and about the need for religious regulation of religion to insure that harmony. Throughout American history, assumptions about the compatibility between religion and reason have bolstered confidence that religion and rationality must be on the same side and that freedom of religious expression will contribute to disclosure of that harmony. Especially in the case of Protestants who have seen themselves as guardians of their nation's destiny, Americans have confidently assumed their own religion to be coextensive with reason, unlike the other religions practiced by their neighbors, which they often imagined to be full of fantasy, superstition and peculiar forms of cultural expression.

Cultural differences between France and the U.S. derive, at least in part, from the different religious histories of the two nations. While religious diversity and notions of limited government originating in Protestant thought have shaped American culture, the interplay between Catholicism and secular rationality in French history has shaped French culture. Thus Baubérot points to the unique role and profound impact of Catholicism in French history and then to the birth of French nationalism "amid a frontal and violent conflict with Roman Catholicism" on behalf of freedom, equality, and reason. He highlights the tension between reason and religious authority in the story of modern France, with reason ascendant through its inscription in law and government.

Blandine Chélini-Pont describes the relationship between Catholicism and *laïcité* somewhat differently, pointing to the emergence of a fusion of Catholic and secular values emerging out of earlier opposition between the two. Chélini-Pont presents that fusion as one explanation for why French voters rejected the EU Constitution earlier this year. "From a country that was clearly divided into two camps, which knew themselves very well and drew on the reciprocal hatred in order to exist, has emerged a country in which each camp is penetrated by the ideas of its firmest enemy." This reformulation of national identity in terms of a distinctive love-hate relationship to the Catholic Church distinguishes French culture from that of other nationalities and works against French participation in a common and more generic European culture. France's troubled but historic role as the Church's eldest daughter contributes to the uniqueness of French culture and to the sense of national pride in that uniqueness, which fills some people eager for European Union "with despair," as Chelini-Pont observes.

French attachment to a distinctive national history in which a love-hate relationship to religion plays a major role is not the only source of French reluctance to endorse a European Constitution. As other essays in this volume suggest, France's pressing need to create public spaces in which religious minorities feel at home may also contribute to this reluctance. A European Constitution that does not acknowledge religious values as resources for public life and public policy would seem to thwart desires for cultural inclusion among religious minorities in France who want French culture to reflect the vibrancy of their religious communities and the reverence individuals feel for those communities. Rejection of the EU Constitution can thus be seen as an acknowledgment of the religious concerns expressed by non-Catholics about their future in France as well as an affirmation of the importance of France's distinctive historical relationship to the Catholic Church.

While Catholic sensibilities exert profound influence in France, American Protestants and their religious sensibilities have exerted powerful influences on the shape of American culture and on structure of American law and government. According to historian William R. Hutchison, "at least 85 percent" of colonists at the time of the American Revolution, were English speakers with religious backgrounds in Calvinist Protestantism. When the Declaration of Independence was proclaimed on July 4, 1776, "this quite homogeneous population had spent" a century and a half "constructing a culture to their own specifications."[1]

David Little is right to point to the connection between Roger Williams and John Locke and to Locke's influence on Thomas Jefferson, and to stress the connection between their view of religious freedom and religious pluralism. Without denying these connections or the admirable qualities of the liberal political philosophy derived from Protestant thought, we need to press the question of its expression in American culture along some other lines that parallel but also complicate Little's eloquent defense. There is no denying that the First Amendment guarantee of religious freedom and prohibition of religious establishment developed as an expression of liberal Protestant thought or that the legalization of these principles has helped Catholics, Jews, and other non-Protestant groups make themselves at home in the United States. But the importance of Catholics, Jews, and other non-Protestants in American society cannot be overstated, especially after 1820 when immigration patterns changed the demographics of American society dramatically. Catholics, Jews, and members of other religious groups—Native Americans, Muslims, Eastern Orthodox Christians, Hindus, Buddhists, Sikhs, B'hai, Wiccans, and others—have contributed to the fabric of American society and to the strength of American cultural resources. At the same time, this diversity of American religious life has provoked considerable hostility and resentment, especially among white Anglo-Saxon Protestants (WASPs) who have felt their hegemony threatened.

Some might even argue that Protestant resentment of Catholics, Jews, blacks, and Muslims in America outweighs the hospitality accorded these groups by American law and custom. Many historians would credit Jews and Catholics as primary actors in the development of American pluralism, along with Hindus, Buddhists, Muslims, and Native Americans more recently, pushing against a Protestant establishment and making pluralism happen. Adding to the problem of conservative Protestant resentment of outsiders is the question of the ongoing strength of liberal Protestantism, the religious and political tradition out of which American ideas of freedom and equality emerged. To what extent has an ongoing tradition of liberal Protestant religion continued to enrich American life? Does that religion not dissolve into secular liberalism? Is not liberal Protestantism post-religious and not very effective at sustaining itself as a religion, as some religious conservatives have pointed out?[2] How much credit should Protestants really get for religious pluralism and multiculturalism?

Scott Appleby's discussion of Catholic swing votes in American elections since 1976 and the influence of conservative Catholics in the current Bush administration offers supporting evidence of the weakness of liberal Protestantism in the U.S. today as well as direct evidence of the importance of Catholicism. Although Appleby does not take it up, the prominence of abortion as an issue in American politics today is an especially visible example of the influence of Catholics in American society and politics. Religious hostility to abortion and birth control are not absent in American Protestant history prior to *Roe v. Wade* in 1973, but was muted and relatively unimportant compared to more public expressions of religious hostility prior to debates over *Roe*. Public condemnations of abortion and birth control derived mainly from Catholic doctrines about the soul and the supernatural origins of life and from twentieth-century Catholic theological claims about human sexuality. Protestant evangelicals embraced Catholic ideas about the origins of life with a vengeance. The success conservative Catholics have had in making opposition to abortion a religious fundamental against which no Catholic can dissent, and then marketing this fundamental to evangelical Protestants in ways that have led them to give opposition to abortion a central place in their public platforms, illustrates the way in which religious ideas are bought and sold in American culture and how closely the politics of religious influence mirrors the market economy. The success of the abortion issue in American politics today reflects the economic and political clout that Catholics wield in American culture and public life today. It also reflects a political approach to religious doctrine that resonates deeply with Protestant fundamentalism and suggests that the political strategies of American Protestant fundamentalism may have had some influence in mobilizing right-wing Catholics against abortion.

The process of indigenization that Liyakut Takim writes about in his essay on Muslims immigrants to the U.S. is also a two-way process. This process is not to be confused, he argues rightly, with assimilation. Like other immigrants to the U.S. before them, Muslims immigrants are reconstituting their religious tradition in the U.S. in response to American culture and law. At the same time, they are changing America, contributing to an increasing linkage between religion and social conservatism and diluting concerns for civil rights and political activism among some African Americans.

Michael Berenbaum's discussion of American Judaism is equally sobering with respect to the correlation between the growth of political conservatism and a strong sense of religious community. Berenbaum's describes the dissolution of traditional European Judaism in the U.S. and the reconstituting of Judaism in the U.S. around the Holocaust and the State of Israel. In addition to a story of religious renewal, this history involves the growing strength of Jewish influence in American politics, especially with regard to American foreign policy in the Middle East. Berenbaum's essay calls attention to the rise of religious conservatism among a religious community in America previously known for its support and advancement of a secular state that guarantees freedom and equality to all citizens.

The essays by Michel Wieviorka, Catherine Wihtol de Wenden, and Sébastien Fath explore the problems and ironies of religious multiculturalism in France. The essays reveal specific differences between multiculturalism in France and the U.S. and also provide evidence of common dilemmas resulting from difficulties involved in harmonizing multiculturalism with equality. As these authors explain, Jews, Muslims, and Protestants in France would all like their religious cultures to have more of a bearing on public life and not simply be relegated to the realm of private religiosity in an overwhelmingly secular culture. The push for communal religious expression among French Jews, Muslims, and Protestants creates a real dilemma, however, not only because of the social tensions and pressures for social change associated with it but also because the push for communal religious expression challenges the way France has traditionally understood equality and freedom.

Wieviorka traces the history of Jewish identity in France, arguing that prior to the 1960s Jews were expected to keep their religious identity private in exchange for full enjoyment of their rights and responsibilities as French citizens. A major change occurred beginning in the 1960s, when French Jews increasingly defined themselves as an ethnic group with a desire for a greater communal presence in public life that reflected a growing sense of dignity and pride in their group heritage and the importance of that religious heritage for world history and civilization. Jews aspired to contribute to French society not only as individuals but also as representatives of an important religious group. Thus Jews felt that remembrance of the Holocaust as a horror that should never be allowed to happen again was an important remembrance not only for them, but for all citizens of France who should be encouraged to protect the rights of Jews as part of their commitment as citizens to liberty, equality, and brotherhood. Although effective in important respects, Jewish communal activism in France also helped to fuel resentment. As pride in the State of Israel developed along with growing confidence in Jewish identity, a modern form of anti-Semitism took greater hold in France, as it did elsewhere. This new and highly politicized anti-Semitism revitalized an older religious tradition of demonizing and scape-goating Jews for social ills, casting that older religious tradition in new political form. As Jewish religious identity became more public in the modern French state, it assumed a political force that mobilized detractors as well as supporters.

Wieviorka calls attention to the dilemma that Jews face in this situation. How do they affirm their rights and responsibilities as individual citizens who happen to be Jewish without undermining the ethnic solidarity that enables them to mount strong public resistance against anti-Semitism? Conversely, how do Jews affirm the ethnic solidarity that makes a significant space for Judaism to develop within French culture and thus enables resistance against anti-Semitism without undermining the individuality that enables Jews to be French citizens and ambassadors of French culture?

The dilemma Wieviorka describes so well is not limited to Jews. French Muslims and Protestants also face the same general problem. Of course, the par-ticular histories of the three groups are distinct in many ways and reflect impor-tant differences in religious beliefs, practices, and social situations. But Jews, Muslims, and Protestants share the problem of negotiating the relationship be-tween the individuality of French citizenship and the affirmation of communal solidarity that enables religious minorities to experience citizenship fully.

Catherine Wihtol de Wenden's essay argues that Muslims have been incor-porated into French culture but not fast enough. In addition to problems of eco-nomic, political, religious, and educational discrimination she discusses, de Wenden calls attention to the integration of Muslims within French society that is occurring and has already occurred. Her essay is valuable for the rich analysis of demographic change it supplies and also for its discussion of the intellectual and political will within French society to respond democratically to immigra-tion and religious difference. De Wenden's argument for the promise of integra-tion is all the more important after the riots in the fall of 2005, which clearly dramatized the failures of integration and the frustration many young Muslims feel in being denied work, education, and political voice. The essay is also help-ful in showing how religion functions in this context as a galvanizing force and means of political protest.

There is considerable irony to this situation. Given the history of France as a modern nation born out of violent protest against an authoritarian religious and political regime, and given the development of *laïcité* as a means of protecting liberty and equality by keeping religion out of public life, it is ironic that relig-ion should figure so prominently in protests against the inequality of French society. Beyond irony, we can see in de Wenden's discussion of French Mus-lims a version of the dilemma Wieviorka called attention to in his discussion of the situation of French Jews. Just as the politicization of Judaism helps to fuel anti-Semitism even as it supports robust collective expressions of Jewish citizenship that enable effective combat against anti-Semitism, the politicization of Islam provokes more of the discrimination and stereotyping against which politicized Muslims protest. As a flamboyant vehicle of social protest, radical Islam undermines the integration of Muslims into French society, even as desire for integration is at least part of what generates protest.

The religious feelings French Protestants express about the character of French society are less militant than those expressed by young Muslims in the *banlieues*, but the underlying dilemma implicit in growing Protestant demands to bring God to the city can be seen as a variant of the same problem. As Sébastien Fath explains, Protestants supported the 1905 law officially separating church and state because that law worked to remove the authoritarian, anti-Protestant influence of the Catholic Church from government and gave Protestants equality with respect to the law they had not previously enjoyed. A hundred years later, a new generation of evangelicals object to the absence of Christianity in French culture and assert the need for Christian influence on public policy and in French society more generally. This new demand to bring God back into the city but in ways Protestants can approve and even control is similar, in certain respects, to demands made by Muslims and Jews for greater recognition of their presence as religious communities within French culture. The new evangelical demand for public recognition brings with it another version of the same dilemma Muslims and Jews present of challenging the focus on individual rights on the basis of which the space for freedom of religious expression was created. But the Protestant case also carries a special irony of its own because of the affinity between *laïcité* and Protestant religious and political thought. The more evangelicals succeed in making a case against *laïcité*, the more *laïcité* fails as a means of protecting religious freedom and pluralism for everyone. If Protestants succeed in putting a dent in *laïcité*, would that success not work against the principles of liberty and equality that Protestant resistance against the Catholic Church at earlier stages of European history played a role in helping to establish?

In the era of the French Revolution and early Republic, Protestant support for the tradition of *laïcité* was perfectly understandable; the principles of *laïcité* involved claims to individual rights to freedom of thought and expression that arose in the milieu of Enlightenment political philosophy developed by liberal Protestant thinkers in England, America, and France as well as by deists with backgrounds in French Catholicism. More pietistic and theologically conservative Protestants went along (with varying degrees of enthusiasm) because they found a haven from Catholic persecution in a republican system that protected their right of religious freedom. But the liberal republican system that protected their rights was inconsistent with more socially aggressive forms of Protestant evangelicalism that developed in the nineteenth century. Because those forms of evangelicalism have been far less prominent and influential in France than in the United States, the interplay between evangelicalism and American ideals of freedom and equality provides a cautionary tale that scholars seeking to understand French evangelicalism might fine interesting. In nineteenth-century America, evangelicals asserted the right to define government and public education with rhetoric that claimed America to be a Protestant nation. In their effort to bring their God to the whole country, nineteenth-century evangelicals worked to affix a pietistic and theologically conservative stamp on a system of government that had been constructed at the end of the eighteenth century out of liberal Protestant principles of republican government. In many respects, recent efforts to call America to her heritage as a Christian nation represent a continuation of this struggle for a religious America, another chapter in a history of controversy over the extent to which Americans should be free, equal, and pluralistic.

Fath calls attention to the generic God of American civil religion that has functioned for some time as a kind of symbolic umbrella over a more or less democratic and religious pluralistic populace. He contrasts this "imagined community" uniting Americans from many different cultures and religious backgrounds under the auspices of a generic God with the relatively "undiversified religious landscape" of French *laicité*. Without denying Fath's insight, I would call attention to the Protestant ancestry of the generic God of American civil religion and the way in which evangelicals in recent decades resuscitated the vigor of this deity, which had waned in the years prior to Ronald Reagan's election as president of the United States. Evangelicals redeployed this deity in the late twentieth century, much as it had been deployed in the nineteenth century as a means of suppressing religious pluralism and dissent. I would stress the contrast between Robert Bellah's depiction of the inclusive, mild-mannered, generic deity of Dwight Eisenhower, Richard Nixon, and John F. Kennedy, and the aggressive and politically pointed deity of the Religious Right. The Religious Right not only worships a more vengeful deity but also deploys the symbols of American civil religion and the principles of religious freedom and equality in ways that vitiate diversity and suppress dissent. At the same time, the Religious Right is extremely enthusiastic about capitalism. But the market economy they love is promiscuous, lured this way and that by money, choice, and new forms of creative expression. If we bemoan the fact that every idea must be sold, we can take some comfort in the fact that bad ideas are so easily ridiculed as well as in the constant churning up of new groups, new movements, and new ways to get ahead that go some way in counterbalancing hegemonic and authoritarian tendencies in American religion and politics.

Although the escalating process of religious politicization is now occurring in both countries, this process is further advanced in the U.S., where religion-saturated identity politics has more free rein. Thus Michel Wievioka refers to the politicization of religion in France as a process of Americanization. The politicization of religion may be less well developed in France, but it is not for that reason less troublesome. If the bulwark of *laicité* resisting that politicization crumbles, the principles of freedom and equality *laicité* is meant to protect are in jeopardy.

As we have seen, differences between France and the U.S. with respect to multiculturalism depend to some extent on the underlying differences in ideas about religion's proper relationship to government authority and reason. While both nations have resisted religious authority in government as a threat to freedom and equality, with government neutrality creating the space for religious pluralism and multiculturalism, the relationship between government and religion in France involves a much stronger emphasis on government and its neutrality than in the U.S. As a result, while some people would take French multiculturalism to be an oxymoron, multiculturalism is commonly acknowledged and often celebrated in the U.S. as the best thing America has going. Even the most right-wing proponents of Christian identity in America accept religious voluntarism, a multiplicity of churches, and separation of church and state.

In some respects, the U.S. offers a model here, as Sebastian Fath suggests. America's greatest strength is its multiculturalism. Religion plays the major role, I would say, in sustaining multiculturalism. Among other things, religion provides affective modes of celebration and it is in the context of these affective practices that people often feel at home in the world and confident to express themselves. It is true that the rhetoric of multiculturalism can exaggerate and sweeten the reality, and minimize the tendencies to oppression and conformity in American culture. But the color, movement, and music of America is her beauty and religious pluralism is often the medium through which that beauty arises. At the same time, however, American enthusiasms for both multiculturalism and for the sovereignty of individual conscience make it difficult for many Americans to think rationally across the boundaries of culture and individual sovereignty, to interact with one another intellectually, and to think seriously, realistically, and deliberately about where we are headed as a nation. This problem has come to a terrible head in the context of our invasion of Iraq; religious impulsiveness helped get us into the war without much realistic forethought about what might actually happen there. In public life at least, Americans talk at each other more than with each other and this is because we lack a strong public discourse of rational neutrality that provides space for sustained analysis of public issues and common problems. Such discourse of rational neutrality is, of course, a French forte.

In France, the tradition of *laicité* has worked to keep religion out of public life by honoring religious freedom as an individual right that must be extended to everyone equally. If Americans acknowledge the essentially communal nature of religion more readily, the French have an admirable substitute for the unifying communal aspect of religion in their reverence for reason. And appeals to human reason may the most straightforward means of ensuring liberty and equality in public life, more straightforward and less easily encumbered than appeals to God. But reason may not offer everyone the effervescent vitality, the feeling of connection to transcendent power, or the sense of belonging that religion does. Religion may offer a matrix for human creativity out of which new solutions for the future may emerge.

As Jeremy Gunn observed, both of our countries are missionary countries with strong feelings of national identity and desires to impart our ideas about government to others. We should have more conversations with each other. It would be nice if France and the United States could bring their respective strengths to each other. In any case, the multiculturalism that is the best part of the U.S. and the capacity for rational analysis that the French are so effective in developing are hardly incompatible; indeed, a more effective combination of the two seems to be a requirement for the future in both countries and in the larger world. In this combination, a kind of soft republican multiculturalism may also be required in which participation in religious community is deliberate and self-conscious and in which the individual feels free to wear or not wear a headscarf. A secular government, a fair-minded legal system, and strong government support for the rational analysis of religion help make spaces for genuine religious pluralism and for a vibrant multiculturalism in which religion serves as a medium for creative expression and moral thought. Equally important, at this time and place in our histories, a full blown fair-mindedness—fair-mindedness that is truly responsive to individuals and to the communities and traditions to which individuals feel tied—requires multiculturalism.

Notes

1. William R. Hutchison, *Religious Pluralism in America: The Contentious History of a Founding Ideal* (New Haven, CT: Yale University Press, 2003), 21.

2. For example, Stanley Hauerwas, "A Christian Critique of America," *The Cresset* 50, no. 1 (November 1986): 5-16.

Index

About the Contributors

R. Scott Appleby is professor in the Department of History and director of the Joan B. Kroc Institute for Peace Studies, University of Notre Dame. He teaches courses in American religious history and comparative religious movements. From 1988-93 he was co-director of the Fundamentalism Project. He is the author of *The Ambivalence of the Sacred: Religion, Violence and Reconcilation* (Rowman & Littlefield, 2000), as well as of *Church and Age Unite! The Modernist Impulse in American Catholicism* (Notre Dame, 1992). He is also co-editor of *Being Right: Conservative Catholics in America* (Indiana, 1995).

Jean Baubérot is honorary president and professor of the History and Sociology of Laïcité (i.e. the institutional separation of church and state) at the Ecole Pratique des Hautes Etudes at the Sorbonne in Paris, where he was the founding director of the Research Group on the Sociology of Religions and Laïcité from 1995 to 2002. His publications include *Histoire du protestantisme* (Presses Universitaires de France, 5th ed., 1998), *La morale laïque contre l'ordre moral* (Seuil, 1997), *Une haine oubliée: l'antiprotestantisme avant le pacte laïque, 1870-1905* (Albin Michel, 2000), *La Laïcité, 1905-2005, entre passion et raison* (Seuil, 2004), and *Histoire de la laïcité en France* (Presses Universitaires de France, 4th ed., 2007).

Michael Berenbaum currently serves as director of the Sigi Ziering Institute at the University of Judaism. Recently named executive editor of the *New Encyclopedia Judaica* (Macmillan, 2006), he was for three years president and chief executive officer of the *Survivors of the Shoah Visual History Foundation*. From 1988-93 Berenbaum served as project director of the United States Holocaust Museum. He is the author and editor of sixteen books and numerous articles. His most recent books include *A Promise to Remember: The Holocaust in the Words and Voices of Its Survivors* (Bullfinch, 2004) and *After the Passion Is Gone: American Religious Consequences* (AltaMira, 2004).

Blandine Chélini-Pont is associate professor in contemporary history and a member of the Interdisciplinary Research Group on Law and Social Change at the Université Paul Cézanne, Aix-en-Provence, France. She directs the series on Law and Religion published by Presses Universitaires d'Aix-Marseille. She has published articles on the effects of globalization in Christianity and on the emergence of religious freedom as an international issue. Her books include *Géopoli-*

tique du christianisme (Editions Ellipses, 2003) and, co-authored with Jeremy Gunn, *Dieu en France et aux Etats-Unis* (Berg International, 2005).

Sébastien Fath is currently a researcher at the National Center for Scientific Research (CNRS) in France. He lectures at the Sorbonne University (Ecole Pratique des Hautes Etudes), and is in charge of a research program on religious change in contemporary Western societies. The author of ten books, he has recently published *Dieu bénisse l'Amérique. La religion de la Maison Blanche* (Seuil, 2004), *Militants de la Bible aux Etats-Unis. Evangéliques et fondamentalistes du Sud* (Autrement, 2004; awarded the Chateaubriand History Prize), and *Du ghetto au réseau. Les protestants évangeliques en France 1800-2005* (Labor et Fides, 2005).

T. Jeremy Gunn is the director of the American Civil Liberties Union (ACLU) Program on Freedom of Religion and Belief and is the Senior Fellow for Religion and Human Rights at Emory University School of Law. He has published, with Professor Blandine Chélini-Pont, *Dieu en France et aux Etats-Unis: Quand les mythes font la loi* (Berg International, 2005), which is a revised version of "Religious Freedom and *Laïcité*: A Comparison of the United States and France," *Brigham Young University Law Review* (2004). He currently is writing and editing several publications on comparative law and is under contract with Praeger to publish a book on religion and American foreign policy.

Alec G. Hargreaves is director of the Winthrop-King Institute for Contemporary French and Francophone Studies at Florida State University and a specialist on post-colonial minorities in France. His recent books include *Racism, Ethnicity and Politics in Contemporary Europe* (Edward Elgar, 1995), *Post-Colonial Cultures in France* (Routledge, 1997), *Memory, Empire and Postcolonialism: Legacies of French Colonialism* (Lexington, 2005), and *Multi-Ethnic France: Immigration, Politics, Culture and Society* (Routledge, 2007).

John Kelsay is Distinguished Research Professor and Richard L. Rubenstein Professor of Religion at Florida State University. His work focuses on the comparative study of religious ethics, especially with respect to issues in political ethics. He is the author of *Islam and War: A Study in Comparative Ethics* (Westminster/John Knox, 1993) and, most recently, of *Arguing the Just War in Islam* (Harvard, 2007). Professor Kelsay also serves as co-editor of the *Journal of Religious Ethics*.

David Little is T.J. Dermot Dunphy Professor of the Practice in Religion, Ethnicity and International Conflict at the Harvard Divinity School. He previously served as senior scholar at the United States Institute of Peace in Washington, D.C., where he directed the Working Group on Religion, Ideology and Peace. From 1996-98, he was on the State Department Advisory Committee on Religious Freedom Abroad. He is the author, with Scott W. Hibbard, of *Islamic Ac-*

tivism and U.S. Foreign Policy (US Institute of Peace Press, 1997), as well as other works.

Amanda Porterfield is Robert A. Spivey Professor of Religion at Florida State University. A historian of American religion interested in the interplay between religion and culture, she has written books on the New England Puritans, Protestant women missionaries in the nineteenth century, and the transformation of American religion after 1960. She also has wider interests in the history of Christianity and in the comparative study of world religions. She is co-editor of the quarterly journal *Church History: Studies in Christianity and Culture.*

Rémy Schwartz is a member of the Council of State, the highest administrative court in France, and a consulting professor at the Université de Paris-I (Panthéon-Sorbonne). He heads the editorial committees of two law journals, *Les Cahiers de la fonction publique* and the *Bulletin juridique des contrats publics.* He has served as the author of a report to the French prime minister on the creation of a National Immigration Museum, as rapporteur général for the High Council on Integration and as rapporteur général of the report produced by the Stasi Commission, appointed by President Chirac in 2003 to review and make recommendations for revising the code of *laïcité.*

Liyakat Takim teaches a wide range of courses on Islam in the Department of Religious Studies at the University of Denver. A native of Zanzibar, Tanzania, he has published over thirty articles/entries in various journals, books, and encyclopedias. In addition, Professor Takim has translated four books and has a book on *The Heirs of the Prophet: Charisma and Religious Authority in Islam,* forthcoming with SUNY press. He is currently translating volume four of 'Allama Tabatabai's voluminous exegesis of the Qur'an. His current research examines reformation of Islamic law in contemporary times. He is also writing on Shi'ism in the American context.

Sumner B. Twiss is Distinguished Professor of Human Rights, Ethics, and Religion at Florida State University, and Professor Emeritus of Religious Studies at Brown University. He is the co-author or co-editor of six other books, including one on religious diversity and American religious history. He is the co-editor of the quarterly *Journal of Religious Ethics* and senior editor of the new book series *Advancing Human Rights* (Georgetown University Press). He has just completed a co-edited book on interpreting human rights atrocities from humanistic perspectives and is working on another co-authored volume on religion and the pursuit of global ethics. He maintains research interests in comparative religious ethics and the phenomena of collective violence.

Michel Wieviorka is Professor of Sociology at the Ecole des hautes etudes en sciences sociales in Paris, where he directs the CADIS (Centre d'analyse et d'intervention sociologiques). He is president of the International Sociological

Association and editor of the *Cahiers internationaux de Sociologie*. His publications in English include *The Arena of Racism* (Sage, 1993), *The Making of Terrorism* (University of Chicago, rev. ed., 2004), and a major study of anti-Semitism in France, *La tentation anti-sémite* (Robert Laffont, 2005) of which an English translation is currently in preparation.

Catherine Wihtol de Wenden is a senior research fellow at the CNRS (National Center for Scientific Research) based in the Centre d'Etudes et de Recherches Internationales in Paris. A specialist on international migration, she has served as a consultant to the Council of Europe, the United Nations High Commissioner for Refugees, and the European Commission. Her publications include *L'immigration en Europe* (La Documentation française, 1999), *La citoyenneté européenne* (Presses de Sciences Po, 1997), *La beurgeoisie* (with Rémy Leveau, CNRS Editions, 2001), *Police et discriminations* (with Sophie Body-Gendrot, L'Atelier, 2003), and *Atlas des migrations dans le monde* (Autrement, 2005).

Made in the USA
San Bernardino, CA
27 January 2018